Mastering Study Skills
A Student Guide

Thomas G. Devine
University of Lowell

Linda D. Meagher

 Prentice Hall, *Englewood Cliffs, New Jersey 07632*

Library of Congress Cataloging-in-Publication Data

DEVINE, THOMAS G.
  Mastering study skills.

  Bibliography: p. 299
  Includes index.
  1. Study, Method of. 2. Report writing.
I. Meagher, Linda D. II. Title.
LB2395.D48 1989   371.3′028′12   88-5805
ISBN 0-13-560021-9

To our students — past and present

Editorial/production supervision and
  interior design: Patricia V. Amoroso
Cover design: Diane Conner
Cover photo: Mark Gibson, The Stock Market
Manufacturing buyer: Ray Keating

 © 1989 by Prentice-Hall, Inc.
A Division of Simon & Schuster
Englewood Cliffs, New Jersey 07632

Printed in the United States of America

10 9 8 7 6 5 4 3 2 1

ISBN 0-13-560021-9   01

PRENTICE-HALL INTERNATIONAL (UK) LIMITED, *London*
PRENTICE-HALL OF AUSTRALIA PTY. LIMITED, *Sydney*
PRENTICE-HALL CANADA INC., *Toronto*
PRENTICE-HALL HISPANOAMERICANA, S.A., *Mexico*
PRENTICE-HALL OF INDIA PRIVATE LIMITED, *New Delhi*
PRENTICE-HALL OF JAPAN, INC., *Tokyo*
SIMON & SCHUSTER ASIA PTE. LTD., *Singapore*
EDITORA PRENTICE-HALL DO BRASIL, LTDA., *Rio de Janeiro*

Contents

Preface

Books such as this are often the result of authors' dissatisfaction with similar books in the field. This one is not. There are already in existence excellent books on college study skills. The writing of this book was not intended as criticism of the efforts of others to prepare students for success in college courses. Like the others, this book is intended to help students more effectively. It tends to differ from them, however, in at least five respects.

1. It is based on the belief that success in college rests more upon knowing how to learn, understand, and remember than upon such hard-to-define attributes as intelligence or academic aptitude. An underlying assumption is that those students we now call "intelligent" or "academically talented" are in fact those who have developed effective study skills.

2. It attempts to reflect the best recent research on how people learn, think, and remember. Its chapters are based on the best modern knowledge in a number of fields. Its underlying theory is derived from a variety of sources, particularly from research findings about study-skills instruction, reading comprehension, vocabulary development, and learning theory. (A list of books and articles, as well as a key to their use, may be found at the back of the book under References.)

3. Its activities are related to the textbooks students are actually using and to lectures they are attending. Rather than extract pages from "typical" college textbooks for exercises, this book sends students to their own books and classes to try out new learning techniques and suggested approaches.

4. It constantly relates reading to writing. Reading and listening skills, for example, are reinforced regularly through appropriate writing activities. Patterns of paragraph organization are learned not only by examining basic patterns in printed materials but also by writing paragraphs using these patterns. The belief that students learn to read more effectively by writing is stressed in every chapter.

5. It is realistic. Although rooted in research and theory, this book is primarily a *practical* guide to the improvement of college study skills. Each of its suggestions grows from work with students in classes, lectures, labs, libraries, and conferences. Each of its exercise activities has been used successfully with a variety of students.

Mastering Study Skills was written for college freshmen and sophomores and college-bound high school students. It is hoped that these readers carry its suggestions for learning, understanding, and remembering into their later college and post-college lives, proving the Chinese adage that serves as this book's theme: "It is better to show a hungry man *how* to fish than to give him a fish."

1

Study Skills and You

INTRODUCTION AND OVERVIEW

Successful college students know *how to study*. They have learned how to manage time, read and listen efficiently, take effective notes, understand and remember course material.

This chapter gets you started on a program of study-skills mastery. It defines key study skills, shows you how to develop a positive attitude toward college study, and helps you identify your own strengths and weaknesses.

SUGGESTED GUIDE QUESTIONS

1. Which study skills are most important?

2. Why is your attitude toward study so important?

3. What are obstacles to a positive attitude?

4. How can you discover your own strengths and weaknesses?

5. What can you do to get your year off to a good start?

WHAT ARE STUDY SKILLS?

Success seems to come easily for many college students. They get good grades each semester, score well on tests, receive invitations to join honor societies, graduate with distinction, and impress interviewers with their resumés. How do such students differ from their less successful classmates? Are their successes in learning due simply to chance? to better home backgrounds? to special abilities? to intelligence?

As more research studies are made of college success, many simplistic views held in the past are rejected. Investigators find, for example, that luck has a minimal influence on academic success. Home background plays a role, it is true, but in itself cannot account for differences between success and failure in college. Investigators are increasingly suspicious of so-called "intelligence tests" and IQ test scores. Many now believe that scores from such tests are misleading or inaccurate or both, and that such tests really measure experience, memory, motivation, and the use of certain cognitive skills rather than intelligence. (See References, p. 299, for more information on these and related points.)

How then can differences between successful and unsuccessful students be explained?

This book is based upon the belief that success in college depends to a large degree on *mastery of study skills*. It assumes that students who know how to study tend to succeed and that students who have yet to learn how to study tend not to succeed.

Its underlying philosophy is that academic success rests primarily upon three aspects of study-skills mastery:

The study *skills* themselves

Study *habits* associated with the skills

The *attitudes* students bring with them to college

What are study skills? They are those mental processes students use to (1) understand new information and ideas found in lectures and textbooks, (2) make sense of and remember the new material, and (3) share this material with others in discussions, in writing course papers and research reports, and in examinations. Related to these cognitive skills are study habits such as managing one's time, selecting the proper time and place for study, and overcoming distractions. Underlying both skills and habits are the attitudes students have about ability to learn, about their personal levels of expectation, and about college life in general.

Can *you* master study skills? All the evidence from research and observations of college students through the years indicates that you can. The specific mental processes associated with learning are all learnable! You can learn the skills needed to listen to lectures attentively, take effective notes, manage reading assignments in textbooks, learn specialized terminology, write term and research papers, and take tests successfully. As you acquire competence in skills, your study habits and your attitudes will improve.

EXERCISE 1

To get a better idea of where you stand now in relation to key study skills, rate yourself by checking the appropriate column.

Study Skills and Habits	Never	Sometimes	Usually	Always
1. I keep a study schedule.				
2. I use a priority list.				
3. I keep an assignment list.				
4. I take lecture notes.				
5. I listen for main ideas.				
6. I look for a speaker's plan.				
7. I outline lectures.				
8. I relate new material to what I already know.				
9. I preview reading assignments.				
10. I check out definitions of unfamiliar words.				

Study Skills and Habits	Never	Sometimes	Usually	Always
11. I invent questions to be answered while reading.				
12. I make predictions about reading.				
13. I outline reading assignments.				
14. I write brief summaries of lectures and readings.				
15. I paraphrase sections I do not understand.				
16. I make up possible test questions while reading.				
17. I use a plan such as SQ3R.				
18. I keep a notebook.				
19. I review lecture material immediately after class.				
20. I keep a notebook list of specialized terms and words.				

    The twenty study skills and habits listed in this exercise were selected from the first chapters of this book. If you found yourself checking "never" or "sometimes," then you probably should read and study these chapters carefully. You seem to be in need of help with basic study techniques. If, on the other hand, you find that you are relatively strong in these areas, read the chapters (on your own or with your group) and note particularly the skills and habits you still need to work on. You may use SQ3R, but not as effectively as you might. You may keep a notebook but not as systematically as you should. Many students know about or have heard of certain study skills without using these skills regularly. You may be one of these people!

WHICH STUDY SKILLS ARE MOST IMPORTANT?

Dozens of separate study skills are described in the following chapters. Each skill is important and can help you learn and remember new material; however, certain skills and sets of skills are more powerful than others. This book will emphasize them.

The first relate to *previewing*, or getting an overview of material to be studied. Research findings indicate that when learners know what it is they are about to learn, they learn it more efficiently. Evidently, such previews activate any prior knowledge of the material and create a mind set conducive to new learning. When students have brief summaries, or advance organizers, of chapters and lectures prior to reading and listening, their learning is maximized.

Previewing also includes advance knowledge of the meanings of words used by lecturers and authors. Because comprehension can only take place when listeners and readers understand words used by speakers and writers, efficient previews focus upon technical vocabulary and unfamiliar words.

How do you preview new material? First, check textbooks for overviews and advance organizers. Survey chapters and lecture notes to see what lies ahead. Specific strategies are suggested in the next chapters of this book.

A second set of skills has to do with *establishing a purpose* for study. Students who read or listen to discover answers to questions tend to gain more from reading assignments and lectures. Students who try to predict what authors and lecturers will say tend to profit more from their reading and listening. When you read and listen to find answers and test predictions, you study purposefully. Your attention is more apt to focus on the material and your new learnings tend to remain in long-term memory.

How do you establish a purpose for learning? You may create personal questions and predictions from your initial previews of the material, or you may develop them from headnotes and titles within assignments. Again, strategies are recommended in the following pages.

The third set of study skills relates to *note taking*. Because new information remains in short-term memory for only a few seconds, readers and listeners need to identify items they want to retain and then capture these on paper for later study. College students need to become efficient in a number of note-taking skills: underlining, outlining, mapping, getting main ideas, and using personal codes and symbol systems.

How can you become a more efficient note taker? You need to understand the advantages of various note-taking techniques, and then you need to practice each until you discover the ones that work most effectively for you. Note-taking techniques are suggested in the chapters that follow.

The final set of key study skills relates to *summarizing.* To understand a lecture or textbook reading assignment, try to rebuild in your mind the message that the speaker or author wanted to put into the talk or chapter. To do this, you must identify the main ideas, distinguish them from supporting points, arrange them in correct order, see the underlying plan, and reorganize the message in your own words. One of the best ways to comprehend either spoken or written messages is to summarize them. In order to improve your mastery of the skills associated with comprehension, you will be given valuable tips throughout the book on developing summarizing skills.

EXERCISE 2

To check your understanding of the last few paragraphs, write out a brief summary to answer the question: "Which study skills are most important?" When you have completed it, go back and reread this section to see how well you comprehended and remembered it.

WHY IS ATTITUDE IMPORTANT TO SUCCESS?

The chief difference between those who succeed in college and those who do not is mastery of study skills. Successful students tend to be those who have learned important study skills and developed effective study habits. However, there is another aspect to college success that you should think about: *your attitude toward study.* If you have a confident attitude toward your college work, it reinforces your use of study skills. On the other hand, if you lack confidence, you may never make the best use of your skills. You need to think early in your college career about answers to such questions as: What are attitudes? What are my attitudes toward study and college? How can they be improved? What dangers typically confront students who have a set of negative attitudes in school?

What Are Attitudes?

One dictionary says that attitudes are mental positions that people adopt toward the world or part of the world. They are similar to feelings or emotions people have, which then tend to guide their thinking about certain topics. For example, one person may have a negative attitude toward, say, golf or ballet. No matter what that person hears or sees, he cannot accept golf or ballet because his views are fixed — and fixed negatively. The attitude acts as a bias or prejudice, shaping what the person feels and thinks. Another person may have a firm, positive attitude toward jogging. No matter what new information she acquires about jogging, she will not be discouraged. She may never win important races, but she gets satisfaction from the sport.

Do your attitudes color your understanding of life, either for the better or worse? Some people carry negative points of view and fail to understand much of what they encounter in their lives. Others have such highly positive attitudes about the world that they tend to be both happier and more successful. Attitudes, then, can deeply influence not only how you understand the world, but how you enjoy it.

What Are Your Attitudes Toward College and Study?

Clearly, how you feel about college will affect your life there. If you believe that college is an unpleasant experience, one that will demand too much of you and make you miserable, then you may not succeed. If you think that the years before you will be full of work, success, and enjoyment, then — generally speaking — you probably will succeed. Students who begin the first semester with a negative attitude toward the college experience start with potential trouble. Even though they may have been introduced to effective study skills and habits before college, their attitude acts as a handicap.

How Can Attitudes Be Changed?

The best way to change attitudes toward college and toward yourself as a college student is to think always in terms of *positives*. Some people dwell on their failures and inadequacies. They become almost obsessed with every problem they have had along the way: "I was in the bottom group in first-grade reading," "I just couldn't pass tenth-grade geometry," or "I can't ever seem to get higher than a C in English composition." By constantly focusing on their failures, over time they build a personal picture of failure. They think in terms of negatives.

To build your self-esteem you must concentrate on the many successes you've had through life. Failure-oriented students forget that they must have had many successes to have attained the spot they've reached! Merely to survive through twelve years of elementary and secondary school and get into college at all indicates a history of successes that they seem to forget. To survive through the first two decades of life shows considerable staying power, which they also disregard. Success-oriented students don't completely forget their failures, but they know that all people have to fail sometimes. They focus instead on their successes.

How can you build a positive attitude toward college? Here is a simple four-part strategy you can try immediately:

1. ***Think for a while about your past successes.*** What achievements stand out in your mind? What special satisfactions have you had in school? Which particular struggles have you won through successfully?

2. ***Take each new task as it comes and do it as well as you can.*** One trick you will learn in this book is to break large jobs down into smaller tasks. As the semester continues, you will find that you can do individual tasks and do them well.

3. ***Take failure in stride.*** Everyone around you (in college and in life) meets failures every day. You need to note your problems and try to figure out what went wrong and what you must do to make things go right the next time. Whatever you do, don't stop too long to think about each breakdown in your success chain!

4. ***Continue to move ahead.*** Take each new challenge as it comes; break large jobs into smaller; and keep moving. In time, you'll discover that you can become a success-oriented student with high self-regard, one whose attitude toward college is positive rather than negative.

Here is a simple exercise to get you started.

EXERCISE 3

Stop now and list here as many of your achievements as you can. Note successes in elementary and high school, in sports, in work, in your family relations, in hobbies, and so forth. You can start, obviously, with the important fact that you were accepted into college!

EXERCISE 4

Early in the semester, you probably should examine your own feelings about the college experience. One way to do this is to write out thoughtful answers to the following questions:

1. Why did I decide to attend college?

2. Do I really want to be in college? Why? Why not?

3. Do I believe I can succeed? Why? Why not?

4. What may cause problems for me? How can I get around such potential problems?

5. What do I have going in my favor? What are my strong points? How may I best take advantage of them?

WHAT ARE OBSTACLES TO A POSITIVE ATTITUDE?

Developing a positive attitude comes with time. During the next few weeks concentrate upon your successes; do each new task to the best of your ability; take any failures you may have in stride; and continue to move ahead. You will find your self-regard increasing as you become more and more success-oriented. However, it is only fair to say that there are obstacles along the way. Let's look at some of them now.

1. **Busyness.**   Many college students fail because they are too busy. They rush back and forth and give the appearance of being occupied with business, but, in fact, they are busy with *busyness*. They simply do not know how to make use of their time. They mismanage time and energies. Some get overly occupied with part-time jobs, some with family and friends, some with social activities. Many use all these as excuses not to work on course assignments, papers, projects, and test preparation.

2. **Procrastination.**   College life is rich: new things to do, new people to meet, new places to visit, and so on. Some students become so engrossed in the activities and excitement of campus life that they become first-class procrastinators, putting off what has to be done now until another day.

3. **Fatigue.**   Work makes people tired — that is a fact of life. Unfortunately, some students use fatigue as an excuse to put off work. They need a rest or a "quick nap." They need a quiet evening in front of the television or a movie. In time, some students get so skilled at using real or imagined tiredness to avoid tasks and assignments that any self-regard they started with disappears.

4. **Inexperience.**   You get experience by doing things. Some students use their lack of background and experience to dodge work that needs to be completed: "I've never done a library research paper before because we didn't have them in high school" or "I can't read a play because we didn't study them." For some students, pleading lack of background becomes another way of justifying potential failure.

5. **Inability.**   Ability, like experience, comes with doing. Too many students say they lack some basic ability and, as a result, are unable to meet responsibilities. "I can't do math" or "I don't know how to spell" are two of the oldest excuses in the world for avoiding assignments. They are also two more ways of insuring that you never acquire a confident, positive attitude.

HOW CAN I DISCOVER MY OWN STRENGTHS AND WEAKNESSES?

Some students have to wait for the semester to end before discovering how well they know how to study. That's too late. You can get a quick estimate now of your present study-skills competence by completing the following Study Skills Checklist.

Read and think about each of the questions, then mark a check in the appropriate column. If you are a first-year college student, much of your information will be based on your experience in secondary school. If you have already begun college, you can base your answers upon recent experiences.

When you complete the entire checklist, you can draw a line with a ruler from check to check and get a profile of yourself as a user of study skills. The profile will show your areas of greatest strength and weakness, and give you an overall picture. Exercises at the end of the checklist will suggest other ways of interpreting it.

STUDY SKILLS CHECKLIST

	Always	Usually	Sometimes	Rarely	Never
1. Do you keep track of assignments in a notebook?					
2. Do you begin study with all necessary tools on hand?					
3. Do you choose a study area free from outside interferences?					
4. Do you have a study schedule that allows a consistent time each day to study for each course?					
5. When faced with many tasks, do you set priorities for yourself?					

	Always	Usually	Sometimes	Rarely	Never
6. Do you prepare for lectures by looking ahead in the textbook?					
7. Do you listen to find answers to your own questions?					
8. Do you listen for main ideas?					
9. Do you take lecture notes?					
10. Do you summarize your lecture notes?					
11. Do you preview reading assignments?					
12. Do you turn headings into questions?					
13. Do you underline or take notes as you read?					
14. Do you check the meanings of unfamiliar words in assignments?					
15. Do you summarize your reading assignments?					

	Always	Usually	Sometimes	Rarely	Never
16. Are you able to find the main ideas in reading assignments?					
17. Are you able to find examples and details that support main ideas?					
18. Can you find main ideas in charts, graphs, and tables?					
19. Do you outline reading assignments?					
20. Do you look for organizational patterns?					
21. Do you read over directions before taking a test?					
22. Do you read all the questions before taking an exam?					
23. When you finish an exam, do you review your answers?					
24. Do you turn multiple-choice items into questions?					

	Always	Usually	Sometimes	Rarely	Never
25. Do you pay attention to guide words in essay questions?					
26. Do you make a rough draft of written work before handing in the final copy?					
27. Do you outline papers before writing them?					
28. Do you edit your papers for spelling and grammar?					
29. Are you able to find what you need in the library?					
30. Do you use an acceptable footnoting and reference system in term papers?					

EXERCISE 5

What are your particular strengths and weaknesses? Analyze your present capacities by completing the following sentences:

1. The Study Skills Checklist shows that my strongest points are

2. I built these strengths in the past because

3. The checklist shows that my weakest points are

4. I am probably weak in these areas because

5. According to the checklist I am also relatively weak in

EXERCISE 6

You can analyze your study skills further by using the following Study Skills Checklist Summary Chart.

Place a plus sign beside the numbers of items you had checked for "Always" and "Usually." Place a minus sign beside those you had checked as "Rarely" or "Never." When you finish, you will have a graphic representation of your strengths and weaknesses. Sum up your observations by answering the questions below the chart.

STUDY SKILLS CHECKLIST SUMMARY CHART

Area	Checklist Items				
Study habits	1	2	3	4	5
Listening in lectures	6	7	8	9	10
Reading textbook assignments	11	12	13	14	15
Finding main ideas and outlining	16	17	18	19	20
Taking tests	21	22	23	24	25
Writing term and research papers	26	27	28	29	30

Questions:

1. Which seem to be your strongest areas?

2. In which chapters of this book will you find more information about your areas of strength?

3. Which appear to be your weakest areas?

4. In which chapters will you find more information about these?

5. How do you account for your strengths and weaknesses in study skills?

GETTING THE YEAR OFF TO A GOOD START

Many students find that the first weeks of college are hectic and occasionally frustrating.

For one thing, the territory is different: buildings, dorms, classrooms, libraries, bookstores, cafeterias, even streets, walks, and passageways. Time must be spent simply in orienting oneself, in mapping out the new territory.

The schedule is different too. Instead of the predictable and comfortable schedules worked out by supportive high school principals and guidance counselors, college students are expected to make out their own, arranging certain classes on certain days, putting one class in one time slot and another in another slot. Energy must be spent these first weeks in simply readjusting one's inner clock.

Most different are the people. Rather than the somewhat homogeneous student body of the high school, college students are apt to represent a wide range of talents, backgrounds, personal styles, and even appearances. Again, time and energy must be spent becoming comfortable with the variety of young men and women who make up the college community.

Your first task in college is to get yourself organized and familiar with the new environment. Here are some suggestions for getting the year off to a good start.

Before Classes Begin

In the days before courses actually start, you can take steps to assure yourself a productive study routine for the semester.

1. Make sure that your living accommodations are livable! Even the most academically sophisticated college students sometimes forget how important it is to be at home in new surroundings. If you are in a dormitory, get acquainted right away with the arrangements, schedules, regulations, and so on. If you are in an apartment, make sure you have basic supplies: kitchen equipment, laundry facilities, hangers for clothes, and so on. If you carelessly postpone fundamental housekeeping tasks until classes are underway, you are placing unnecessary burdens upon yourself.

2. Get to know the campus. Locate in advance classroom buildings, administrative offices, the college bookstore, cafeteria, snack bar, and so forth. It will not help your confidence much if you cannot find your first class!

3. Get the latest copy of the college catalog. This contains information about college rules and regulations, graduation requirements, major fields of concentration, core courses, dates for midterm and final examinations, the names of faculty, and other important information. While you have time, go through the catalog and check out key data on your institution.

4. Look for student newspapers and other sources of campus information. Often found in the student center, the library, or administrative offices, these publications will tell you about special interest groups, social events, church functions, clubs, and so forth. You may also learn of tours of the college or community arranged for new students. Don't forget to check bulletin boards!

5. Pick up your class schedule. If you do not get a copy of your schedule at registration, obtain it now from your advisor, the departmental office, or the administrative offices. This is the ideal time to organize your days and weeks. Determine exactly how much time you have available for sports, recreation, or part-time work.

During the First Week

Some tasks need to be completed during the first week of the semester.

1. Get your textbooks. Sometimes it is unwise to purchase books before classes actually begin because instructors make changes in book requirements or note in class that certain books are "suggested" or "recommended" rather than required. Check out this kind of information at your first class session before spending large sums of money for books and supplementary items. However, it is equally unwise to postpone book purchases for too long. Bookstores sometimes run out of textbooks for popular courses, and it may take several weeks for orders to be filled.

2. Start a notebook. One of the basic tools needed for success in college is a good-quality loose-leaf notebook for your class and reading notes. A loose-leaf book is better for your purposes than a spiral-bound one because in it you can also keep course outlines and other handouts. (It is wise to purchase a small paper punch when you buy your loose-leaf notebook.)

3. Buy a pocket assignment book. In it you can copy assignments, due dates for papers, test dates, and other essential information. You need a record of this kind of data, written neatly and kept in one place. One of the worst things that can happen to you as a beginning college student is to lose track of course assignments. You need to know exactly what is due for each class and exactly when it is due. Don't be one of those students who simply tries to remember assignments or who jots them down on scraps of paper!

4. Strike up an acquaintance. Naturally, you will want to meet many other students and extend your circle of friends and acquaintances. During the first weeks and months of college you will probably do that. However, you need to get to know at least one person in each class immediately. You will find it valuable to have one person with whom you can discuss assignments or course material. If you have to be absent from a class during the first week or two, you can also check this person's notes and make sure you get all assignments.

5. Get to know your advisor. Find out as soon as possible the name and office location of your faculty advisor. As questions about your program or schedule come up you will need an experienced person to consult.

During the First Month

As you grow accustomed to your new environment and schedule, most problems seem to diminish. However, you need to watch for certain potential problem areas.

1. Punctuality.   Make sure you get to all your classes on time. Few behaviors are more annoying to college instructors than persistent tardiness. They begin lectures, demonstrations, and discussions assuming that all students are present and actively taking notes. They do not like to be interrupted, nor do they like to think that some students don't care enough about the course to come on time.

2. Attendance.   You must be present at all classes for information, explanations, and discussions of course material. You cannot rely on the textbook alone, nor on reading someone else's notes. You must be engaged in the lecture listening process if you are to get the most from courses.

3. Assignments.   As noted earlier, you need an assignment record to keep track of daily and weekly tasks. *You also need to do those tasks on time.* Putting off assignments ("I'm tired" or "I have all these other things to do first") is dangerous. The more you postpone jobs, the more difficult they become.

4. Tact.   Because of the newness and strangeness of the college situation, some students seem to forget all they ever knew about good manners and civilized behavior. Remember to conduct yourself like a mature adult. You should speak up in discussions, but don't overdo it and talk all the time. And, of course, you should not carry on conversations during class time or otherwise be disruptive. Always try to make a good impression not only on your instructors but on your fellow students.

EXERCISE 7

From the following list of suggestions, choose the three you believe are most important for students beginning their college careers. Write a brief paragraph explaining your choices.

1. Pick up your class schedule.

2. Get your textbooks.

3. Purchase a jacket or T-shirt with the college insignia.

4. Make sure your living accommodations are comfortable.

5. Find out procedures for adding or dropping courses.

6. Get a good-quality notebook.

7. Buy envelopes and letterheads with the college name and logo.

8. Get to know some people in each class.

9. Discover the college policy on drugs and alcohol.

10. Buy a pocket assignment book.

EXERCISE 8

Here are some common problems that arise during the first weeks of the semester. Choose what you think is the best solution.

1. During the first week of school José found that he had two classes scheduled at exactly the same time. What should he do?

    a. Attend the one he likes better and stop going to the other

    b. Make an appointment with the chairperson of his department

    c. Visit his advisor

    d. Check with the dean of the college

2. At the end of the week, he discovered that one of the courses on his schedule had been cancelled. What should he do now?

    a. Continue without that particular course

    b. Consult with his advisor

    c. Obtain an Add/Drop form from the office and add another course

    d. Use that time for additional study and recreation

3. Susan paid tuition for five rather than four courses and decided that she should drop one course. How can she find out which course is not required in her program?

    a. Check the bulletin board in the student center

    b. Consult the college catalog

    c. Ask each course instructor

    d. Ask an upper-class student who knows the program

4. Susan would like some money back for the course she dropped. What is her best source of information on tuition refunds?

    a. The departmental secretary

    b. The course instructor of the course she plans to drop

    c. An upper-class student familiar with the college policy on such matters

    d. The college catalog

5. You need to see your advisor about the schedule change, but find that her office hours are at a time when you have a class. What's the best way to get to see her?

    a. Skip your class.
    b. Leave a note asking for an appointment.
    c. Explain your problem to the course instructor.
    d. Go to the department chairperson.

WHAT ARE MY RESPONSIBILITIES IN CLASS?

Many unsuccessful students blame the college or their instructors for their problems. It is wise to remember, however, that success begins with you — and it begins the first days of the semester in your classes.

Here are some questions to examine carefully:

1. How are assignments made? (Does the instructor tell the class what students are to do for the next session? Are assignments printed on a course guide or syllabus? Are they written on the board?)

2. When are assignments due? (Is it assumed that each assignment is to be prepared for the next class? Are some assignments scheduled for later in the course?)

3. Are there special assignments? (Am I expected to do a term paper? A research paper? Brief reaction or response papers? When are these due?)

4. What form is expected for written work? (Is there a handbook that spells out the format for papers? What is it? Where do I get a copy? Must everything be typed? Are there special requirements for papers?)

5. What part does attendance play in grading? (Is perfect attendance expected? Am I allowed cuts? How many?)

6. How will grading be done? (Is the course grade based on daily recitations? On a midterm plus final? On a final examination alone?)

7. What role does discussion play in the course? (Am I expected to respond regularly? Will part of my grade be based on class participation? If so, how much of a proportion of the final grade is based on participation?)

8. Am I expected to read more than the course textbook? (Is there a supplementary reading list? If so, how much of it am I responsible for? Must I buy some of these books? Is there a "reserved" section in the library for supplementary reading books? Am I expected to read articles suggested in class? Which ones? How will I know?)

9. What do I need to know about labs and field trips? (Am I expected to attend labs? When? Where? How are these scheduled? Are field trips planned? Must I go? When are they scheduled?)

10. Am I expected to sit in a certain seat each day? (Does the instructor use a seating plan? Is attendance taken according to a seating plan?)

EXERCISE 9

Answer one of the following questions in a brief essay.

1. What are study skills?

2. Why is it important to: Preview assignments? Establish a purpose for reading and listening? Take notes? Summarize lectures and reading assignments?

3. What are some study habits associated with college success?

4. Why is attitude so important to success?

5. What are obstacles to a positive attitude?

6. How may attitudes be changed?

7. What particular study skills do you need to improve?

8. Why is it important to have a good-quality loose-leaf notebook?

9. In what ways can an assignment book help you?

10. What steps can you take early in the semester to make sure your year is successful?

POINTS TO REMEMBER ABOUT STUDY SKILLS

1. Effective study skills lead to success.

2. Study skills can be acquired.

3. Good study habits are essential.

4. Attitudes affect success.

5. Your attitudes may be changed for the better.

6. Know your strengths and weaknesses.

7. Begin the year with a good loose-leaf notebook.

8. Get a pocket assignment book at once.

9. Learn your schedule and college routines early.

10. Start the semester positively.

1
MASTERY TEST

To discover how well you understand Chapter 1, choose the best answer for each of the following questions.

1. What are study skills?

   a. Mental processes used to understand and remember new material
   b. Thinking skills used in reading
   c. Mental processes used in college courses

2. Which study skills are most important?

   a. Listening and reading skills
   b. Previewing, establishing purpose, note taking, and summarizing
   c. Keeping notes in a loose-leaf notebook

3. What is a study habit associated with college success?

   a. Managing your time
   b. Believing you can succeed
   c. Summarizing lecture and reading notes

4. How can negative attitudes toward study be changed?

   a. Think of past successes.
   b. Learn to take effective notes.
   c. Schedule your time carefully.

5. What are some obstacles to a positive attitude?

   a. Poor time management
   b. Inadequate thinking skills
   c. Procrastination and being overly busy

6. Why is it better to use a loose-leaf rather than a spiral-bound notebook?

   a. It fits more easily into a locker.
   b. It can hold course outlines and other handouts.
   c. It resists wear better.

7. What can you note in an assignment book in addition to assignments?

   a. Names and addresses of other students

   b. Birthdays and important dates

   c. Due dates for course papers

8. What can you learn from the college catalog?

   a. The names of advisors

   b. Graduation requirements

   c. Titles of required textbooks

9. What task should you attend to early in the semester?

   a. Get to know your advisor.

   b. Discover the college policy on plagiarism.

   c. Purchase stationery with the college insignia.

10. What is one of your responsibilities in every class?

   a. To attend social events

   b. To sit in the same seat every day

   c. To discover what part attendance plays in grading

2

Learning to Make the Best Use of Your Time

To keep up with regular assignments, you need to study approximately thirty hours each week. Special projects, term and research papers, and preparation for quizzes, midterm and final examinations add many hours of study to your schedule. To cope, you need to manage your time efficiently and follow a well-designed plan of study.

This chapter shows you how best to organize and manage your time by using a daily activities schedule, a weekly and monthly schedule, a priority list, and an assignment calendar. It also includes valuable advice on improving your concentration and organizing your study environment.

SUGGESTED GUIDE QUESTIONS

1. Why is it important to organize and control your study time?

2. In what ways does a simple priority list help?

3. What is an assignment calendar?

4. Why do you need to set realistic goals for study?

5. How can you avoid distractions and improve your concentration?

HOW CAN I BEST SCHEDULE DAILY ACTIVITIES?

The first step in building a plan of study is to determine how much time you have available for study. To do this you must evaluate your day from the time you get up until the time you go to bed. You are looking for the number of hours you use efficiently and the number you tend to waste.

The following are typical daily activities to consider:

Washing and dressing

Working

Eating meals

Attending classes

Traveling

Socializing

Taking care of household responsibilities

Relaxing

Sleeping

Before you evaluate your daily activities, look at the sample daily activities chart that follows and see if you can find the four hours of study time most students need each day.

SAMPLE DAILY ACTIVITIES CHART

6 to 7 A.M.		Wake up, wash, dress, breakfast
7	8	Take bus or walk to class
8	9	Biology
9	10	Meet with friend
10	11	Chemistry
11	12	Lunch
12	1 P.M.	English
1	2	Sociology

2	3	Biology Club meeting
3	4	Part-time job
4	5	Part-time job
5	6	Part-time job
6	7	Dinner
7	8	Talk with friends
8	9	Housekeeping chores (washing, shopping, etc.)
9	10	Relaxation (TV, listening to records, etc.)
10	11	Writing English paper for next day's class
11		Bed

Examine this sample schedule critically. You may not need to worry about some parts of it, because you don't have a part-time job, don't do housekeeping chores every day, or skip TV. You can look at it objectively. Ask yourself what might be changed, deleted, added, shifted, or combined.

EXERCISE 2

What can you do to organize each day more effectively? Using the schedule you have just completed, answer each of the following questions.

1. What single item seems to take the biggest chunk out of your day?

2. What items can be eliminated from your day most easily during the next weeks?

3. What items must stay? Why?

4. What important items can be shortened?

5. In what ways can you immediately change your daily schedule to obtain more study time?

After you have critically examined this sample schedule, try one of your own following the format in the next exercise.

EXERCISE 1

Make your own Daily Activities Chart. The time column on the left is blank so that you can fill in half (or even quarter) hours. Fill in your actual activities in the column on the right.

Time	Activities

HOW CAN I PLAN FOR THE WEEK OR SEMESTER?

As you have seen, the first step in building a plan of study is to determine how much time you have available for study. The second step, which we will examine now, is to build a study schedule that will show you when and what to study, as well as how much time to spend on each course.

The following suggestions will help you build a study plan that really works.

1. Remember to set aside *two hours of study time for each class per day.* Anything less than an hour does not give you adequate time to read and understand assignments or to write and rewrite papers.

2. You must plan your study hours so that you are studying the same subject *at the same time each day.* Some students can't see the logic behind this suggestion, but experience indicates that when people focus

on the same subject at the same time each day, they build a habit that becomes a natural part of their daily routine.

3. Schedule breaks between study hours. Studies have shown that students who take breaks before changing subject matter emphasis or before going into a second hour on the same subject are more alert and more effective than students who do not take such breaks.

4. When you schedule your study time, you should try to include study periods before and after classes. This gives you an opportunity to review materials before going to class, a matter of major concern when you have an exam or a report. It also gives you an opportunity to review the lecture notes after a class while you still have material fresh in your mind.

5. If you schedule study time in the evening, you should put the subjects that require the most work *first*. Some subjects are more challenging than others — because the course is more difficult, the professor more demanding, or because students have had less experience with the subject in secondary school. Clearly, you should schedule those subjects early, when you are less fatigued, and postpone those subjects you are comfortable with for later.

6. Don't forget your personal and social time! Study time is crucial, but students who omit time for normal recreational activities and exercise tend over a period of time to have more trouble concentrating on their assignments. Wise students build recreational time into their schedules.

Before you plan your weekly or semester schedule, remember the purposes behind this planning:

- You want to control and organize your time so that you always know not only where you are going but when you are leaving and how you are getting there.

- You need to build into your plan at least one hour of study time for each hour of class time if you expect to succeed in college.

- You must also schedule time for recreation and exercise in order to succeed.

In essence, you want to control your time rather than having your time control you.

EXERCISE 3

Examine the following weekly schedule and note what may be wrong with it.

Time	Monday	Tuesday	Wednesday	Thursday	Friday	Weekends
6–8	------------------------- breakfast, dress, and travel -------------------------					
8–9	English	Sociology	English	Sociology	English	
9–10	Study Chemistry	Study	Study Chemistry	open	Study Chemistry	
10–11	Chemistry	Psychology	Chemistry	open	Chemistry	
11–12	Calculus	Study Psychology	Calculus	open	Study Psychology	
12–1	--------------------------------------- Lunch ---------------------------------------					
1–2	Study Calculus	open	Study Calculus	open	Study Calculus	
2–5	----------------------------------- part-time job -----------------------------------					
5–6	--------------------------------------- dinner ---------------------------------------					
6–7	------------------------------------- recreation -------------------------------------					
7–10	--------------------------------------- study ---------------------------------------					
10–11	------------------------------------- recreation -------------------------------------					

What advice might you give the student who follows this particular schedule? Using the following questions to guide you, write a short letter to the student suggesting changes in his or her personal study plan.

1. What is being neglected in this plan?
2. What, if anything, is being overemphasized?
3. Can corners be cut? Where?
4. What hours has this person left unaccounted for?
5. In what ways might the study plan be improved?

EXERCISE 4

At this point, you should be able to set up an efficient study plan for yourself. Try one using the following grid:

Time	Monday	Tuesday	Wednesday	Thursday	Friday	Saturday	Sunday
7–8							
8–9							
9–10							
10–11							
11–12							
12–1							
1–2							
2–3							
3–4							
4–5							
5–6							
6–7							
7–8							
8–9							
9–10							
10–11							
11–12							
12–1							

WHAT MUST BE DONE FIRST?

Once you have established a plan of study for the day or week, you find yourself in a familiar predicament: Several jobs pop up at once in a given time slot. What should you do? Which comes first? Which can be postponed? The way out of this all-too-frequent dilemma for many students is to make a *priority list*.

A priority list, as used by many successful students, is a list of items that must be done by the day's end. Some items on the list are very important, while others are not quite as important but nevertheless must be attended to before going to bed. The point is that with a schedule as busy as yours, a number of details must be taken care of, and it is up to you to set reasonable priorities.

Here is an example. One person's list may contain the following items:

1. Get car fixed.

2. Set up new ride back and forth to school.

3. Buy notebook paper.

4. Return call to friend by 5:00 P.M.

5. Write rough draft of composition.

6. Make dentist appointment.

7. Read Chapter 4 in sociology textbook.

8. Check game score on late news.

All these items are important to the person who made the list, but some clearly are more important than others. To get ahead in college, this person needs to place numbers 5 and 7 at the top of the list. However, if the student has a broken car, getting a ride to class the next day must come first. Each priority list is unique, but each demands considerable thinking.

You can make a daily priority list as well as a weekly one. Experiment to discover which works best for you. Once you have made the list, remember to carry it with you — perhaps inside the front or back cover of your notebook. As you complete a job, you check it off. As new tasks confront you, you can add them to your list and later work them into a reasonable order according to priority.

The values of such lists are:

You get the most important jobs done first.

You tend to get more done than if you functioned without any system at all.

Most important, you will find that a priority list frees your mind of annoying details that can hinder your concentration when you are studying.

HOW CAN AN ASSIGNMENT CALENDAR HELP ME ORGANIZE MY TIME?

An assignment calendar gives you a clear picture of what is expected of you daily, weekly, and monthly during the term or semester. It should reflect *all* short- and long-term assignments and examinations. The calendar should be hung in a place where you will see it each day, so it will serve as a constant reminder of what needs to be done and when.

Here is an example of a typical student's assignment calendar:

OCTOBER

Sunday	Monday	Tuesday	Wednesday	Thursday	Friday	Saturday
1	2	3 History quiz	4	5	6	7
8	9	10	11 Calculus exam	12	13	14 Computer available
15	16	17	18 Psychology midterm	19	20	21
22	23 Oral report History	24	25	26	27	28
29	30	31 English paper due				

EXERCISE 5

Begin your own personal assignment calendar. Either purchase a large wall calendar or draw one of your own based upon your pocket calendar. Make sure the individual day blocks are large enough to write in more than one assignment or examination. (Unfortunately, sometimes two or more tests or papers are due on the same day!)

EXERCISE 6

Many students prepare a Course Organization Sheet for each of their classes.

Here is the form for such a sheet. Complete it for one of your classes, and consider doing one for each of the others.

COURSE ORGANIZATION SHEET

Course title: _____

Instructor and office hours: _____

Textbook(s): _____

Course requirements: _____

_____

_____

_____

_____

_____

Grade Breakdown   **Dates Due**

quizzes =   _____   _____

exams =   _____   _____

midterms =   _____   _____

finals =   _____   _____

Additional

papers =   _____   _____

projects =   _____   _____

labs =   _____   _____

other =   _____   _____

HOW CAN I MAKE THE BEST USE OF TIME SET ASIDE FOR STUDY?

You can learn to organize your time by developing a personal plan of study with daily and weekly schedules, priority lists, and an assignment calendar. However, you still may find yourself unable to make the best use of the time set aside for study.

Imagine this situation: You are reading a twenty-page psychology assignment for a class discussion the next day. You find that your mind keeps wandering every few pages at first and then, later, every few paragraphs. Noises in the study area, people seen from the corners of your eyes, even words in the printed text — all cause your attention to stray from the task of studying.

What can you do to keep your mind on the job? To improve your concentration? There are several techniques you can try.

First you must adopt a positive attitude about the assignment. You must decide that this reading and study is what you are going to do no matter what else is happening around you. Once you have made this commitment, you are halfway there! The second step is to establish a purpose for reading and study; by doing this you become an active rather than a passive participant in your learning. You can concentrate more easily on predetermined activities such as searching for answers to questions that you made up before reading. The third step is to preread the material. When you skim the assignment before actual reading, you get a rough overall view of what the author plans to discuss and what the assignment is all about. The last step is to try to see relationships between the new material you are reading and information you already have. Looking for relationships helps you to focus attention on the pages of the book.

In the chapters that follow you will have several opportunities to experiment with these steps and others. You will learn to use them as you tackle more and more difficult assignments.

Now let's examine some specific suggestions for helping you make the most of your study time.

1. Set realistic goals for study.   Decide what you are going to do and how long you think it will take you to complete the activity. For example, you decide to do ten problems in calculus, allowing yourself five minutes per problem. Since you know from experience that this is a realistic goal, you will find it easier to focus your attention on the task before you.

2. Take a short break after completing each study goal.   As you learned earlier, short breaks give your mind a chance to rest and refocus.

3. Break down large tasks into small ones.   At times you will have assignments that are so long you will feel there is no end in sight! For example, you may have to read and outline three 30-page chapters in your chemistry textbook for the next class in order to have the background to understand the lecture. You may realize at the last minute that you have only a day and a half to do this job. If you try to do the whole job at one sitting, your mind will surely wander. However, if you set the more realistic goal of dividing the task into three separate parts, you will find each manageable and your concentration improved.

4. Combine different types of study activities.   Often, doing *all* reading or *all* writing activities will cause your mind to wander. Too much of the same activity becomes fatiguing and annoying. Schedule your work so that you spend one sitting on a writing task and another on a straight reading job. Some students, turn reading assignments into writing activities by writing out notes, making summaries as they go along, or writing out main ideas as they read.

5. Don't forget to maintain a positive attitude.   When you are forced to complete an assignment that you do not enjoy, you may find it difficult to concentrate. Make sure you have broken the large task into smaller, more reasonable ones. You can keep telling yourself that the next chunk may be more enjoyable!

EXERCISE 7

Many students space their study time by using a study cycle plan. They study for sixty minutes, take a fifteen-to-twenty-minute break, review for fifteen minutes, and then continue the cycle.

Examine the study cycle presented below, then try it during your next study session. Complete the exercise by writing a one-paragraph description of your experience with the plan.

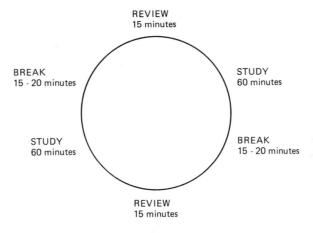

Figure 2-1

HOW CAN I IMPROVE MY CONCENTRATION WHEN STUDYING?

You may schedule your time carefully and do all you can to make the best use of it, but still have problems concentrating on the material. You may be bothered by *outside distractions* such as people walking by or someone playing your favorite song in the next room. You may be bothered by *inside distractions* — such thoughts going through your head as, "I need a date for the party Friday night'' or ''I need thirty dollars for that textbook.'' Your concentration may also be put off by lack of interest — you find yourself saying, ''Ten more pages to go . . . six more . . . three more'' or ''I already know this.''

Because these sources of poor concentration can cause you major problems in college, you need to examine each carefully.

Outside distractions.   These tend to come from the physical surroundings; they can break your train of thought instantly. They range from a passing ambulance with its sirens on full blast to the ticking of a nearby clock. The best thing to say about outside distractions is that *you can control them*. Close windows, put the clock in the bureau drawer, shut doors, and so on. Most important, you can deliberately seek out areas that are relatively free from distractions. You can, for example, sit at a table in a back corner of the library where few people go rather than sit next to the busy front door. You can also choose to study at a time of day when other people are not about making noise. You do not have to be a victim of most outside distractions!

Inside distractions.   Inside distractions come from your own mind and are harder to control. They include thoughts of home and family, personal responsibilities, assignments, work, friends, and so on. The best way to control these distractions is to prepare a priority list. Get down on paper those tasks you *must* do at once — and *do them* if they outrank study at the moment! You will find that writing down the thoughts that pop into your head will help you to control them. Once you have jotted down your concern (about family, social life, work, money), the problem will not go away, but it will recede from the fore-front of your mind and free you for the study task.

Lack of interest.   This is the worst problem of the three. What can you do when you lack interest? Maybe you should think about dropping the course. (You can come back and take a required course at a later time when perhaps you will be more able to cope with it.) The advice given earlier about being an active rather than a passive reader may help. When you read to find answers to questions or test predictions, your mind is more apt to be active. When you take notes, your body is busy and your mind tends to follow along. More suggestions for becoming an active rather than a passive student follow in other chapters of this book.

Study Tips to Improve Concentration

1. **Study alone.**   Usually it is best to work by yourself. As you continue through this book, you'll see there are times when it pays to exchange

ideas with other students so that you can all better understand and remember material. However, most of the time you'll find it far more productive to work solo, free from distractions of social chitchat, music, eating, and so on.

2. Position your body for alertness.   Some people learn while studying in bed or on the floor or stretched out in a comfortable recliner chair. However, you will find that your mind functions better most of the time when you sit at a table or desk in a straight-backed chair. The more you relax your body, the more inclined it is to doze off or go to sleep.

3. Choose a good study area.   You should study in an area that provides you with a good table or desk and a proper chair. You also need good light and ventilation. Lots of space is a help so you can spread out your books and papers. Items that should *not* go into your study area: television sets, radios, phonographs, newspapers, magazines, and any other potential distractions.

4. Check your physical condition.   If your physical needs have not been met, they can be a cause of distraction. It is almost impossible to study effectively while your stomach is rumbling from hunger or your throat is dry. It is difficult to study when you are tired. Your mind cannot process new information while you are nodding off because of fatigue. Regular meals, sleep, and exercise are crucial to efficient study.

5. Keep study materials handy.   There are certain basic materials you should have on hand while working. Having them within reach prevents unnecessary trips out of the study area with all the diversions and distractions such trips always seem to include. You may need:

Dictionary

Textbook

Atlas

Paper of all kinds (typing, tracing, carbon, graph, lined, etc.)

Pencils and pens

Calculator

Colored markers

Paper clips

Scissors

Elastics

Tape

Glue

Compass and protractor

Typewriter

Each person's list will vary. The important point is that you should come to your study area well supplied. Think in advance of all the things you will need, and make sure you have them available.

What else can go wrong? Despite all their precautions, many college students report other study interferences. Some of these are noted here with some possible solutions for you to consider.

1. You think of other things to do.   This happens to almost everyone. In the middle of a chapter, something pops into your mind: "Oh, I must remember to do that before I leave the library," "I need to speak to so-and-so about next week's assignment," or "I promised to call home and forgot." Such thoughts take your attention away from the printed page. *The solution*: Keep one page at the back (or front) of your notebook for "Things to Do." When these distracting thoughts come to mind while studying, write them on the list for later consideration and free your mind for work. Some students keep *two* lists: one for tasks that must be completed at once and the second for jobs that can wait a day or two. Writing them down, simple as that sounds, does help you to concentrate on study.

2. You start to worry about a problem.   A word or phrase in a book or something in the room may remind you of a real, often personal, problem that needs your attention. Because the problem is serious to you, it takes your mind from study. *The solution*: Write it down, possibly on another notebook page reserved for "Problems." Decide at once whether it deserves immediate attention or can be considered at another time. If you decide the problem is of major importance in your life, *stop studying*. Take care of the problem as best you can, or at least take the first steps in solving it. You cannot study otherwise. On the other hand, if the problem has no immediate solution, write it down on your "Problems" page and go back to work.

3. You lack the confidence needed to do the assignment.   Remember, everyone sometimes doubts his or her ability to do a job. Dwelling on these doubts takes time and energy from jobs that need doing. *The solution*: Break up major tasks into smaller parts and concentrate on doing these smaller parts one at a time. Put all your time and energy into completing the parts; as each is completed, your confidence will improve. The most challenging jobs in life are done this way: one step at a time.

4. You are nervous.   Nervousness is caused usually by excess energy generated by your body to help you do important jobs. All students get nervous at least once in a while. *The solution*: Divide jobs into smaller parts and do one at a time, worrying only about the one you are doing at the moment. As you complete more and more, your nervousness should go away. In extreme cases, jogging or walking or other exercise may help, as does a hot bath or shower. One thing for sure: In the long run pills don't help, and, may do damage to your body and mind.

5. You are depressed.   Depression may be caused by loneliness, homesickness, money problems, grades, friends, and so forth. The list sometimes seems endless. Depression may also be caused by a variety of physical problems. If you are sometimes depressed, you should accept the condition as part of normal life. If you are always depressed, you should check with a physician or counselor. *The solution*: For temporary depression, try exercise or a change of activities. Plan a more regular schedule, keep regular hours, make sure you eat correctly and get exercise. If your depression lingers, check with the college health office or your own family physician. You may need some medication or other professional intervention.

6. You are blocked.   Workers in all fields sometimes are blocked, and find that they simply cannot work. Writers, both professional and student, talk about writer's block. During the semester, you may find yourself in this predicament: You just can't get going! *The solution*: Again, break the task up into small chunks. You may not be able to write an entire research paper, but you can — no matter how blocked — write one page, one paragraph, or one sentence. You may not be able to complete a lab assignment in its entirety, but you can at least start and do one small chunk of it. Once you have completed a part, it is often necessary to force yourself to do one other small part. Whatever you do, don't say, "I'll come back to this later, when I feel better about doing it." That is *not* the way to overcome a block.

EXERCISE 8

Think about each of these questions, then write out your answers for later discussion.

1. Why is it important to organize and master your time?
2. What are some of the problems you will encounter if you do not follow a master schedule?
3. Should you study alone or with others?

4. What is the value of occasionally studying with others?

5. What can you do to improve your concentration while studying?

6. In what ways does your present study area need to be changed?

7. What changes can you make now to improve your study habits?

8. What outside distractions bother you? What can you do about them?

9. What inside distractions bother you? What can you do to control them?

10. What can you do when you lack confidence in your ability to complete an assignment?

EXERCISE 9

To help you evaluate your study areas, complete the following chart by writing "yes" or "no" under each heading. When you finish, examine your responses and decide which place is best for effective study.

	Library	Dorm Room	Home
1. I spend time talking to friends.			
2. I listen to music.			
3. There is a great deal of movement.			
4. People interrupt me.			
5. The lighting is poor.			
6. The chairs are too comfortable.			
7. It is either too warm or too chilly.			
8. I can spread my materials out on a table or desk.			
9. I am comfortable and alert here.			
10. The phone disturbs me.			
11. I can keep all my study materials handy.			

	Library	Dorm Room	Home
12. I can maintain a good sitting position.			
13. I can be alone.			
14. I seem to tire more quickly here.			
15. I seem to do my best work here.			

POINTS TO REMEMBER ABOUT TIME MASTERY

1. Maintain a weekly and semester study schedule.
2. Divide and balance study time and social activities.
3. Be consistent in your plans.
4. Use an assignment calendar.
5. Study in a proper setting.
6. Study alone.
7. Know what is expected of you and when assignments are due.
8. Carry a priority list.
9. Divide big jobs into smaller ones.
10. Keep a positive attitude toward study.

2
MASTERY TEST

To check how well you understand Chapter 2, complete the following true-or-false test by circling the correct response beside each statement.

1. A priority list tells you exactly what to do first. **T F**

2. A daily activities chart shows you where you are wasting your time. **T F**

3. You should set aside two hours of study time for each hour of class time. **T F**

4. You should study the same subject at the same time each day. **T F**

5. You need to study routine, mechanical material first, before you study more difficult material. **T F**

6. Once you start, keep studying without taking breaks. **T F**

7. Break down large tasks into smaller ones. **T F**

8. Outside distractions cannot be controlled. **T F**

9. It is best to study in a group. **T F**

10. It is possible to study when you are hungry. **T F**

3

Learning to Listen to Lectures and Class Discussions

INTRODUCTION AND OVERVIEW

Much college instruction occurs in lectures and class discussions. You need to listen to pick out main ideas, note important information, and organize the ideas and information in such a way that they make sense to you and will be more easily remembered.

Learning to listen is one of the most valuable skills you can acquire as a college student. Your success in the next years may be directly related to your ability to gain the maximum amount of information and understanding in oral language situations.

This chapter examines some of the characteristics of classroom listening and suggests a variety of ways for you to improve your college listening skills, as well as techniques for better note taking in lectures and discussions.

SUGGESTED GUIDE QUESTIONS

1. How can you improve your lecture listening skills?

2. What can you do to better focus your attention during a lecture?

3. What steps can you take to remember more of the material presented in lectures and discussions?

4. How can you take more effective notes in lectures and discussions?

5. How can you improve your listening skills and participation in group discussions?

HOW DOES LECTURE LISTENING DIFFER FROM REGULAR LISTENING?

Most people listen a great deal. Various studies have shown that the average person devotes as much as 45 percent of the time spent each day in verbal communication listening (compared to only 30 percent in speaking, 16 percent in reading, and 9 percent in writing). However, most ordinary verbal communication is unstructured and spontaneous; much of it is intended to establish good relations with other people and facilitate the business of life. A person does not need to learn to do this kind of listening.

Classroom listening, whether in discussion groups or in the lecture hall, is different. Speakers tend to have specific messages. They think through their communications beforehand and structure them in some way. If they are experienced speakers, they also tend to use certain signals and follow certain plans. In such situations, listeners should learn how to follow the plans, pick up the signals, note the structures, and figure out the intent of the speakers.

Much of your college learning will take place in lecture halls. Professors will prepare rather formal talks that are intended to catch your interest, share information not in the textbooks, and add other information from different points of view. Many college students ask why professors lecture at all: "Can't material be presented through films? demonstrations? outside readings?" The answer, of course, is that course material can — and often is — given in a variety of ways, but through the years lecturing has proven to be one of the best ways of getting lots of information across rapidly. A teacher can outline the basic principles of the course and *say* these more effectively than most students can get them on their own. By presenting information orally, a teacher can emphasize what is especially important in a course and add explanations that are not always available in books. The teacher can pace an oral presentation to fit the needs of students in the class; that is, information and ideas that seem puzzling to a group may be highlighted and discussed in greater depth, while other information that everyone seems to understand may be passed over more quickly. A good lecturer has another advantage over a printed book. He or she can actually see how learners respond: Expressions of puzzlement or frustration may be noted at once and adjustments made in the lecture. That eye-to-eye contact allows the speaker to take advantage of the feelings and immediate responses of listeners, interjecting serious-ness or humor or, when necessary, repeating or reemphasizing.

Classroom listening, the kind you will have to do in lectures and discussion groups, is a special variety of listening. As in ordinary social listening, you must pay attention and try to make sense out of the language you hear. However, in the classroom you are expected to do more. You must:

Pay especially careful attention.

Be aware of the speaker's plan and purpose.

Set purposes for your own listening.

Note main points and important information.

Be able to retell the gist of the speaker's message in your own words.

EXERCISE 1

To obtain an approximate evaluation of your own lecture listening skills now, have someone read aloud to you this section taken from a college lecture. When you have listened, take the brief test given below.

Listening and reading are dissimilar in a number of ways and these differences need to be examined in order to understand better the ways in which the two seem comparable and, perhaps, mutually reinforcing.

It may be noted first that situations or communications contexts are different in a number of respects. Readers are usually alone with the printed page. They can neither ask it questions nor pick up signals apart from the print the writer has indicated. Listeners, on the other hand, can interrupt, cajole, insist upon clarification. They can also take advantage of visual signals such as facial expressions, eyebrow movements, subtle bodily twitches, and so forth. They can also note the ways speakers stress certain words in sentences. They know, for example, that when a speaker stresses *boys* in the sentence, "The boys on our street like Tom," he or she is implying strongly that the girls and/or the adults on the street do not like Tom. The use of italics, capital letters, or underlining never quite replace the simple tricks of emphasis that speakers and listeners know from childhood.

The whole speaking-listening context is influenced also by considerations that rarely influence readers. Listeners can be powerfully affected by the loudness or softness of the speaker's voice, by the speaker's politeness or rudeness, by seemingly trivial and nonverbal features such as eye color, taste in clothes, hair style, even jewelry. All these nonverbal features actually shape the actual message that listeners pick up. As one psychologist has noted, when you deliver a public speech against a backdrop of imposing martial band music and fluttering flags, you get an impression of dignity and power you might not otherwise get.

There is another way in which listening differs markedly from reading: Each takes place in a very different *time* context. Readers can go back to check on facts and interpretations of facts. They can stop when fatigued. They can look ahead to check the writer's plan and direction. They can even refuse to engage in the communications act by shutting the book. Listeners can do none of these things. They may sometimes be able to interrupt a speaker, but they cannot go back in time to discover what they missed. They must trust memories which may be spotty or inaccurate. They cannot go forward to see where the speaker is headed.

Reading and listening, then, are not the same, but rather two different modes of language reception, each influenced by different factors and each following a different game plan. Learning to be an effective and efficient reader does not necessarily make one an effective and efficient listener.

After you have listened to this "lecture," try to answer the following questions to see how well you are able to get a speaker's message. The answers are all within the above paragraphs, so you can check your skills by rereading what you have just listened to.

1. What three features may be found in a speaking-listening situation that are not found in a reading situation?

2. What three features may be found in a reading situation but not in a lecture situation?

EXERCISE 2

After careful thought, write out your answers to the following questions. These will help you better understand the next section on improving your lecture listening skills.

1. Did your mind wander at all as you listened? Why? Why not?

2. What might you do to help you focus your attention better on the lecture?

3. Did you remember everything you heard in the lecture? Why? Why not?

4. Why do you think you remember some points and not others?

5. What can you do to remember more?

HOW CAN I IMPROVE MY LECTURE LISTENING SKILLS?

There are four definite strategies you can use to improve your listening skills in the classroom. You can prepare for lectures in advance, listen with a well-defined purpose, take notes, and summarize the speaker's main points. These four strategies are discussed in detail here.

Prepare Yourself

Considerable evidence from research supports the belief that when learners have an overview of what they are going to learn before they learn it, they learn it better. Army sergeants used to say of recruits, "First, you tell 'em what you're going to tell 'em; then you tell 'em; and then you tell 'em what you just told 'em." Recent research findings say those overviews provide learners in advance with an approximate idea of the learning task, thus helping them define it more clearly before they begin learning. Some research also shows that overviews serve to remind learners of information they may already have about the topics to be learned, thus making learning easier and faster. (For more information about this research, see the books suggested under References, p. 299.)

You can prepare to read and study a textbook chapter by previewing it quickly to get an overview, but this is not possible in the case of a lecture. What can you do to prepare for a lecture?

First, you can find out in advance what topics will be treated in the lecture. Usually, lecturers distribute a list of course topics during the first week of the course. You can check the list to discover what is coming next. Many instructors remind students of the subject of the next class or provide enough clues so that they can predict the area to be covered.

Once you have identified the topic or topics, you can prepare yourself by reading ahead in the textbook. If you know, for example, that the next lecture will deal with "The Beginnings of Capitalism," you can scan the appropriate pages of the book to give yourself an overview. If your own course text seems too difficult, you can obtain an overview of the topic in the library by quickly reading appropriate sections of other textbooks.

You can also prepare by rereading your previous notes. These will contain references to points the lecturer believes are important, and will help you develop a "mind set" to learn the new material.

Proper preparation can introduce you to important words and terms. When you spot specialized terminology in your reading overviews, note such words in your notebook with definitions obtained from either the textbook's glossary or a dictionary. Your learning during the lecture will be greater when you know the specialized vocabulary of the lecturer.

Set a Purpose for Listening

Sitting through a course lecture may seem to be a learning experience for some students; for most, it is not. As you listen in class, you need to listen with a definite purpose. This helps you focus your attention on the material and often serves to assist you as you process the new information and try to make sense of it.

Where do you find a purpose? One way is to listen to find answers to questions you have about the subject. The time you spent in preparation should have led you to a variety of questions. For example, most of the headnotes and subtitles in the textbook may be turned into questions: "The Causes of the Great Depression" may become your personal question, "What were the causes of the Great Depression?" Often your quick preview of the textbook material will lead you to other questions: If you noticed that the textbook author discussed political causes, you ask the question, "What were the political causes?"

As you prepare for the day's lecture, write down in your notebook questions that come to you. Then, as you sit in the classroom, listen to find answers. Your note taking will tend to be more systematic. You can still jot down other things the teacher says, but now you have a real reason for listening: You want to find out how the teacher answers your questions. You will find that you can focus your attention more easily on the material; you are no longer a passive listener sitting there while words flow over your head (or "in one ear, out the other," as one student puts it).

Another way to establish a purpose for listening is to try to predict possible test items. In your survey of the related reading you can note topics, ideas, and items of information that might lead to test items; then, as you listen to the actual lecture, check to see if this data is repeated or stressed. After class, when you review your notes, try to create good test questions from the material you have collected. When you have listed several questions, turn these into multiple-choice items, true-false items, or sentence-completion test items. Try, too, to reword some of your questions as directions for essay tests.

Listening to generate test questions is not only an excellent way to improve lecture listening skills, but is also an effective approach to test taking. With practice, some students become extremely proficient at predicting test items, using these as they study and review for examinations. As they have opportunities to compare their own items with test items actually appearing on an instructor's examinations, they learn to rephrase, sharpen, and refine their questions while at the same time becoming more aware of the kinds of questions certain teachers tend to ask. (For more information on test taking, see Chapter 10, "Learning to Take Tests in College.")

Make Notes as You Listen

There are a number of important reasons for note taking during lectures and class discussions. Eight are described briefly here.

Note taking helps you focus attention.   Your mind may wander during even the best lectures. You are less apt to be distracted if you are keeping a record of the lecture in your notebook.

It is an indispensable memory aid.   Most people retain only a fraction of the information they hear. By writing key ideas and recording important information you can keep these in memory longer. You can also go back to your notes later to make sure data is retained in memory.

It helps you note main points.   Most lectures are organized around one or more main ideas. As you listen with a pen in your hand, you are more apt to note and record these key ideas.

It helps you see the speaker's plan.   Speakers tend to structure their lectures according to some plan. They may present material in chronological order, enumerate (or list) items, compare and contrast, or explain causes and effects. When you take notes, you become more aware of speakers' plans and, therefore, more likely to see the underlying structure of the lecture.

It helps you keep track of specialized vocabulary.   Often a speaker will use terms and phrases that you do not yet understand. By copying these (even with phonetic spellings), you can later check them in your textbook's glossary or a dictionary. Remember, you cannot really make sense of a message, whether spoken or written, when you do not know the meanings of the words used.

It provides you with a record of course lectures.   By dating your notes and keeping them in careful order, you give yourself a record of the course.

You can tell what topics were and were not covered, which were emphasized, and which the instructor seems to consider of less importance.

It gives you a valuable source of information for test preparation.   If you have taken careful notes, you have built for yourself a repository of data for test preparation. You can use your notes to refresh your memory prior to midterm and final examinations.

Note taking gives you more control over your own learning.   As you take notes, *you* decide what is and is not important; *you* record the main points and key information; *you* organize the data of the course in a way that is meaningful to you. Good notes provide you with a personal summary of your learning experience.

Specific suggestions for better note taking are given in the next section. These should enable you to better understand and remember material you encounter in your lectures.

Listen to Summarize

One of your responsibilities as a learner is to make sense of what you learn. One way to make sense of your learning is to retell it or explain it to someone else. By listening with this purpose in mind, you enhance the probability of understanding. (For more information on summarizing as a comprehension strategy, see References, p. 299.)

How can you listen to summarize? Four suggestions are made here. (Other ideas for summarizing are found in the next two chapters.)

Immediately after the lecture, carefully tell yourself what you have just heard in as much detail as possible.   Recall: What was the main point of the lecture? What were the most important points? How was the lecture organized? What were the speaker's intentions? What was he or she trying to get across? Some students say that they cannot conveniently sit down after a lecture to make a quiet mental summary. However, you can often find quiet time as you walk from building to building or as you drive home or to work.

Tell someone else what you have just heard.   Some students make it a regular practice to tell a roommate, friend, or relative about their experiences of the day. Retelling the gist of a lecture, however briefly, may often be incorporated into such communications. When another person is not available, imagine one and retell the main points of the lecture to him or her.

Write a summary.   As you will learn in subsequent chapters, writing a summary is one of the most powerful learning tools available to you. When you write a summary, you are forced to decide which ideas are basic and which are peripheral, you must determine the central idea of the lecture, you must sequence your material in a sensible manner; you must, in short, make sense of what you have just heard. Some students make time for summary writing by including it in their end-of-day study schedule; they regularly block off thirty to sixty minutes each evening for a review of the day's notes and the writing of brief recapitulations of each day's lectures.

Make up a news story.   Soon after the lecture, pretend you are a news reporter covering the event. Decide on a headline (usually the main point of the lecture) and which details you will include. The old reporter's format can guide you: Provide answers to the questions *who, what, where, why, when,* and *how.* The "5 *W*'s plus *H*" format gives you a structure for a news story that summarizes the material.

EXERCISE 3

Once you understand the four suggestions made above for improving your lecture listening skills, complete the following Response Sheet for an actual college lecture.

RESPONSE SHEET

Topic of lecture:

Date:

Course:

Preparation

Write here the steps you took to prepare for the lecture. Tell how you knew what the topic would be, give the title of the textbook you used, note the pages you read, and list those vocabulary items you noted.

Purpose for Listening

Write here the questions you developed during preparation time and any predictions you made.

Note Taking

Include here the notes you took during the lecture. (Were you able to answer your questions? Check out your predictions? Did you note main points? The speaker's plan? What specialized terms did you note?)

Summarizing

Write a summary of the lecture.

SUGGESTIONS FOR TAKING EFFECTIVE LECTURE NOTES

Note taking is a highly personal, individualized process. Students take notes in different ways, and what works for one person does not necessarily work for another. You will have to experiment with a variety of techniques before you decide which serve you most effectively. Here are some suggestions to get you started.

Note Answers to Your Own Questions

The previous section emphasized the value of prelistening preparation. Before a lecture, you should check over the appropriate section of your textbook to get a rough idea of what the speaker will discuss. When you do this, you can create for yourself a few questions that you want answered in the lecture. For example, your schedule says that the topic for tomorrow's economics class is capitalism. You can walk into that class cold or you can prepare. If you choose to prepare, you look at your course notes and discover that the reading assignment is a chapter called "Pure Capitalism and the Circular Flow." Before the lecture you should skim the chapter and either (1) make up some questions of your own that you would like to have answered by the speaker, or (2) convert chapter headings into questions. To convert headings into questions, you can follow a simple plan such as the following:

Textbook Headings	Your Questions
Capitalist Ideology	What is "ideology"? What is "capitalist ideology"?

Textbook Headings	Your Questions
Private Property	I know what it means, but what do economists include under this category?
Freedom of Enterprise	What is the meaning of this phrase?
Role of Self-Interest	What is the role of self-interest?
Competition	Do economists define this the same way I do?
Markets and Prices	What are they? What do they have to do with capitalism?
Limited Government	What does government have to do with capitalism? What is "limited" government?

You may also make up questions by examining the previous class's lecture notes. Look at what was discussed and the ways the speaker approached the topic. Devise questions of your own that you think will be useful for tomorrow's class. If the speaker seemed to take a certain point of view about the topic, try to predict what he or she may say about the new topic and then invent appropriate questions.

No matter what your questions are, or how many questions you have, you will find that listening to answer them will focus your attention on the lecture and help you better understand its flow. It is less easy to be distracted when you listen with a clearly defined purpose.

Try to Note the Speaker's Main Ideas

A beginner in a field cannot always discriminate between main and minor ideas, but the process of looking helps him or her to start to weed out the details from the key points. One simple technique is to listen carefully and copy only those ideas that appear to have significance. You may miss some important points, but you are trying. Take your ten or fifteen main ideas away from class and check them against the assignment in the textbook. Compare them with those of other students. It is the active process of trying to find main ideas that will make you a successful student. Here are some clues.

- The speaker may tell you directly: "One important thing to remember is . . ." or "A key point to remember is . . ." Sometimes college teachers hint that a certain item may be a good examination item. Clearly, that is a clue.

- He or she may write on the board. Some teachers make it a point to write key words or phrases on the board. When this happens, you may have been given a powerful hint.

- The speaker may list main points for you. Sometimes he or she may say, "We have three points of importance here" or "Five causes are . . ." Take advantage of these clues; they may be the best of all.

- The speaker may change voice pitch, emphasis, or rate of speed. Such clues are subtle but worth catching. Good lecture listeners are always on their toes to pick up such vocal giveaways.

Look for a Plan

Lectures are not like conversations; they usually have some underlying plan or structure. Students who watch for the plan have a much better chance of grasping the ideas presented. Here are two suggestions to guide you:

Look for familiar organizational patterns. Speakers as well as writers tend to organize their materials according to certain basic, widely used patterns. When you spot a familiar pattern, you can usually get a sense of where the speaker is going and what to look for next. Chapter 6 describes in detail the organizational patterns found in reading assignments. Here they are described briefly so that you may be more aware of them in lectures.

Speakers frequently organize their material in simple *lists*. In other words, they enumerate. For example, a lecturer may say, "There are five important characteristics we need to note," and then discuss them, one at a time. The speaker almost always signals each point by saying "first," "second," "next," or "finally."

Sometimes they follow a simple *sequence*. When the material falls into a time order, for example, speakers may tell what happened first, then what happened next, and so on. They signal their intentions with words such as "first," "second," and so on. The sequence pattern is important; it is also used when speakers want to give directions or explain how to do something.

Speakers often use the *generalization* pattern. They make a general statement about the topic and then provide details or examples. A history professor may say, "The early decades of the century were a time of great social change," and then give several examples to support this statement. The signal words and phrases used with this pattern are "for example," "for instance," "specifically," or "thus."

Sometimes lecturers follow a *cause-and-effect* pattern. They present a cause and its effects, various effects and possible causes, or other cause-effect relationships. You can often spot the cause-and-effect plan when you hear "because," "therefore," or similar signals.

Another familiar pattern is *comparison and contrast*. The speaker tries to explain one item by comparing or contrasting it with another. In order to explain life in colonial America, a history professor may compare it with life in twentieth-century America. The signal words and phrases to watch for are "on one hand," "in comparison," "similarly," "in contrast," and so on.

Often speakers find that the best way to organize certain material is by a simple *question-answer* plan. They ask questions and provide their own answers. You can note these by the obvious signals: "who," "what," "how," "why," or similar question introduction words.

As you look for familiar organizational patterns to guide your listening, remember two important points:

- **Speakers may shift from one pattern to another.** They may start with a simple enumeration pattern and then shift to comparison and contrast or to a generalization supported by examples. They may start with cause and effect but then further develop some of their material using a sequence pattern. You cannot be expected to follow every pattern used in a lecture, but you can take advantage of your knowledge of organizational patterns to better follow and understand a lecture and to take more effective lecture notes.

- **Speakers usually signal patterns with familiar words and phrases.** "First," "second," and "finally" signal both the enumeration and sequence patterns; "because" and "therefore" signal the cause-and-effect pattern. After you have become familiar with commonly used signal words and phrases, it is easier to recognize widely used patterns of organization. (You will find a complete list of signal words and phrases in Chapter 6.)

Use a "plan guide" as you take notes.   To do this, you block off your paper into four sections as follows:

- **Introduction**   This may serve as an attention getter. It is that part of the lecture when the speaker connects the talk with previous class lectures or relates it to textbook reading assignments. Often it includes an overview or some guide questions. Jot down pertinent comments in the Introduction block.

- **Main Idea**   At some point at the beginning of the lecture the speaker may indicate the main idea or thesis of the talk. Write this down. If it is not indicated early in the lecture, leave your Main Idea block open and try to fill it in later in the class.

- **_Body_**   Here is where the main body of material is noted. Write down the key ideas, supporting details, examples, and references. This is the section that may be organized according to one of the organizational patterns. Watch for a sequence, an enumeration, cause and effect, comparison and contrast, or generalization. Often speakers shift plans as they speak, so be wary.

- **_Summary_**   Allow a block at the end for a summary. Sometimes lecturers provide a brief summary to pull their discussion together; at other times you will need to fill this in yourself.

Outline

Many people recommend outlining as a good note-taking technique. However, you should remember that outlining works better with reading assignments than with lecture note taking. When you read you have the book in front of you and can take advantage of subtitles, headings, and paragraphs. You can also reread to check on the outline as you go along. In a lecture you have no typographical clues and no time for checking because a speaker moves along rapidly. Sometimes a speaker will share an outline with a class and actually write notes in outline form on the chalkboard. When a speaker does this, consider yourself fortunate and take your notes in outline form. Otherwise, be wary; outline if you can. If you cannot, then take your lecture notes in your personal system and later reorganize them into an outline form.

There is another form of outlining you may like to try for both lecture and reading note taking. It is called _mapping_ and is done as follows: Jot down the main topic in the middle of your page. As the talk proceeds, write down the various points the speaker makes in relation to the main topic. As the speaker adds more information, write this in relation to the topic and subtopics. When you make notations, try to relate them to one another with straight lines or arrows. A "map" of the section you have just read might look something like Figure 3–1 on page 60.

Keep Track of Key Words

You cannot understand spoken or written communications when you do not understand all the words. In a reading situation, unfamiliar words can be checked in the glossary of the textbook or in a dictionary. When confronted by a term you do not know, put down your book and obtain a meaning before you continue. However, this is rarely possible in a lecture situation. What should you do?

- Copy down new words as you hear them. Because of the spelling problems, you may need to copy them phonetically — _but copy_

LECTURE NOTES

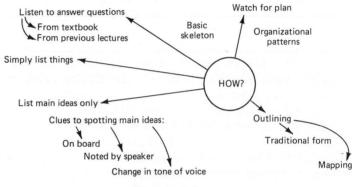

Figure 3-1

them. You can check the correct spellings later as you look up the meaning.

- When the lecturer writes a new term on the chalkboard, copy it immediately into your notes. When a definition is provided, copy that too. On those occasions when the lecturer takes the time to note a word, you can be fairly sure it is important for understanding the material.

- During the time you set aside for lecture preparation, watch for specialized vocabulary. When certain terms and phrases are used in the chapter, you can assume that many of them will be used in the lecture too. Make sure you check out their definitions in the glossary or dictionary.

Allow Space in Your Notes for Summaries

We have emphasized the value of summarizing as a study tool. When you take lecture notes, you do not have time to summarize each new section of the lecture. However, you can set space aside in your notes for later summarizations. When you realize that the speaker has completed one part of the lecture and is about to move into new territory, block off several lines so that you can later write a brief summary. It is during the process of writing in summaries afterward that much of the lecture material is comprehended and taken into memory.

One final note needs to be made about lecture note taking: *Do not try to copy everything!* Some students, in their eagerness to succeed, try to get down on paper every remark made by a lecturer. This is a dangerous practice for at least two reasons. In the first place, you will miss large amounts of material while you are trying to write. Speakers move rapidly. As you try to catch every word, they move ahead to explain other matters. You cannot win at this game. In the second place, note taking is recommended as a *process*. Its purpose is not to capture on paper the speaker's every word, but rather to give learners an opportunity to better process incoming information. It is in the note-taking procedure that you force your mind to note main ideas, recognize key words and concepts, and make sense out of the speaker's language. Instead of copying everything, listen to answer questions, note key ideas, outline, map, and identify important new words and phrases.

NOTE TAKING IN MATH AND SCIENCE LECTURES

The above suggestions for better note taking will help you in all your classes. However, in your science and mathematics lectures you may need to do the following:

1. In addition to copying the problems that instructors may place on the chalkboard, make sure you also copy the *explanations* that accompany the presentation of problems. Get the basic material from the board into your notebook; in addition, get all the directions and comments instructors make as they discuss it. You'll need the explanations as you go over the problems later.

2. When instructors move too rapidly for you, leave *blank spaces* in your notes. These will remind you later that you did indeed miss important explanations and encourage you to go back after class to fill them in, either by talking to the instructor or another student.

3. If possible, get each step in a process down in your notes *in sequence.* This means that your notes will often be numbered: 1, 2, 3, and so on. When you realize later that you missed one or more steps, you can again call for help. ("What's step 5?" "I missed number 6 — what is it?")

4. Continue the practice of *summarizing*. Leave space in your lecture notes so that you can go back later and write brief summaries. Ask yourself about a particular problem: What is this really all about? Then, in your own words, write a two- or three-sentence summary that pulls the new ideas together. The actual process of writing a summary is a powerful tool for understanding. The summaries themselves will be valuable when you review and study for an examination.

5. Make sure you keep track of *vocabulary*. When instructors use technical words that are new to you, write them down immediately. Definitions may be given for them in class, but sometimes not. When you have no meanings for unfamiliar words, you cannot hope to comprehend the lectures. Your job is to check the course textbook after class and make sure you have definitions that you understand placed beside all technical terms in your notebook. (Look in the book's glossary, and then go back to the chapter to note how the unfamiliar words are used by the author in discussion.) In math class, you need to be especially careful because many common English words have specialized meanings in math (*cone, angle, point, field, group, set, mean, radical, plane, degree*, and so on). Make sure you get these, too, in your notebook list of technical words and terms.

6. Learn how the *symbol systems* work. The languages of mathematics and science includes highly evolved, arbitrary symbol systems. Just as you must know the technical vocabularies of these fields to understand the material, so must you know their symbol systems. It is wise to keep a section of your notebook for a "dictionary of symbols." Many of these are explained in the textbook; many will be explained in class. You need to keep track of them and make sure you learn them as the course moves ahead.

WHAT'S THE BEST WAY TO KEEP LECTURE NOTES?

Note taking is a highly personal matter. Each student develops his or her own approach. Some approaches incorporate all the techniques suggested here; others may focus on only two or three; some may be based on a single technique such as mapping.

However, no matter what kind of note-taking approach you develop, you will need a *record-keeping system*. To take effective notes day after day, in class after class, and not have a system for keeping track of your notes could be disasterous.

Here, then, are ten suggestions for organizing a record-keeping system:

1. Keep your notes in a loose-leaf notebook. Spiral-type notebooks, pocket-size booklets, tablets, and folders of separate pages do not work as well for your purposes as a standard, full-sized 8½-by-11-inch loose-leaf, hardcovered notebook that holds lined paper with full margins.

2. Set aside a separate page for each lecture, date it, and record across the top the topic for the day.

3. Write the assignment down as soon as it is given.

4. When the instructor distributes duplicated study guides, bibliographies, or assignments, punch holes in them and place them immediately into your notebook so they cannot be misplaced.

5. Take notes only on one side of each page. Allow ample margins and space at the top and bottom of each page for further notes and comments as you study.

6. Write as legibly as you can.

7. Use a simple abbreviation system such as the following:

e.g.	for example	+	and
ex	example	$\therefore$	therefore
w/	with	$\Rightarrow$	implies
info	information	def	definition
$\leftarrow$	results from	$\rightarrow$	leads to

In time, you will develop personal symbols and abbreviations of your own in certain fields of study: *rdg* for *reading*, *comp* for *comprehension*, *wr* for *write*, and so on. In scientific fields you will find commonly used abbreviations; get these from your science books and note them as your instructors use them in class. Some dictionaries also offer lists of widely used abbreviations. Do not hesitate to use them.

8. Mark dates for examinations.

9. Keep notes from different courses separated by cardboard dividers.

10. Make sure your name, address, and telephone number are clearly printed in the front of the notebook.

This book becomes a major key to college success! Losing it can be a disaster.

LISTENING SKILLS IN DISCUSSION GROUPS

Some of your classes will be discussions rather than lectures. Many students ask, "In what ways are these different? Do I need to learn other kinds of listening skills? Do I need to take notes? Will my notes be different?"

The lecture-type class we have been discussing here is ideal for professors presenting information to large groups. It allows the professors to organize data and share it rapidly, to both supplement the textbook and suggest alternative points of view. When used well, the lecture method personalizes course content. However, not all courses lend themselves to large group lectures. Often a professor wants to give her students opportunities to respond to information, share opinions, discover points of view on their own, or evaluate controversial issues. The listening you will have to do in such classes *is* different. What are some of the differences?

1. You need to prepare more beforehand.   Prior to a lecture, you need to review the appropriate textbook readings and check your previous lecture notes. However, most of your actual work is done during the lectures as you take new notes, and after the lecture as you study your notes. For discussion groups, on the other hand, you need to prepare carefully *before* the class. For example, you need to read and think about the topic, develop questions, and come into the class with a point of view about the topic. In practice, you need to take notes *before* the discussion session. Here are some of the notes you might take:

- List those points you do not understand in the reading. This list becomes a guide for you to create original questions as well as a checklist to discover how much you learn as the discussion proceeds.

- List those items you disagree with. You can then begin — in advance of the class — to think through your reasons for disagreement. Once you have these written out, it is easier to introduce them into the discussion.

- Get down hard data! Most participants in discussion groups have opinions but are not always able to back them up. In your notes, you should list as much data as you can find in your reading: dates, statistics, names, figures, and so on. You'll find that other people pay more heed to your comments when you can support them with solid evidence.

2. You need to participate.   Of course you may sit and listen to others talk — but that is not the point of a discussion. You must involve yourself in the talk, and you may do this by preparing beforehand. Here are some specific ideas for getting involved:

- Come with questions you want answered and make a point to ask them.

- When a question is asked that *you* can answer, don't hesitate; speak up and share your information.

- If you have information (from your hard data list), share it. Provide those dates, names, and statistics. After all, you have done your "homework." Let everyone know.

- When you have an opinion, voice it. The whole purpose of a discussion is to share opinions and points of view.

- If you are shy, make it a point to say something early in the discussion. The longer you postpone speaking, the more difficult it becomes. (One survey several years ago found that the greatest fear of most Americans was speaking in public! Don't think there is anything wrong with you because you don't like to speak out in public. Rather, circumvent this fear by making a contribution early. After you have spoken the first time, the next time becomes less awkward.)

- Don't say too much. No one in a discussion group likes a long-winded participant. Students in the group want to talk and often have comments to make after you have spoken. Many actively resent one who "makes a speech." Be brief and to the point.

- Don't argue. Make your point, present your argument briefly, and provide the supporting evidence (hard data). Try not to get up on a soapbox. Never get into direct arguments and disagreement with individuals; always speak to the group as a whole.

- Keep track of the discussion in your notebook so ideas that come to mind do not get lost. One person's comments may trigger ideas that need to be expressed later when she has finished speaking; you may lose your train of thought if you fail to keep a record.

3. Etiquette is especially important. As noted, you should avoid arguments and disagreements with other students in the group. There are a few other points to remember about group discussion etiquette:

- Look at people when they talk. Group discussions are formalized efforts at effective human communication. One component of good oral-aural communication is eye contact; people generally speak better when they know that listeners are paying attention. Looking at a speaker does not always mean that you understand or even that you are paying attention, but it does indicate that you are attempting to grasp the speaker's meanings.

- Never talk when someone else is speaking. A good discussion can be quickly ruined by social chitchat and private conversations.

- Try not to distract a speaker. Talking while someone is speaking is clearly distracting, but there are other forms of distraction as well: fiddling with your pen, cleaning out your notebook, rearranging your clothes, doing isometric exercises, tapping your foot, and so on.

4. Note taking remains important.   Even in discussions you take notes. These will not be as formal and organized as those you take in lecture classes, but they should reflect the flow of the discussion. Some of the suggestions made earlier apply more directly to discussion groups:

- Make lists of items that come up in the discussion. As various people contribute, jot down in a simple list form those pieces of information, key words, questions, and statements that seem to stand out for you. Later, you can use these to refresh your memory and help you recall the main flow of the talk.

- Copy down the main ideas. You cannot always tell which is a main idea and which a minor, but you can make the attempt. As the discussion moves along, write down what you think are the chief points. These may be valuable later as you think through the ideas discussed during the session.

- Note what you need to check out later. Often, individual students will bring new points of view or fresh information into discussion. Note these items quickly for further research.

EXERCISE 4

Read the following questions carefully before you attend another discussion group. Afterward, write out answers to each and be prepared to share these with the group.

1. Can you identify people who are clearly prepared for the discussion? What leads you to believe they are prepared?

2. Are there students who talk too much? How do others in the group seem to respond to them? Why do you think they talk so much?

3. Can you spot shy people? Do they talk at all? How do others respond to them? Why do you think they are reluctant to speak?

4. Do any speakers come prepared with hard data? Do they seem to have notes? How do others respond to them?

5. Does anyone argue or disagree on a personal basis? How do others respond to them?

6. Can you find any examples of poor group discussion etiquette? What are they? How do others respond? How did the instructor react? What might you do if you were the instructor?

7. Do people take notes? What kind of notes do they seem to take?

8. Where do people sit? Do reluctant speakers tend to sit in the back? Are "soapboxers" up front? How is the room arranged: chairs in lines? In a circle? In a horeshoe? What arrangement do you recommend for maximizing discussion participation?

9. What causes group discussions to get out of hand?

10. What do you think makes for an excellent class discussion? Why? What recommendations do you make for better discussion groups?

EXERCISE 5

Chapter 3 discusses several strategies for improving your listening skills for lectures and class discussions. In the space provided below, write one paragraph about the strategy you think can help you most. In it, note the reasons why you have selected that particular strategy.

POINTS TO REMEMBER ABOUT COLLEGE LISTENING SKILLS

1. Prepare for lectures and discussions.
2. Come with questions.
3. Arrive early and sit up front.
4. Listen with pen in hand.
5. Watch for the speaker's purpose and plan.
6. Jot down unfamiliar words.
7. Leave wide margins.
8. Note key points.
9. Summarize afterward.
10. Keep notes securely in loose-leaf notebook.

3
MASTERY TEST

Check your understanding of college listening skills by completing this multiple-choice test. Choose the response that best completes each statement.

1. Listening in lectures is different from listening in conversations because speakers

    a. may use facial expressions.

    b. tend to be organized.

    c. may use humorous explanations.

2. When listening to lectures, students must

    a. set a purpose for listening.

    b. take notes in outline form.

    c. arrive before the class begins.

3. When listening to lectures it is important to

    a. take notes in outline form.

    b. remain until the end of the lecture.

    c. note the speaker's main points.

4. You can prepare yourself for a lecture by

    a. reading about its topic in your textbook.

    b. checking definitions of specialized vocabulary to be used.

    c. outlining in advance.

5. When preparing for a lecture you should

    a. master the specialized vocabulary of the course.

    b. make up questions to guide your listening.

    c. make a careful study of graphs and charts in the textbook chapter.

6. Note taking helps you

    a. focus attention.

    b. think of original interpretations.

    c. compare your learning with that of others.

7. Summarizing helps you

    a. think of original interpretations.
    b. prepare for term papers.
    c. think through the speaker's message.

8. Signal words indicate a speaker's

    a. attitude toward students.
    b. predications.
    c. organizational patterns.

9. Mapping is

    a. a form of outlining.
    b. a device for organizing your study time.
    c. a technique for learning chemistry.

10. When taking notes, it is important to

    a. leave space for later additions and comments.
    b. copy everything down.
    c. develop detailed outlines.

4

Learning to Manage Textbook Reading Assignments

INTRODUCTION AND OVERVIEW

Textbooks are required reading in many college courses. They provide a basic structure for courses as well as sources for much course material. They often serve as foundations upon which instructors develop lectures, class discussions, and other leading activities.

To succeed in college you need to know how your textbooks are organized and what kinds of help they can give you. You also need to have strategies for managing textbook reading assignments so that you expend a minimum of effort to obtain a maximum of learning.

This chapter presents suggestions for becoming better acquainted with course textbooks as well as four specific strategies to better understand and remember reading assignments. You will learn how to prepare for assignments by previewing effectively, how to set yourself a purpose for reading, how to take better notes, and how to learn more efficiently by summarizing. The chapter concludes with a description of an alternative approach to reading assignments and some important tips.

SUGGESTED GUIDE QUESTIONS

1. What specific steps can you take to become better acquainted with your textbooks?

2. Why is it important to preview assignments?

3. How can you set yourself a purpose for reading?

4. What note-taking techniques are most effective for reading assignments?

5. Why is summarizing a key study strategy?

CHECKING TEXTBOOKS BEFORE YOU STUDY THEM

Most people check over a book before buying it. They note the title and author's name, skim any quotes from reviewers printed on the back cover, and often read a page or more from the front. Many would-be book buyers examine illustrations and read randomly selected paragraphs; some even check out a book's index and table of contents before buying it.

Because most college textbooks are required, many students fail to give them the careful scrutiny they deserve. Textbooks need to be examined systematically, even though you are required to purchase and study them.

The time you spend checking over your textbooks before you study them pays off in a number of ways:

You get an overall picture of the course.

You can see what will and what will not be covered.

You see what study helps are provided (maps, graphs, questions, summaries, etc.).

You begin to develop the confidence that comes with perspective: You know where you are going and how you will get there.

How can you become acquainted with your textbooks quickly? The following eight suggestions should help you get perspective on the books you will be studying during the semester.

1. Read the title page, both back and front.   On the front you will find the full title of the book with any subtitle, the name of the author (or authors), plus some indication of where he or she comes from (usually university affiliations). At the bottom you will find the publisher and the city in which the publisher is located. On the back of the title page are the date of publication and, usually, the publication data used in cataloging the book in the Library of Congress. All this information can help you pinpoint the book in time and place.

2. Read through the table of contents carefully.   This gives you an idea of the scope of the book. It not only reveals what is treated but also what is not discussed in the book. Because many college courses follow the plan of the books chosen, you get a good notion of what the course will be about by reading the table of contents.

3. Check the index.   Many students use a book's index only when preparing a research paper, but a careful examination of the index before you read the book actually helps to activate knowledge you already have in a field. You can quickly discover topics you know about and those that are new to you. You gain an overall perspective on the weeks ahead.

4. Examine the glossary.   Here you will find definitions of terms the author thinks are important to a study of the subject. By noting these words you can sometimes gain a sense of the course and any special language used by scholars in the field.

5. Read all the introductory and prefatory material.   Many students ignore introductions and prefaces; by doing so they miss the stated intentions and purposes of the author. The few minutes you spend with this material can help you gain insights into the way the author's mind works, while at the same time providing you with an overview of the general plan (and limitations) of the book.

6. Read the first and last chapters.   This may seem a time-consuming activity, but nothing will give you a better perspective on a book. You begin to see what the course is about, where it begins, and where it ends. The information you gain in the process helps you to put your study of specific chapter assignments into perspective.

7. Skim through the entire book.   Your examination of the table of contents allows you to see the plan of organization, but a quick look at the book itself helps you to see some of the actual material you will be studying. When you do individual assignments in the book during the semester, you will have a sense of how each fits into a larger whole.

8. Check for study helps.   Look at illustrations, maps, charts, and graphs. Note the headings and subtitles, the marginal notes and questions. Look to see if there are summaries for chapters and headnotes for sections of the chapters. All of these aids are valuable; knowing about them in advance will encourage you to use them regularly.

EXERCISE 1

Before doing your next actual textbook reading assignment, get to know the book better by completing the following exercise.

1. What is the full title? Subtitle (if any)?

2. Who is the author (or authors)? Is any information about the author provided in the book itself? What does it tell?

3. When was the book published? Is it a revision? (A revised book has been updated and rewritten.)

4. How are the topics organized? (Chronologically? By topics? By major areas?)

5. Does your book include:

    graphs?

    charts?

    maps?

    tables?

    illustrations?

    cartoons?

6. What is your opinion of the quality and quantity of these supplementary aids?

7. Does the book include:

    headnotes?

    questions?

    guides?

    typographical aids?

    a glossary?

    an index?

8. What is your opinion about the quality and quantity of these study aids?

EXERCISE **2**

Once you have a general idea of the book you are studying, check other aspects of it.

1. What does the introduction tell you about the book's purpose? Is this statement in harmony with your purposes for taking the course? What are points of disagreement, if any?

2. Does your examination of the glossary indicate many unfamiliar terms? Does this tell you anything about the course? (Will it be necessary, for example, to master a whole new vocabulary? If so, what steps should you take immediately to learn the new vocabulary of the subject?)

3. Does your examination of the index indicate that the course content will be entirely new to you, or is it somewhat familiar territory? In what ways will this information influence your study habits in the course? Could you be misled into believing that familiar material does not have to be studied as carefully as new material?

4. What do you learn about the author's style by reading the first and last chapters? Does he or she use many new and unfamiliar terms? Are sentences unusually long and complicated? What does this information indicate about the study procedures you need to use in learning from the book?

HOW CAN I READ TEXTBOOKS MORE EFFECTIVELY?

In the previous chapter on lecture listening, you were advised to (1) prepare for a lecture, (2) set a purpose for listening, (3) take notes, and (4) listen to summarize. Each of these approaches to classroom listening can be applied effectively to textbook reading assignments. They can be used by you as four powerful strategies for better understanding and remembering what you read in your textbooks and related assignments.

Strategy 1 — Previewing

You check over your textbooks to get an overview of the course and to see better its individual topics in a larger perspective. You prepare yourself for a lecture by reviewing previous notes and preparing your mind to better understand its new material. Such *previews* have long been believed valuable by psychologists of learning. (See References, p. 299.) Previews — whether of books, lectures, or individual reading assignments — can:

Help you see separate topics in relation to the larger whole.

Prepare your mind for new learnings.

Help you understand and remember better by showing you roughly what you are going to learn before you actually start to learn it.

How do you preview a textbook reading assignment? Here are six techniques that work for successful students at all levels.

1. Read the title.   This may seem like an obvious first step, but many students simply read the assigned pages. Their instructor says, "Read pages 99 to 123," and that is what they do! However, titles and subtitles are important: They signal the topic and help you narrow it down and see the limits the author has set. Sometimes they can also help you see the particular approach the author is taking.

2. Read the introductory material.   Often the first paragraph gives you an overview. Sometimes chapters contain specific introductions which also give overviews and provide clues to what follows. Sometimes, too, authors provide *headnotes*, short paragraphs that label the information and help you get an idea of the material to follow. No matter how a particular book handles the introductory material, you should spend some time reading it, because, as has been noted, you understand assignments better when you know what's coming.

3. Note the headings.   In textbooks, unlike most other kinds of books, publishers and authors provide definite headings. These are labels to clue you in on the ways the material has been set up in the book. They signal what is included, marking off boundaries so that you will know that one group of paragraphs talks about one thing and the next set talks about another. Often these headings are in a different type of print: They appear in italics, capital letters, color, or heavy print called boldface.

4. Look for typographical aids.   When headings are set off in a different type of print, they are typographical aids. However, publishers and authors use other kinds of aids, such as sentences or phrases printed in margins (called *marginal aids*), questions inserted in the paragraphs or margins, boldface, italics, and color. One popular textbook in general psychology has a chapter titled "Memory and Language." It is carefully subdivided by headings into areas (or subtopics) such as "Three Kinds of Memory" and "Recall and Recognition." These are marked in the left margin by blue capital letters. Each of these is subdivided by subheadings: "Short-term Memory," "Long-term Memory," "Free Recall," and "Recognition." These are further subdivided into separate sections on the page by titles printed in blue italics: "The Great Herring Caper: You Are There" and "Acoustic Representations in Short-Term Memory." Once a student has become acquainted with this simple system of signaling important information in the text, reading and study become easier. Most important, the system allows you to preview quickly and see what the chapter is about before you read it.

   5. Read the end.   At the conclusion of a chapter or section of a chapter, the author frequently places a short summary of what has been said. It may be the final paragraph or it may be clearly labeled "Summary." Reading it is crucial. Some authorities on learning say that having a summary statement of what you are supposed to learn *before* you try to learn it can make a major difference in the quality and quantity of your learning. Sometimes the headnote will give you a summary, but you cannot always be sure. You need to read the summary material before you read the assignment.

   6. Check the illustrative materials.   Often books contain good photographs, maps, charts, and other illustrative material. These can give you a good overview of what's coming. Spend a few minutes before you start reading to examine this material. It can provide clues to the contents of the actual reading assignment and do what an effective overview should do: prepare you for what is coming while it reminds you of what you already know.

EXERCISE 3

To gain practice in previewing, select a textbook assignment from one of your courses and answer the following questions about it.

1. What is the title? How does it help you define the topic?

2. Where is the introductory material? Where does it begin and end? How is it set off from the rest of the paragraphs?

3. How are the headnotes set off from the rest of the printed page? How do they help you get an overview?

4. What are the main headings? The minor headings? How are they distinguishable?

5. What other typographical aids are used in your book? How do they stand out from the printed page? In what ways do they help you get an overview?

6. What summary material is provided? Where does it begin and end? Is it made to stand out? How?

As you preview an assignment, you should also check out unfamiliar words. Obviously, you'll never understand a reading assignment if you don't know the words the author uses. Imagine, for example, trying to read an assignment entitled "Ecology and Contemporary Problems in Society" without knowing the meaning of the words *ecology* and *contemporary*, or trying to figure out a chapter that uses the word *eclectic* several times when you don't have a meaning for it.

Because the study of vocabulary is so important to success in college, Chapter 8 is devoted to the subject. However, you will need some way to deal with unfamiliar words immediately, so here is a quick and easy technique you can apply as you do your assignment previews.

This technique, sometimes called the SSCD approach to vocabulary, asks you to check for Sound, Structure, Context, and then the Dictionary. It is based on the fact that you actually have several vocabularies. Some words are in your listening vocabulary; that is, you have heard them spoken and understand them, but you have never seen them in print. Other words are in your reading vocabulary: You have seen them in print and know what they mean, but you have never actually spoken them. Other words may be in your spoken vocabulary: You say them frequently but have never seen them in a book.

Here is the way SSCD works: When you encounter a new word in your reading,

- ***First, sound it out.*** It may be a word that is already in your listening vocabulary. By applying the simple phonics skills you learned in elementary school, you probably can sound it out. This is the first S.

- ***Next, look for structure clues.*** Structure clues deal with those parts of words that you may already know. For example, if you know the word *structure*, then *structural* is easy. If you know *continent*, then *transcontinental* is easy. If you also know that *trans-* has the meaning of *across*, and that *-al* usually turns a noun into an adjective, then you are in business. Many words in your assignments are like these; you don't need to check your dictionary. You simply need to look closely to discover familiar word parts. This is the second S.

- ***Next, try the context.*** When a new word is not in your listening vocabulary and does not contain familiar word parts, guess at its meaning from the way it is used in the sentence. This is the way most successful readers figure out the meanings of unfamiliar words: They guess. This is the C in SSCD.

- ***Finally, check the dictionary.*** When sound, structure, and context clues all fail you, look the word up in the dictionary. This, of course, is the *D* in SSCD. Many words in college textbooks are supposed to be new to you; you'll have to look them up in order to make sense of the assignments.

When you do your preview of an assignment, note unfamiliar words. Especially watch for those that appear in titles, headnotes, italics, or boldface. As you scan the assignment to discover what topics it covers, note words that seem to be used repeatedly. Copy all such words in your notebook and use the SSCD approach to save time and improve your understanding.

Strategy 2 — Setting a Purpose

When you have a purpose for listening to a lecture, you listen better. You pay attention and your mind focuses more clearly on the material. The same holds true for textbook reading. When you read with a purpose, your mind is less apt to wander and you begin to distinguish between various ideas, note significant details, and grasp the meaning of the author's message.

Previewing helps you get a handle on an assignment. It gives you some idea in advance of what an author is trying to say. That is important, but not quite enough. You also need to define in your own mind what you are looking for in the book. Defining your purpose helps you relate the material on the printed page with your personal goals.

An example may make this clearer. You preview a chapter and find that the author is planning to discuss memory. Your preparation for reading reveals that the author will distinguish between *short-* and *long-term memory* and also between *recognition* and *recall*. Once you have a rough idea of the topics, you can begin to make up questions you want answered in your reading. Some of these might be: What's the difference between short- and long-term memory? How do I get information from short- to long-term memory? When did I last recognize something but found myself unable to recall more about it? What's the difference between these two kinds of memory? Can I improve my memory?

When you read an assignment with such clear-cut questions in mind, your mind is active. You are less inclined to daydream. You now read to find answers to your questions. You, in short, have a purpose for reading.

How can you set purposes for reading? As noted in the discussion of lecture listening, you can make up questions you want answered or you can make predictions about what you think the author will say and then read to check your predictions. Here are some ways to give yourself purpose:

1. Turn headings into questions. For the introductory psychology textbook mentioned earlier, you can take each of the headings and create your own personal questions. The heading *Short-term Memory* can become "What is short-term memory?" *Recall and Recognition* may become "How do these two differ?" A sociology textbook with the heading *Limitations of Polling* can become "What are the limitations of polling?" A heading in a history book, *Causes of Peasant Revolt*, may become "What were the causes of the peasant revolt?" The same headings may lead you to personal questions such as "How do *I* get information into long-term memory?" or "What might cause *me* to revolt if I were a peasant?"

2. Turn headings into predictions. Many efficient readers take headings and make predictions about what they think the author may say. *Limitations of Polling* leads to the prediction "I bet he'll say that a certain number of people must be included in the sample of those polled." *Causes of the Peasant Revolt* might lead to "The author will mention the cost of bread." These predictions provide purposes for reading the assignment. Students who make them read to discover how accurate their predictions are.

3. Turn titles into questions.   Titles tend to give you more questions. The title "Memory and Language" may lead you to several questions, such as "What is meant here by memory? How does it relate to language? Can't I remember things that aren't in words?" and so forth. "Recent Advances in Microbiology" may lead to "What is microbiology? What are some of its advances? What discoveries have been made recently? How do these affect me? What is still unknown in this field?" and so forth.

4. Turn titles into predictions.   Check the titles and subtitles and try to guess what you think the author will say about each topic. "Recent Advances in Microbiology," for example, may lead you to predict that the author will discuss research, mention certain recent studies, note the limitations of the studies, and probably say something about work that still needs to be done in the field. Once you have identified your predictions, you can read to discover how successful you are as a predictor.

5. Use questions modeled on the "5 W's plus H."   Take the pattern used by many newspaper reporters and create questions based on *who*, *what*, *when*, *where*, *why*, and *how*. You will find that the questions based on *who*, *when*, and *where* are the easiest to answer from your reading. *What*, *why*, and *how* questions tend to be more difficult. All textbook assignments do not lend themselves to this technique, but it is valuable when headings are vague or missing. For example, *Causes of the Peasant Revolt* may lead you to the question, "What were the causes?" The heading *Peasant Revolt*, however, may lead you to ask: "Who started it? What happened? Where did it happen? When was this revolt? Why did they revolt? How did they go about it?" You may not always find answers to all your questions, but you are more apt to read with purpose and, thus, greater attention.

6. Make predictions based on the "5 W's plus H."   You can easily take the same technique and use it to make predictions: "I think it happened during the Middle Ages" or "It probably happened in Europe." Such predictions will also help you to be a purposeful reader of even the most routine assignments in your textbook.

7. Get questions from first sentences.   Sometimes the title is too vague, there are no headings, and the "5 *W's plus H*" technique is not appropriate. What to do? One trick is to read the first sentence in each paragraph and concoct a question from it. For example, a book on the history of ideas might present problems: The assigned chapter is entitled "Politics in a New Key," it has no headings or typographical aids of any kind, and to make matters worse, the "5 *W's* plus *H*" approach seems to lead nowhere. However, by reading the first sentence of each paragraph, a student can come up with some questions:

- "It was too late and Herzl soon realized it"

    leads to

    Who is Herzl?

    Why was it too late? Too late for what?

- "A strong personal ingredient, more accessible to the psychologist than to the historian, unquestionably played a crucial part in his espousal of the redeemer's role"

    leads to

    What was the "strong personal ingredient"?

    Why was it more accessible to the psychologists?

    What part did it play?

    What does *espousal* mean? *redeemer*?

    To whom does *his* refer? Herzl?

EXERCISE 4

One way to create questions for note taking is to turn headings and subtitles into questions. Here are the headings from a college textbook on economics. (Notice how the headings themselves form an outline.) Turn each one into a question that you could use to guide you in taking notes from this chapter.

THE SIMPLE ANALYTICS OF ECONOMIC GROWTH

Growth Economics *What are growth economics?*

    Two definitions *How may the term be defined?*

    The importance of growth *Why is growth important?*

    Arithmetic of growth *What is the "arithmetic of growth"?*

Ingredients of Growth

    Law of diminishing returns

    The production possibilities curve and diminishing returns

    Diminishing returns: arithmetic example

    Optimum population

    Malthus and misery

    Rising productivity and growth

Aggregate Demand and Growth

    Keeping pace with capacity

    Full-employment growth model

Allocative Efficiency and Growth

EXERCISE 5

To check your ability to set a purpose for reading, select one of your reading assignments and complete the following exercise before *you begin to read it.*

1. Read the title of the chapter or section assigned. What questions or predictions can you make from it?

2. Read the headnotes. What questions or predictions can you create from them?

3. Try the "5 *W*'s plus *H*" technique. Skim the assignment and make up questions that begin with *who, what, where, when, why,* and *how.*

4. Take a paragraph from the assignment and read only the first sentence of it. What questions can you invent from this sentence? What predictions?

5. What *personal* questions come to mind from your previewing?

6. Read the assignment now. Answer the questions as you read. Check

the predictions as you read. Be prepared to discuss your responses to these techniques for setting purpose.

Strategy 3 — Note Taking

As you have learned (see Chapter 3), note taking helps you focus attention, note main points, see a speaker's or author's organizational plan, and keep track of specialized vocabulary and unfamiliar words while serving as an indispensable memory aid, providing you with a record of your new learnings, and giving you a valuable source of information for test preparation.

As you read textbook assignments, you need to keep accurate notes in a secure notebook. You can follow many of the suggestions previously given for lecture listening:

1. Write down the answers to the questions you asked as you set a purpose for reading.   If you noted ten questions, write these into your notebook with the answers you located as you read.

2. Write down the main ideas you found as you read.   Sometimes a twenty-paragraph assignment will lead to twenty separate main ideas. Often you will find only a few ideas that you consider crucial in the assignment. Your notes may consist only of these key points or main ideas.

3. Outline the assignment.   Often you will be able to find a well-defined main-idea sentence and supporting sentences with examples and details. You may then write out an actual outline (see the next chapter for information on outlining). At other times, you may develop a "map" such as was described in Chapter 3.

4. Write down important words.   You need to keep a record of technical and specialized vocabulary as well as words unfamiliar to you. In some assignments, your notes may consist entirely of new and technical words.

5. Write summaries.   Often you may choose to write brief summaries of sections of a chapter assignment or a single summary of an entire assignment.

In addition to these suggestions, which may be followed in either lecture listening or reading assignments, there are at least three others to follow as you study textbooks:

1. Underline.   When you own the textbook, you may choose to underline main-idea sentences or key words and phrases. This technique is valuable in that it forces you to identify those ideas you believe are crucial to understanding the assignment. It also allows you to review quickly before a test. Unfortunately, some students underline too much. They draw lines under almost every sentence, thus losing the value of discriminating between main and minor ideas and of saving time in later test preparation.

2. Use a coding system.   Many students develop personal codes to note important material in their books. They use stars, crosses, exclamation points, minus signs, and other marks in the margins to focus their attention on key points. They can then review the material by following their own code signs to note main points for test review. Students who use this note-taking system say that it helps them focus attention, note main ideas, and highlight important vocabulary words, and that it takes less time than other systems. Like underlining, it should only be used with books you own.

3. "Block."   Blocking is another effective way to make your note taking help you better manage reading assignments. Here is how it is done.

- Divide your notebook pages into three columns, approximately two inches, two inches, and four inches wide.

- As you read the assignment, note in the *second* column the topic of each paragraph or set of related paragraphs.

- In the third column (the four-inch one) jot down ideas and information you think are important. For example, when reading an assignment about the first Roosevelt administration, you may note in the second column such topics as Major Legislation, Problems Abroad, or Economic Crisis. In the third column, next to each of these topics, you would write the names, dates, and brief descriptions of pieces of legislation, problems, or specific crises, plus other information that you believe is important.

- In a second reading of the assignment, you can recheck the topics column to make sure you have selected correct ones and to add more data to the third column.

- If the instructor has lectured about the material, you may go back to your lecture notes and add material from the lecture that fits into the third column. For example, information not in the textbook may have been given about specific problems abroad. Because you can easily locate the topic (Problems Abroad), it is relatively simple to add this lecture material to your reading notes.

- After you have gathered all information (from reading and lectures), go over your material and create questions for the first column. These questions will not necessarily be the same ones you created when you were setting a purpose for reading; they are created *after* you have read. The questions you write in the first column are designed to help you review and study your notes.

Here is an example of a set of notes based on a reading assignment in a biology textbook.

EXAMPLE:

ASSIGNMENT: THE HUMAN DIGESTIVE SYSTEM, PP. 145-167

Questions	Topics	Data
What is a stomach?	stomach	stomach — pouch in the abdominal cavity — has millions of gastric juices — secretes gastric juices after each meal
What are the 3 kinds of gastric juices?	kinds of gastric juices	There are 3 kinds of gastric juices: 1. pariental cells 2. "chief cells" 3. mucus-secreting cells

Strategy 4 — Summarizing

How do you know when you have understood a reading assignment? Do you have to wait until the test? Many authorities now agree that you can test yourself as you read by *retelling*, or summarizing, as you go along. For example, you may read five pages of the textbook and wonder if you are really getting the author's message. You can check your list of main ideas, or you can go one step further and try to retell what you think the author is saying. Simply tell yourself in your own words what you have just read, or, even better, summarize the textbook assignment in your notebook.

Summarizing is one of the most difficult of all study skills. Many students shy away from summarizing because it takes time and effort.

However, those students who make a regular practice of pausing as they read to tell themselves what they have read tend to understand assignments better. Those students who actually write out brief summaries in their notebooks find that the practice forces them to think through the author's message. The process of writing makes them discover what the author is saying. Those who write out summaries also find that their summaries become an important aid for later pretest review and study.

Here are some suggestions for summarizing:

1. Use your list of main ideas as a jumping-off place. If you have kept track of the main points in the assignment, these can provide you with the basis for the summary.

2. Make sure you retell the main ideas in sequential order. The author probably had a plan to guide him or her. If you follow the same sequence, you will approximate the original plan. This helps you get a better picture of the organization underlying the assignment.

3. Use your own words, not those of the author. A retelling is not a collection of quotes! Simply stringing together words, phrases, and sentences from the assignment does not help you reinterpret the author's message. You need to use your own words.

4. Pretend that you are telling a fellow student what was discussed in the assignment. Start by saying, "In this section the author explained that . . ." You'll find that you either can retell or you cannot. If you cannot, then clearly you have yet to understand the assignment yourself; you should go back and reread, using the four strategies described here.

5. Pretend you are a writer for a digest magazine. Your job is to condense the material from the textbook assignment. Your readers will be people who have not taken the course and you have to tell them — in simple language — what the material is all about. As noted before, this kind of retelling on paper is difficult. It will take time and energy. However, it may be one of the best ways to make sure you know what you have read.

EXERCISE 6

Now is the time to try these four strategies on an actual textbook reading assignment. Select an assignment from one of your courses, use each of the strategies as you read the assignment, and then complete this Record Sheet.

Course: _____

Textbook: _____

Assignment: _____

Date: _____

1. Preview

Indicate here the steps you took in previewing the assignment. Note unfamiliar words and specialized vocabulary you needed to check on before reading.

2. Setting a Purpose

Note here the questions you created from titles, headings, first lines, illustrations, or your preview. Note too any predictions you made prior to reading.

3. Note Taking

Note here the type of note taking you tended to use: underlining, outlining, mapping, main ideas, or summarizing. If possible, attach your actual notes to this Record Sheet.

4. Summarizing

Write a one-paragraph summary of the reading assignment. If you used a series of summaries as your primary note-taking technique, you may attach these.

PROBLEMS WITH INDIVIDUAL SENTENCES

Sometimes individual sentences in reading assignments present problems that either slow you down or prevent further reading. You cannot be expected to make sense of an assignment when this happens.

What can you do when individual sentences are unclear? Here are some suggestions.

1. Read the previous and the following sentences.   Often there are clues in these that help you figure out the difficult sentence.

2. Go back and reread the paragraphs that precede the troublesome sentence.   Again, there may be clues available to help you interpret the problem sentence.

3. Read ahead.   Often when you realize where the author is going and what the general approach to the topic is, you can make better sense of the trouble spot.

4. Check the words.   It may be that one or two words are unfamiliar or are being used by the author in a specialized way. Check for alternate meanings of familiar words.

5. Look for subjects and predicates.   Sometimes you can ask yourself, "What is this sentence about? What is its subject? What is being said about the subject (in other words, what is its predicate)?" Such grammatical analysis can often help you figure out meanings.

6. Look for sentences within sentences.   Writers and speakers frequently insert one sentence within another in the form of a subordinate clause. Sometimes these are used to describe or modify (adjective clauses); to indicate a condition, time, or place (adverb clauses); or to serve as a subject or object in another sentence (noun clauses). A brief look at possible sentences within sentences often unlocks the meaning of a difficult sentence.

7. Check pronoun antecedents.   When you see pronouns such as *they* or *it*, for example, be wary. Make sure you know what these pronouns represent: What does *it* stand for? Who or what are *they* supposed to be? Many troublesome sentences are troublesome because readers need to search for pronoun antecedents.

8. Paraphrase.   When stopped by a particularly troublesome sentence, try saying it in your own language. For example, "Semantic memory represents knowledge of conceptual relations about the world that are shared within the culture or subculture" may be paraphrased as "Semantic memories are those that most people share." Your paraphrase may not always be exactly correct, but rewording helps you get the meaning of a difficult sentence. The process of paraphrasing encourages you to think through the author's meaning.

9. Supply examples.   Try to fill in, from your memory and experience, examples of what you think the author is saying in a sentence. For example, if you are troubled by "Episodic memory represents one's personal record of individual experiences," search for an example from your record of individual experiences. You may repeat the sentence but add, "such as my own memory of the day it rained on the lake while I was on the raft." Your own example may help you see the meaning more clearly.

10. Ask someone.   When confronted by especially difficult sentences, readers may need help from an outside source. Another student can often help. You may need to ask your instructor. Remember, it is all right to ask. You cannot grasp the meaning of a paragraph or assignment when you are held up by a single important sentence.

THE SQ3R STUDY SYSTEM

There is another approach to textbook reading assignments you should understand. It is a five-part system in which you first *survey* the assignment, then make up *questions* that you want answered, and then *read*. After you have read, you then *recite* or check the answers you have found to your own questions, and finally *review* to make sure you will remember the main points of the assignment.

Here is how SQ3R works:

1. Before you actually read the textbook assignment, survey the pages.   Check not only the title but all subtitles and headings. If the book gives marginal notes, survey these too. The five minutes or so you devote to this activity will give you an overview of the material and an idea of what the author is discussing.

2. The most important step in the system comes after your survey: You now make up questions.   These should not be questions given in the book by the author, but ones that you personally want answered. They are the kind of questions you would ask the author if he or she were present in the room with you while you study.

The questions you create need to be written down because they serve to guide you through the actual reading of the assignment. They may be written on a separate sheet that you keep by your desk as you read or they may be written directly into your notebook. Many students favor the second technique because they can later use the same questions for review purposes before a test.

Where do these questions come from? Five or six good questions may pop into your head as you do the initial survey. You may wonder why the author made a certain statement or what will be said about a certain issue. You may get more questions by turning subtitles and headings into questions. For example, a heading such as "The Causes of the French Revolution" may give you the question: "What were the causes of the French Revolution?" Try to get ten or more questions to guide you through the actual reading.

3. Now you read, with the goal of finding answers to your questions.   The questions serve to guide you through the assignment. The great value of the SQ3R system is that it provides your reading with a focus. You are no longer "just reading"; you are now reading with a specific purpose.

4. After your reading, recite to yourself the answers to the questions.   If your reading has been successful, you should be able to recite answers effortlessly. Sometimes your questions may not be answered. When this happens, star the unanswered questions for a second reading. If you cannot find the answers to certain questions after a second reading, bring them to class. They may serve as good discussion material.

5. Your questions can serve as the basis for your review.   Prior to a class discussion or a test, go over your questions to check that you have retained the information. Many students write out their answers as part of the previous step, *recite*. They can then not only check to see if they have remembered the answers found in reading, but can double-check their answers to avoid another reading of the assignment.

In what way is the SQ3R system different from the approach suggested in this chapter? As you can see, *survey* is the same as Strategy 1 — Previewing. You make a quick trip through the assignment to discover what the author plans to discuss, getting an overview of the material in the process. *Question* is similar to Strategy 2 — Setting a Purpose. Readers can set a purpose through questioning or predicting. Purpose is important because it helps focus your attention and gives you some guidelines for the actual reading. *Recite* and *review* are like Strategy 4 — Summarizing. Here you make sure you have retained and understood the new material.

SQ3R is a tried-and-true approach to reading textbook assignments. You may find it more effective with certain assignments than with others, or simply as an alternative to the approach recommended here of Previewing, Setting a Purpose, Note Taking, and Summarizing.

MANAGING READING ASSIGNMENTS: SOME IMPORTANT TIPS

Clearly, there's more to textbook reading than "going over the pages the night before"! Here are some important suggestions to follow as you begin your college career.

1. Make sure you have copied the assignment correctly.   There are few misadventures more annoying than having spent two hours doing the wrong assignment. Make sure you get the exact pages and that you understand the directions: Should you read the entire chapter or just pages 129 to 158? Are there questions to answer? Are you expected to write out and pass in your answers? Is an outline expected?

2. Do more than read.   "Just reading" is rarely enough; you need to engage your mind actively in the reading process. This means that you need to ask and answer questions, check for unfamiliar words, preview, outline, summarize, and so on. These activities help you focus your attention on the material and keep your mind working as you read.

3. Read with a pen and notebook.   One way to keep your mind (and your body) active during the reading process is to read with pen in hand. Note taking may consist of formal outlines or one-sentence summaries of every paragraph; it may simply be a time line or graph that you make as you read. The key point about note taking is that it tends to promote active involvement in reading.

4. Find the right work area.   If textbook reading is an active mental activity, it cannot be done well in casual circumstances. You must make sure to find an appropriate place: a table in the library, a quiet room, or a study carrel. You need a table or desk for your notebook and as much freedom as possible from social interruptions.

5. Begin reading by reviewing the four recommendations made in this chapter:

Preview to get an overview and note unfamiliar words.

Set a purpose for yourself (such as reading to find answers to your questions).

Take notes as you read.

Summarize, either mentally or in writing, to make sure you understand the material.

6. Change approaches once in a while.   The four-strategy approach recommended here works. However, you may want to try an alternative occasionally as a change of pace. The SQ3R study system offers a good alternative. After you have become comfortable with both approaches, you may want to develop one of your own!

EXERCISE 7

Chapter 4 suggests several study strategies to help you better manage textbook reading assignments: becoming acquainted with your textbook, previewing assignments, setting a purpose for reading, taking notes, summarizing, and using the SQ3R study system. Check over these strategies again, and select the one you believe can help you most.

In the space provided, describe that strategy briefly and tell why you selected it.

POINTS TO REMEMBER ABOUT READING ASSIGNMENTS

1. Be familiar with the book as a whole.
2. Preview assignments.
3. Note unfamiliar words.
4. Look up technical words and specialized vocabulary.
5. Make up questions from headings.
6. Ask: who, what, where, when, why, and how.
7. Predict what the author will say.
8. Summarize.

4
MASTERY TEST

To discover how well you understood Chapter 4, answer each of the following questions.

1. Why is it important to be familiar with your textbooks before you do individual assignments?

2. What specific techniques help you preview an assignment?

3. What are *typographical aids*?

4. Why should you note unfamiliar words before you begin to read an assignment?

5. How can you set a purpose for reading?

6. Which note-taking techniques can be used in reading but not in lectures?

7. What are some disadvantages of these techniques?

8. What are the values of summarizing as a study technique?

5

Learning to Note and Use Main Ideas

INTRODUCTION AND OVERVIEW

Textbook writers organize their material around certain key points or main ideas. These basic ideas serve as hubs around which the information of paragraphs and chapters may be arranged.

When you can identify main ideas, you gain an immediate advantage as you try to understand paragraphs and chapters. You begin to see how the various parts fit together and how each contributes to an overall plan. Once you note the main ideas, you can start to make better sense of reading assignments.

This chapter helps you identify main ideas and then use this knowledge to better comprehend textbook reading assignments. It focuses on three areas: (1) finding main ideas in paragraphs, (2) using main ideas in outlining, and (3) finding main ideas in charts, graphs, and tables.

SUGGESTED GUIDE QUESTIONS

---

1. Why is it important to identify main ideas in reading assignments?

2. Where will main idea sentences be found in paragraphs?

3. In what ways will your skill at identifying main ideas help you summarize reading assignments?

4. What are the values of outlining?

5. In what ways can you deal with troublesome sentences found in your reading?

FINDING MAIN IDEAS IN PARAGRAPHS

Textbook writers tend to organize their paragraphs and chapters around certain main ideas. To make better sense of their work, you need to be able to identify these ideas quickly and accurately.

Here are some suggestions for spotting main ideas in reading assignments:

1. They usually come early, in introductory sentences or paragraphs.

2. They are sometimes indicated in the titles and subtitles.

3. They are sometimes found in headings.

4. They are often repeated, sometimes in different words.

5. They are sometimes called to your attention by the author, who may use phrases like "one important characteristic is," "primary causes are," or "important to."

If you use the strategies recommended in Chapter 4, you help yourself perceive the main idea of an assignment. As you *preview* to gain an overview of the chapter or section of the chapter, you force yourself to read headings, subtitles, and illustrative material; you begin to see the central point or points underlying the assignment. Then, as you set up a *purpose for reading* (using questions or predictions) and *read, taking notes*, the main idea of the entire assignment becomes clearer. Finally, as you *summarize*, you are forced to think through the main idea of the material. (This main idea becomes, as we shall see, the main idea sentence for your one-paragraph summary of the assignment.)

Noting main ideas in individual paragraphs may be more difficult because the main-idea sentences often appear in different positions within paragraphs.

You can locate these main idea sentences more easily if you remember the following:

1. Individual paragraphs are usually made up of two things: a main idea and the details that support it.

2. A writer, in most cases, builds paragraphs around one main idea or in some instances two closely related ideas. The main idea is usually stated at the beginning, in the middle, or at the end of the paragraph. In some cases the main idea may be stated elsewhere in the paragraph or may not be stated at all.

The geometric shapes below represent paragraphs and the straight lines across represent the main ideas. The empty spaces in the shapes represent the details that support main ideas.

FIRST SENTENCE

The first place to look for the main idea is in the first sentence. The author states it and then gives details to support it.

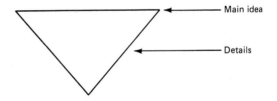

EXAMPLE:

The freezing points of liquids may be changed to some extent by the application of pressure. Those that contract when freezing have their melting points raised by pressure. Most materials behave this way. A few materials, however, expand when they freeze. Water is one of these. Increased pressure decreases the freezing point of these materials also. Thus, the pressure of an ice skater's skate upon the ice can cause the ice to melt. In such a case, a skater is actually skating on ice that has been lubricated with a thin film of water.

LAST SENTENCE

The second most common place to find the main idea is the last sentence. The author uses details and examples to build up to the main idea and then states it.

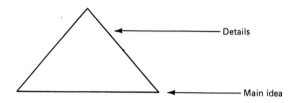

EXAMPLE:

It is clear that the sun warms the earth. It is clearly our major source of heat. However, we can also see that this heat from the sun cannot be transferred to us by either conduction or convection, because there are no molecules in the space that separates us from the sun. Vibrational transfer by conduction or circulatory transfer by convection are, therefore, impossible. Heat transfer from the sun to the earth occurs through a vacuum, that is, through nothing. *This method of heat transfer is called radiation.*

MIDDLE SENTENCE

Another place to look for the main idea is in the middle of the paragraph. The author sometimes uses details and examples to build up to the main idea, states the main idea, and then continues to support it with more information.

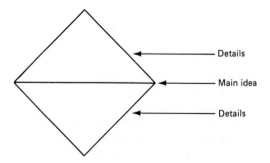

EXAMPLE:

Notice that only the wave travels to the right. The pieces of string simply move up and down. *A wave such as this, with the wave traveling in a direction perpendicular to the direction of motion of the particles, is called a transverse wave.* You can remember this by recalling that *trans-* means "across" and that the particles actually travel across the direction of the propagation of the wave.

FIRST AND LAST SENTENCES

At times an author states the main idea twice. It appears in the first sentence, is supported by details and examples, and then is restated again at the end of the paragraph.

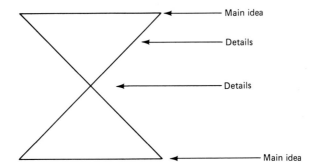

EXAMPLE:

Electrochemistry is concerned with the chemical transformation produced by the passage of electricity and with the production of electricity by means of chemical transformation. It is one of the oldest branches of chemistry, and yet the modern uses of electrochemistry are constantly expanding with the development of many new practical applications. The fact that electricity can be produced by means of chemical reactions allows the storage of electrical energy of the chemical reagents. This internal energy can be used to produce electrical energy at a more convenient time or place. Electric automobiles are being developed and tested as a possible means of avoiding air pollution caused by products from internal combustion engines. Among the sources of power used in space vehicles are solar batteries, which change the energy from sunlight into electric energy, and fuel cells, which produce electrical energy from the chemical energy of fuels. *Electrochemistry also provides insight into such diverse phenomena as the corrosion of metals, the refining of metals, the transmission of nerve impulses in animals, and the interactions of ions in solutions with each other and with the solvent.*

UNSTATED MAIN IDEA

There will be times when the author does not state the main idea. When this happens, the reader must infer or figure out the main idea.

In this type of paragraph there are only details and examples which relate to a specific topic and also which support an unstated main idea.

EXAMPLE:

Such emotions as love, anger, and hate are known to all cultures of the world, yet each allows its members to reveal these emotions in different ways. In some southern European cultures, for example, anger may be shown directly. In Japan, anger may be shown to a child or servant but never to an equal. Yet some Japanese do express anger toward their equals, and some French and Italians rarely demonstrate anger.

One important point to remember: *Main ideas are not the same as topics.* The *topic* is what the paragraph is about; the *main idea* is the position or point of view the writer expresses about some aspect of the topic.

You can make this distinction clear for yourself by first thinking of some topics and then making up sentences expressing an idea about each one. For example, *television commercials* may be a topic; an idea about the topic may be "Television commercials are often more entertaining than the actual programs." *Music* may be a topic; main-idea sentences that express writers' particular views of the topic might be "Music reflects its time" or "The lyrics of the Beatles' songs expressed the mood of the sixties."

As you read paragraphs, distinguish between the topic (what it's about) and the main-idea sentence that states the writer's position about some aspect of the topic.

EXERCISE 1

Read the following selection, "Fix-Up Strategies," taken from a textbook on improving reading comprehension. As you read, look for the main idea in each paragraph and note where it appears in the paragraph. When you finish reading, complete the exercise that follows the selection.

FIX-UP STRATEGIES

1   What happens when readers realize that they are not comprehending what they read? They may give up on the reading task, telling themselves, in essence, that the book or assignment is simply too difficult for them. If they are determined for some reason to discover what the author is saying, they may use one or more of the following "fix-up" strategies recommended by certain reading specialists.

2   They may ignore problems in the reading and continue to read. Good readers tend to do this all the time. Poor readers evidently do not realize that they are ignoring problems. Several research studies have found that successful readers regularly skip over parts of a book that they do not understand and read ahead in hopes that other parts will help them make sense of the material. Unfortunately, this particular strategy works best with trivial obstacles. When readers fail to understand larger pieces of a text, they need to try another strategy.

3   They may not be getting a large enough sample of the author's writing to guess his or her overall plan. Therefore they may deliberately speed up to look ahead, or conversely, slow down for places that appear more difficult. Many poor readers do not realize that changing pace is "allowed." They think that every line must be read at exactly the same rate. Another basic fix-up strategy, then, is this: When you fail to understand an assignment, change your rate of reading.

4   Readers may also suspend judgment. They may continue to read ahead in hopes that the author will fill in gaps, add more information, and clarify points in the text. This is good strategy. When puzzled by an item, read along — maybe increase your rate — and perhaps the author will explain the puzzling item.

5   When readers are puzzled by individual words, sentences, or even paragraphs, they should make a habit of guessing: "I think that word means _____" or "I think this sentence is supposed to mean _____." Readers should hypothesize. Reading is largely a matter of testing out hypotheses: "If I think this word means _____, then I should read along and see if my guess, or hypothesis, makes sense."

6   Another fix-up strategy is rereading. Some readers shy away from this obvious technique because they believe it to be time-consuming and disruptive. They need to know that good readers reread frequently, checking back to see if their hypotheses about word meanings were accurate or if their guesses about an author's statements were correct. Several studies in reading have shown that rereading is especially useful when readers perceive contradictions, irrelevancies, or too many interpretations.

7   Sometimes none of these strategies work. Readers reread, skip ahead, change rates, ignore problems, suspend judgment, or hypothesize; they still fail to understand. The fix-up in such cases is to go to another source. Good readers regularly check outside references; they go to encyclopedias, dictionaries, other books, friends, or teachers. Such a fix-up is time-consuming and disruptive, but often necessary. When all other strategies fail, it is all right to ask someone!

Directions: *Check the sentence that best expresses the main idea of each paragraph. Then, in the space provided, indicate where the main idea appears in each paragraph. Remember, it may be (1) the first sentence, (2) the last sentence, (3) the middle sentence, (4) both first and last sentences, or (5) an unstated main idea.*

Paragraph 1

_____ 1. Readers may give up reading when puzzled.

_____ 2. Readers may use a fix-up strategy when puzzled.

_____ 3. Readers may be determined to discover what an author is saying.

Where does the main idea appear? _____

Paragraph 2

_____ 1. Readers may ignore problems and continue to read.

_____ 2. Good readers do this all the time.

_____ 3. This particular strategy works best with trivial obstacles.

Where does the main idea appear? _____

Paragraph 3

_____ 1. Readers may not be getting enough of a sample.

_____ 2. When you fail to understand, change your reading rate.

_____ 3. Poor readers do not realize that they may change pace.

Where does the main idea appear? _____

Paragraph 4

_____ 1. Readers may suspend judgment.

_____ 2. This is a good strategy.

_____ 3. Perhaps an author will explain a puzzling item.

Where does the main idea appear? _____

Paragraph 5

_____ 1. Readers may be puzzled by individual words.

_____ 2. Readers should hypothesize.

_____ 3. Readers may be puzzled by individual paragraphs.

Where does the main idea appear? _____

Paragraph 6

_____ 1. Rereading is another fix-up strategy.

_____ 2. This strategy is time-consuming.

_____ 3. It is useful when readers perceive contradictions.

Where does the main idea appear? _____

Paragraph 7

_____ 1. Sometimes none of these strategies work.

_____ 2. Another fix-up strategy is to go to another source.

_____ 3. Encyclopedias are a good source of information.

Where does the main idea appear? _____

EXERCISE 2

One of the best techniques for managing reading assignments successfully is *summarizing*. Summarizing forces you to figure out the central points of an assignment. It helps you distinguish between main and minor ideas and place the key ideas in a logical sequence.

A good way to summarize a longer assignment is to locate the main idea of each paragraph and then combine these in a sensible paragraph. Start with the main idea of the first paragraph, as this is probably the main idea for the entire selection. Then present each paragraph's main idea consecutively until you have summarized the complete reading assignment.

Write a summary here for "Fix-Up Strategies" by copying, in paragraph form, the seven main ideas of the seven-paragraph selection. You may need to insert words of your own to make the writing flow smoothly.

EXERCISE 3

Search in one of your textbooks for paragraphs in which main-idea sentences may be found as the first sentence of a paragraph, as the final sentence, or somewhere in the middle. Provide the appropriate information in the following spaces.

1. Main idea sentence at the beginning

   Textbook: _____

   Page(s): _____

   Main idea sentence: _____

2. Main idea sentence at the end

   Textbook: _____

   Page(s): _____

   Main idea sentence: _____

3. Main idea sentence in the middle

   Textbook: _____

   Page(s): _____

   Main idea sentence: _____

EXERCISE 4

You can learn to identify main ideas in the paragraphs of a reading assignment more readily after you have had more experience writing paragraphs yourself. Once you organize and write paragraphs you will begin to see where authors place their main-idea sentences and how they develop them with appropriate details and examples.

Try writing an original paragraph. Select one of the main-idea sentences suggested below, and develop it with at least three examples and details. You may start with the main-idea sentence or place it in the middle or at the end of your paragraph.

SUGGESTIONS:

1. Some college textbooks are unnecessarily difficult for readers.

2. The government needs to increase the import tax on Japanese automobiles.

3. Some teachers make learning fun.

4. Marijuana should be legalized in the United States.

5. College athletics need to be de-emphasized.

A Word of Caution

Identifying main ideas can help you better understand paragraphs and reading assignments. However, you should remember that *not all paragraphs include main ideas*. There are occasions, for example, when authors require more space than even a ten- or twenty-sentence paragraph provides in order to develop a single idea. In such instances, they may write a three- or four-*page* paragraph and then divide it into shorter, more readable segments by arbitrarily indenting. To the eye, accustomed to indented paragraphs, the single, long paragraph appears to be three or four shorter, separate paragraphs.

When you find such paragraphs in a reading assignment, do not be misled. Find the main idea. It is there — at the beginning, in the middle, or at the end. The surrounding paragraphs contain supporting, subordinate examples and details. Often, formal outlining allows you to detect such situations more readily than simply looking for main ideas in each paragraph.

There are paragraphs that do not include main ideas because their authors failed to organize their material. Sometimes authors present information in such a manner that it cannot be outlined. Occasionally you will find paragraphs that are unorganized collections of information lacking a single unifying main idea.

When you encounter paragraphs that lack even implied, or unstated, main ideas, you may be forced to create main ideas to help you make sense of the material presented. However, the process of searching for nonexistent main ideas and then creating your own to superimpose on the author's material can be extremely valuable. It encourages active thinking, which in turn assists you in comprehending new material.

USING MAIN IDEAS IN OUTLINING

Outlining is a valuable note-taking technique. It helps you to understand reading assignments because it encourages you to look for main ideas and see them in relation to other sentences in a paragraph. As you outline, you force yourself to distinguish between main ideas and supporting details and examples.

What is a formal outline? It is a summary in skeleton form in which letters and numbers are used to show (1) main ideas, (2) supporting examples and details, and (3) relationships among all these.

Usually, main ideas are indicated by roman numerals: I, II, III, and so on. Supporting or subordinate examples and details are shown by capital letters: A, B, C, and so on. When other examples and details are needed to support or further describe these, they are indicated by arabic numbers: 1, 2, 3, and so on. If further details are needed to describe or explain these items, small letters are used: a, b, c, and so on. Each new set of letters or numbers is indented, so that a completed outline usually looks something like this:

I. _____

   A. _____

      1. _____

         a. _____

A highly detailed formal outline might look like this:

I. Main Idea (top level of importance)
    A. Supporting example or detail (second level of importance)
        1. Additional example or detail (third level of importance)
            a. Further additional example or detail (fourth level of importance)
            b. Further additional example or detail (fourth level of importance)
II. Next Main Idea (top level)
    A. Supporting example or detail (second level)
    B. Supporting example or detail (second level)
        1. Additional example or detail (third level)
        2. Additional example or detail (third level)
    C. Supporting example or detail (second level)

Remember: Each individual outline may look different. In the above sample, the author needed only one second-level support under the I, but two fourth-level items. Under roman numeral II, however, the author needed three second-level supporting items but nothing under capital letters A and C. Another reading assignment would probably lead to an outline that looked quite different.

Here is the way an actual paragraph may look when outlined:

THE PARAGRAPH

     The governor is reputed to work incessantly. One aide tells of staff meetings that extend into the early hours of the morning. She says that one conference lasted until 2:00 A.M. One planning session, according to her, went through until breakfast the next day. Another assistant says he usually picks the governor up at his home at 5:30 A.M. and drives him to the executive office. Once at the office, he reviews the day's schedule while munching toast and drinking the first of many cups of coffee. After this quick refreshment, he plunges at once into his first meetings of the day.

THE OUTLINE

I. The governor is reputed to work incessantly.
    A. Meetings extend into early hours.
        1. One lasted until 2:00 A.M.
        2. Another until breakfast the next day.

    B. He starts his day at 5:30.

        1. He reviews schedule while eating.

        2. After this, he begins first meeting of day.

This is a simple, well-organized paragraph from a weekly newsmagazine, one that is relatively easy to outline. Paragraphs from college textbooks are not always as tightly organized and, consequently, may not lead to such neat outlines.

Examine this paragraph from a psychology textbook and the outline based upon it:

THE PARAGRAPH

Both semantic and episodic memory are aspects of long-term memory but reflect different kinds of memories. Semantic memory represents knowledge of conceptual relations about the world that are shared with other people. Episodic memory represents one's personal record of individual experiences. For example, Bob's knowledge that carrots grow underground is part of his semantic memory, but Sally's knowledge that she is destined to have them for dinner (and that she hates them) is part of her episodic memory. Her knowledge that clouds contain water is part of her semantic memory, and his knowledge that he got caught in a rainstorm yesterday is part of his episodic.

THE OUTLINE

I. Semantic and episodic memory reflect different aspects of long-term memory.

    A. Semantic memory represents knowledge of the world shared with others.

        1. Bob's knowledge that carrots grow undergound.

        2. Sally's knowledge that clouds contain water.

    B. Episodic memory represents one's personal record of individual experiences.

        1. Sally's knowledge that she is to have carrots for dinner.

        2. Bob's knowledge that he got wet in a rainstorm yesterday.

Outlining the paragraph about the governor is easy because its author presented the material in a consecutive manner: Roman numeral I is followed, as expected, by capital letters A and B, and both A and B are followed by the examples 1 and 2, 1 and 2. The paragraph from the psychology textbook is more difficult to outline because its author presented the A and B to support roman numeral I immediately after the I, and the supporting 1 and 2, 1 and 2 together at the end of the paragraph. However, in both cases, outlining is a valuable study technique in that it encourages you to identify the main ideas and distinguish them from supporting examples and details.

EXERCISE 4

To gain further practice in outlining, read the following selection, "How Do Words Get Meanings?" As you read, try to identify the main ideas and distinguish them from supporting examples and details. At the end of the selection, complete a brief outline of it.

HOW DO WORDS GET MEANINGS?

We all take words for granted. We assume that the words we use were created with meanings attached. Actually, this is not true at all.

Few words were created with firm meanings attached to them. When Edwin Land invented the process for developing film within the camera, he made up a name for his new camera: the *Polaroid*. This is an example of a word made up with a meaning already attached. Another example is *radar*. Scientists during World War II invented a system for bouncing ultrahigh-frequency radio waves from incoming aircraft back to land bases in order to warn of enemy air attacks. At first they called their system "*radio detecting and ranging*," then shortened it to *radar*. When other scientists later figured out a way to bounce signals back from undersea craft, such as submarines, they invented the word *sonar* for "*sound navigation ranging*." Other "made-up" words include *Coke*, *antibiotics*, *television*, and *rock-and-roll*.

Most of the words we use each day are not like these at all. Most are simply convenient symbols to which we attach meanings. If they originally had one specific meaning, we cannot be sure what it was. Take, for example, the word *record*. Originally, as near as scholars can say, it came from the Latin word for "remember." People, in order to remember things,

wrote them down on a piece of paper. In time, to-write-something-down-
to-remember-it became "to record." A record was the written information.
People for years have talked of "court records," "hospital records," and
"school records." When the phonograph was invented, a name was needed
for those cylinders used to capture sounds on shellac. People called them
records. And when cylinders proved less efficient than rounded disks,
people began to call the new shellac disks *records.* The word *disk* itself is
another example of how meanings get attached to words through usage.
Originally, scholars tell us, disk came from an old Greek word for
"throwing." The ancient Greeks threw thin, flat plates, something like our
modern Frisbees. People in more modern times used *disk* for rounded,
thin, flat phonograph records; even more recently, we have begun to use
the same term for one component of the computer (you've heard of "floppy
disks").

Meanings are in the heads of speakers, listeners, readers, and writers.
They are symbols that speakers, listeners, readers, and writers use to stand
for their knowledge of objects, situations, events, actions, and ideas. They
represent the thoughts people carry in their heads about these objects,
situations, events, actions, and ideas. When all people agree about the
meanings they give to words, they understand one another easily. When
they have different meanings for words, communication breaks down.

How would you outline this brief article? Below is an incomplete
outline. Fill in the blank lines with the appropriate information.

HOW DO WORDS GET MEANINGS?

I.   _____

      _____

II.   Few words were created with firm meanings attached to them.

      A. _____

          1. Made up by Edwin Land

          2. Needed for new camera.

      B. _____

          1. Made up by scientists in World War II

          2. Needed to describe _____

          3. Originally called _____

C. Sonar

    1. _____

    2. _____

D.

III. Most words are convenient symbols to which we attach meanings.

A. Record

    1.

    2.

    3.

    4.

B. _____

    1. Originally meant _____

    2. From ancient Greek

    3. _____

    4. _____

IV. _____

_____

A. _____

B. _____

C. _____

D. _____

There are two important points you need to note about this outline:

1. The main idea in the first short sentence is *implied*. You should have written "Words are not created with meanings attached," or something similar. The author did not say this exactly, but he or she expected you to figure out the main idea from what was said in the three sentences of the short paragraph.

2. The items under the capital letters (that is, the Arabic numbers 1, 2, 3, and so on) may vary from reader to reader. This is all right. You may find three or four points you want to write in; someone else may find only two or three. What you list depends on how much information you want to record.

EXERCISE 5

Now try traditional outlining from a textbook chapter. Take the next assignment you have to do and outline it formally, using the plan described here. You should have major headings (with roman numerals) to indicate information at the top level of importance, supporting examples (with capital letters) to indicate the second level of importance, and so on. Your completed outline may not look exactly like those done by other students, but it will help you better understand how the assignment has been organized; later it will help you review for a test.

EXERCISE 6

Try one of the mapping outlines described in Chapter 3. Place the general topic of the assignment on the top of your page, and then write the various main ideas at the ends of lines coming from it. Subordinate ideas and information will be placed on the outline at the ends of lines also. Each line will indicate the relationship of the subordinate material. Your completed outline may look something like this:

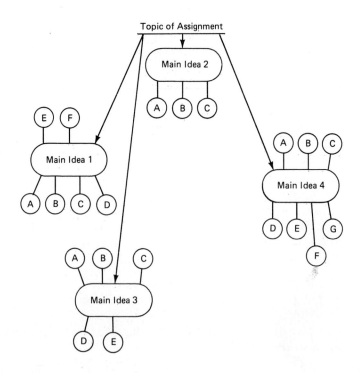

FINDING MAIN IDEAS IN CHARTS, GRAPHS, AND TABLES

Authors often use charts, graphs, and tables to clarify and organize information pictorially. They find that some ideas and information are more easily conveyed to readers in relatively nonverbal forms. You need to identify main ideas in these pictorial representations just as you need to find them in paragraphs.

A *table* is simply a display of data. It may be written, printed, or typed. When an author has material that seems more easily understood in a basic outline form, he or she may present it as a table. The Table of Contents in the front of this book is such a table. You can see that if all this information has been presented to you in paragraph form it would have been difficult to read. In table form you can see the topics and chapter titles at a glance and easily locate sections within chapters as well as page numbers. Tables are a convenient way to display certain kinds of information.

A *graph* is also a visual display, but it usually shows some relationship between two sets of figures. The table of contents for a book could not be presented in graph form, but if for some reason the author wanted to show you how many chapters of a book on study skills dealt with listening compared to, say, reading skill, he or she could present this information in a graph. For example, if the author wanted to show that out of fourteen chapters, two dealt with listening and four with reading skills, he or she could draw a *line graph* as follows:

Total number of chapters   1 2 3 4 5 6 7 8 9 10 11 12 13 14

Listening chapters   ——

Reading chapters   —————

A *bar graph* for the same information might look as follows:

Total number of chapters   1 2 3 4 5 6 7 8 9 10 11 12 13 14

Listening chapters

Reading chapters

A *pie graph*, or *circle graph*, for the same information would show a circle (or "pie") divided into fourteen segments with listening and reading chapters colored in:

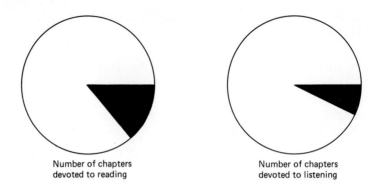

Number of chapters
devoted to reading

Number of chapters
devoted to listening

A *chart* can be any drawing, either a table or a graph, that presents material visually. However, certain kinds of charts are frequently used in books.

A *process chart* displays the steps in a procedure. For example, the SQ3R study system might be shown visually in a process chart this way:

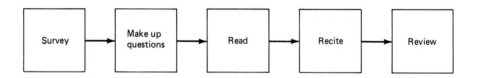

An *organizational chart* displays a plan of organization for different types of institutions, systems, or programs. For example, the academic study-skills program in a college might be shown this way:

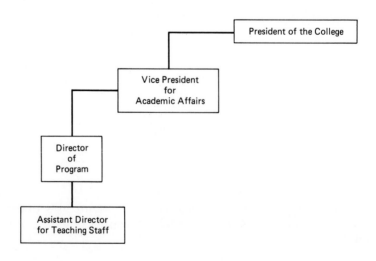

A *flowchart* displays a related series of items and their relationship in a process or procedure. A flowchart for the SQ3R study system might look like this:

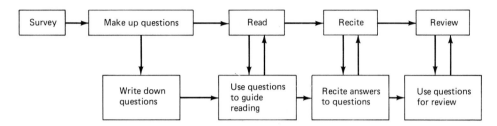

A *tree chart* displays how a number of items in a group relate to one another. A tree chart for a study-skills book or course might look like this:

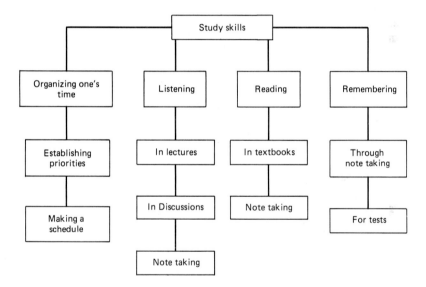

Charts, graphs, and tables can all help you better understand the material in an assignment. Here are some suggestions for dealing with any you encounter in your textbooks:

1. Read the title.   The title (and subtitle) serves as a summary of the total display. You'll not make any sense of it if you cannot see what it is about and how it fits into the total chapter.

2. Read introductory information.   Charts, graphs, and tables are rarely presented by themselves. Usually the author introduces them with a sentence or two (often a short paragraph). You need this basic information to help you interpret the display.

3. Identify its purpose. The author has a definite purpose for presenting a pictorial presentation. Ask yourself Why: Could this information be presented in ordinary sentences and paragraphs? What purpose is served by this particular display? If you turn the title of the display into a question, often the purpose of the display is to answer the question.

4. Identify its type.   As you have seen, various types of graphs, charts, and tables serve different purposes. Is this a pie graph? A bar graph? A flowchart? A simple table? Knowing the type helps you identify its purpose.

5. Read all information given on the display.   The information given at the top, along the sides, and at the bottom provides you with vital clues to your interpretation. If you fail to pick up these clues, you may misunderstand the point of the display.

6. Make sure you know what is being measured.   Does the display compare people, places, things, ideas, or numbers? You need to know in order to make sense of the display.

7. Look for codes or keys.   In order to save space, special codes or keys are sometimes used. As you examine the introductory material and the lines of print under the display, watch for information that reveals the use of such space savers.

8. Relate the display to the text.   Read all printed material carefully so you can relate what has been said in sentences and paragraphs to what is shown pictorially. The chart, graph, or table should help you better understand the assignment. If it does not, you need to go back and read carefully the preceding pages and the display a second — or third — time.

9. Find its main idea.   After you have studied a chart, graph, or table, think again about its purpose in the chapter: Why is it there? What purpose does it serve? Then try to state its main idea in a sentence or two.

10. Summarize.   The real test of how well you have understood any visual representation comes when you try to tell someone else what it means. After you have studied a chart, graph, or table, either write out a brief summary or tell someone (even yourself) what it means.

EXERCISE 7

Read the following graph and answer the questions that are given.

HEIGHTS OF MALE STUDENTS
IN FRESHMAN ENGLISH CLASS
AT WESTERN UNIVERSITY

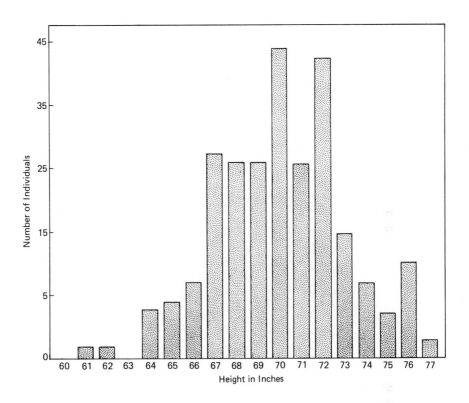

1. What kind of graph is this?

2. What is its purpose?

3. What kind of information is presented by the vertical bars?

4. What is the tallest height noted?

5. How many students are in this category?

6. How many students are 70 inches tall?

7. What is the difference between the tallest and the shortest groups?

8. How many students are 63 inches tall?

9. How many individual students are in the whole population of students shown in this graph?

10. Using the information provided by this graph, tell what is the average height of secondary school seniors.

EXERCISE 8

*Review the graph in the previous exercise, "Heights of Male Students."
Then write a paragraph that presents the same information. Your task
is to transform a pictorial presentation into a verbal one. Start with a
clear expression of the main idea, and then support it with sentences
containing the appropriate information.*

EXERCISE 9

Select a chart, graph, or table from one of your textbook assignments and answer the following questions about it.

1. What type of display is it?

2. What is its purpose?

3. What items are compared?

4. Could this information have been presented in sentences and/or paragraphs? Why? Why not?

5. What is its main idea? Summarize in three or four sentences what you have learned from this display.

EXERCISE 10

One of the best ways to discover what you have learned in a reading assignment is to summarize it. In the space provided, write a one-paragraph summary of Chapter 5, Learning to Note and Use Main Ideas.

POINTS TO REMEMBER ABOUT MAIN IDEAS

1. Identifying main ideas helps your comprehension.

2. They are often indicated in titles and headings.

3. Main ideas in paragraphs often come at the beginning.

4. Sometimes they appear in the middle or at the end.

5. Sometimes they are unstated, or implied, and you have to infer them.

6. You can often summarize an assignment by listing the main ideas in its paragraphs.

7. Outlining helps you see main ideas in relationship to supporting examples and details.

8. Mapping is sometimes a good alternative to formal outlining.

9. Authors often use charts, graphs, and tables to clarify and organize information pictorially.

10. You need to look for main ideas in charts, graphs, and tables as well as in paragraphs.

5
MASTERY TEST

Check how well you read and understood this chapter by completing the following statements.

1. Most paragraphs tend to have a main idea and

    _____ .

2. Their main ideas may be found _____ ,

    _____ , _____ , and

    _____ .

3. Sometimes, however, the main idea of a paragraph is

    _____ .

4. You can often summarize a reading assignment by

    _____ .

5. Formal outlining helps you see main ideas in relation to

    _____ .

6. In a formal outline, supporting or subordinate examples and details
   are indicated under roman numerals by _____ .

7. When a fourth level of importance is needed, you should use

    _____ .

8. In a mapping outline, you indicate the relationships of main ideas
   and supporting items by _____ .

9. Reading the previous and following sentences is a good way of

    _____ .

10. Paraphrasing is _____ .

6

Learning to Recognize and Use Organizational Patterns

INTRODUCTION AND OVERVIEW

Writers tend to organize their material. Rather than simply present material in random fashion to readers, they organize their information and ideas according to some plan or pattern. When there is a plan, writers find it easier to write and readers find it easier to understand what has been written.

This chapter examines six basic patterns writers use. Knowing these patterns provides you with at least two advantages: (1) You will more readily perceive how authors organize their material, and (2) you can use these plans in your own college writing. Thus, knowledge of basic patterns benefits you as both a reader and writer.

SUGGESTED GUIDE QUESTIONS

1. What are organizational patterns?
2. Why do writers use them?

3. Which organizational patterns are most widely used?

4. What are signal words and phrases?

5. In what ways does knowing patterns help readers?

WHAT ARE ORGANIZATIONAL PLANS?

When writers need to present large amounts of material, they adopt a plan to guide them. They must do so if they expect readers to make sense of their ideas and information. Imagine how difficult it would be to understand a textbook reading assignment if the author simply gave you all the information on a topic strung together across the page in a random fashion: first this, then that, then something else — all without any logical connection between one point and another. As a reader, you would be puzzled and frustrated. Clearly, some plan is essential if communication is to take place between writer and reader.

Six patterns widely used by writers to organize material are:

1. Enumeration

2. Sequence

3. Generalization

4. Cause and effect

5. Comparison and contrast

6. Question-answer

Enumeration

In writing about ways to improve reading comprehension, an author may note six specific strategies readers can use to better understand a difficult passage. Rather then jump back and forth from one to another, saying a little bit about this strategy and then a little bit about another, the author may decide simply to *list* the strategies, describing one first, another second, another third, and so on. When a writer organizes material in such a way, he or she is following an enumeration pattern.

Here is an example of the enumeration plan taken from a spy story done in a college creative writing class:

There were four places in the cellar in which a radio might have been hidden. I asked myself where I might have hidden it. It could have been hidden behind the sliding door that led into the furnace area. A second good place might be on the shelves about the work table, mixed in with tools and discarded appliances. A third good spot might be in a drawer under the table, for each seemed big enough to hold a radio transmitter. The fourth place — the one I'd have chosen myself — was the furnace. Who would ever look within the furnace at this time of the year?

Notice that the student writer tells readers that there are *four places* in which a radio might be hidden; then she systematically describes each. As she moves from one to the other, she signals readers by saying "a *second* good place," "a *third* good place," "the *fourth* place." This is the enumeration plan in its basic form as it is found in much writing: The writer tells you what is going to be listed and then gives the list.

Enumeration can be more complicated. Here is a student paper in which the writer enumerates reasons for a certain decision. The writer is telling readers why she came to the decision, but presents her material in the enumeration pattern.

Although I realize that there are more law school graduates than there are openings in law firms, I plan to attend law school. One of my general goals in life is to be a financial success. I may reach this goal through work in business, industry, banking, real estate — or law. My decision to go to law school rather than business school is based on three advantages offered by legal training.

In the first place, I understand that legal training sharpens the mind. My mental abilities will be challenged and I'll be forced to think through difficult problems daily, thus developing all my critical thinking and problem-solving powers. In the second place, much education in law school is gained through reading and writing, and these skills are needed for success in all other kinds of high-level professional work. I'll be forced each week to read difficult law cases and write analyses of them, thus gaining constant practice in these important skills. Finally, I think the competition in law school will be good for me. Having to compete with other top students from other colleges for grades and honors will give me an edge that I can carry into other fields.

As you read these two paragraphs, you should note that the writer *tells you her plan* and then *signals each item on her list*. In the last sentence in the first paragraph, she says "My decision . . . is based on three advantages offered by legal training." As a skilled reader, you now look for the three advantages. In the next paragraph she signals each advantage by saying, "In the first place," "In the second place," and "Finally." As you read, you know that each of these signals will be followed by one of the advantages.

To be a successful reader, you should be aware of this widely used pattern. Sometimes it serves as the basic plan for an entire article or textbook chapter. More often it serves as the structure underlying a paragraph or a section of an article or chapter. To be a successful writer, you should know how to use this plan because it can frequently provide you with a structure for your own paragraphs or papers.

There are three points to remember about using this pattern in your own writing:

- ***The material must lend itself to the pattern.*** You can use it in many papers, but not all. Sometimes, as will be shown in this chapter, other patterns are more appropriate for your purposes.

- ***You need to tell your readers what you are doing.*** You need to write: "There are three advantages," "Five events led to the revolution," or "Several explanations may account for this condition."

- ***You also need to signal each new item.*** Let readers know that new items are introduced by writing "first," "second," "the third reason," "the fourth explanation," or "finally." Such transitional words and phrases, or *signal words*, keep readers informed of your plan of organization.

EXERCISE 1

Read the following paragraph from a student paper and be ready to indicate (1) how the writer lets readers know which pattern underlies the plan of the paper, and (2) the specific signal words used to guide readers through the paper.

Pornography is anti-woman. One can easily list at least three reasons to support this belief. The typical pornographic magazine, for example, treats women as objects. In these publications, they are possessions to be owned, borrowed, or leased. They are never treated as human beings. A second reason is that nine out of ten magazines on display in the typical "adult" bookstore focus on women and girls rather than on men. The numbers should make it clear that the vast majority of pornographic magazines are truly "girlie" magazines rather than sex publications. Finally, such publications never describe feelings of love or tenderness but only physical, sexual behaviors. They describe a world without human emotions in which women, not men, are objects for play and amusement rather than human beings with human aspirations and ideals.

Answer the following questions to discover how well you recognize the ways the pattern of enumeration is used here.

1. What is the thesis or main-idea statement upon which the paragraph is based?

2. What phrase does the author use to let you know the underlying plan or pattern?

3. What signal words are used to note the first reason?

4. What signal words note the second and third reasons?

5. What changes might you make to improve this short paper? (Indicate them here.)

EXERCISE 2

Go through one of your course textbooks and locate three examples of the enumeration plan. Note how the author indicated the plan and the signal words used.

Example 1

1. From (give title of book and page numbers):

2. Topic of the paragraph or section:

3. Words used to indicate pattern:

4. How many items enumerated:

5. Signal words used:

Example 2

1. From:

2. Topic:

3. Words used to indicate pattern:

4. How many items enumerated:

5. Signal words used:

Example 3

1. From:

2. Topic:

3. Words used to indicate pattern:

4. How many items enumerated:

5. Signal words used:

EXERCISE 3

Write a paragraph on any topic you choose, following the enumeration plan. Make sure to indicate your plan to readers and signal each item with appropriate words.

Sequence

Sometimes items on a list need to be sequenced in some way. To make better sense to readers, they must be arranged in some order, such as first to last, smallest to largest, or least important to most important. To present a list of historical events, one writer may decide that readers would understand them best if presented in the order in which they occurred. In writing about events that led to the civil rights movement of the 1960s, another author might choose to sequence items in either chronological order or of significance. A chemist telling about an experiment may sequence items carefully so that another chemist can replicate the same experiment.

Chronological sequence is used when relating events about the past. It is used in history books, stories, anecdotes, even jokes. It is also used when predicting the future, and in science fiction and directions. Other kinds of sequencing may be found in articles, essays, reports, and other forms of writing.

To understand simple sequencing patterns, it may be useful to examine two examples of freshman writing. One is an account of a personal experience; the other is a set of directions for changing an automobile tire.

A.

The midyear break was a disaster story for me. Here's what happened. First, I couldn't get a flight home and had to fly standby. I waited for five hours at the airport before I could get on a plane home. Next, I discovered when I got there that the airline had somehow misplaced my luggage. I had all kinds of things I wanted to bring home and show the family, but — no bags! Then, when I gave up on the luggage and decided to take a cab home from the airport, I discovered that the cabbies were on strike. Next, I tried to call home to get a ride from the airport and realized I had no change for the telephone. When I finally walked in the front door, ten hours after I'd left school, no one was home!

B.

To change an automobile tire is a snap. Let me explain. First, you jack up the end of the car with the flat tire. Then you take off the hubcap and tire lugs. Next you remove the wheel with the flat tire and replace it with your spare from the trunk. Finally, you remove the jack and off you go!

Notice that in each paragraph these students let readers know their intentions and plans. The writer of the first says the midyear break was a disaster story and then "Here's what happened." The writer of the second tells the readers at once that the paragraph is about tire changing and notes that he will explain how to do it. In both, signal words are clearly evident: *first*, *next*, *then*, and *finally*. Each writer is enumerating items from a list but giving them in a chronological sequence.

When you use the chronological pattern in your own writing be sure that you:

Have material that naturally falls into a time sequence.

Give your readers an indication that you are using such a sequence pattern.

Use appropriate words to signal them when you introduce new items in the sequence.

Sequence patterns tend to be more complicated than those used in the two examples given here. As you read your textbooks, watch for variations in use of the pattern.

EXERCISE 4

Read the following paragraph from a history book. Watch for the signal words and be prepared to answer the questions that follow.

> The British Eighth Army was stationed in the desert about 35 miles from Tobruk. Rommel had to oust the army to regain control of Africa. He began his attack on May 26 with a feint in the north designed to distract the British from his main force on the southern flank of the British strong point. Unfortunately for the Germans, the British held the southern flank and were able to isolate a sizeable German force, leaving it exposed to air attack and deprived of fuel, food, and water. Because the British failed to seize the opportunity of counterattacking, two-thirds of Rommel's troops escaped. These troops later joined with the remainder of Rommel's army to return on June 20. Their mass attack on Tobruk succeeded and almost the entire British garrison was captured along with valuable supplies, including the much-needed fuel. Less than a month later, Rommel, now promoted to Field Marshall, entered Egypt triumphantly.

1. What is the main idea of the paragraph?

2. What sentence or phrase helped you realize that this paragraph was arranged according to a sequence pattern?

3. What words or phrases signaled you that the author was moving from one point in time to another?

4. What other kinds of signal words beside *first*, *second*, or *finally* are used here to indicate the next steps in a sequence?

5. Which items in this sequence are not signaled at all?

6. How might you outline this paragraph? Use the main idea as your title and then list each step under it.

EXERCISE 5

Write out a favorite joke or humorous story using the sequence pattern. Underline the sentence or phrase by which you tell readers you are using a sequence. Circle all your signal words.

EXERCISE 6

Give directions to readers, telling them how to make or find something. Again, underline the words you use to indicate sequence and circle the words that signal the steps in the sequence.

Generalization

One of the most widely used patterns, one you should understand thoroughly, is the *generalization-plus-examples*. The writer makes a general statement about the topic, usually the sentence that expresses the main idea of the paragraph. Because the writer wants readers to accept the statement, he or she immediately sets out to prove it. This plan is frequently found in speech as well as writing. For example, a speaker says, "This is the worst winter we've had in years." She then supports her statement with two pieces of evidence: "Our pipes froze for the first time in all the years we've lived in the house" and "We have also paid the highest heating bill we've ever had."

This informal example from conversation represents the generalization pattern in its purest form: a generalization supported by two examples. Found regularly in daily speech, this pattern is also used frequently in writing, particularly textbook writing. Authors make statements about their topics and then support them with specific examples from their research.

Here is an example from a history textbook:

As the war continued, the Nazi Party itself began to fall apart. First, Rudolf Hess, one of Hitler's most trusted aides, flew himself out of Germany to Scotland, where he parachuted from the plane to ask British authorities to make common cause with the Nazis against the USSR. Second, Himmler, head of Hitler's dreaded SS, sent representatives to a religious conference in Stockholm to sound out the possibility of an overthrow of Hitler by the SS. Finally, of course, was the nearly successful attempt in July, 1944, of a group of German officers to plant a bomb under the Führer's table in his East Prussian headquarters.

Notice that the first sentence, the main idea of the paragraph, is a generalization. The next three sentences offer proof or evidence to support the generalization. At first, a paragraph or paragraphs may appear to be either enumeration or sequence but, once readers note the generalization, or main idea, they realize that the following items are offered as evidence, not as items in a series.

This pattern, like enumeration or sequence, may be used as the basis for longer passages or sections of a chapter. Another recent history textbook takes the information given in the single paragraph above and develops it as a ten-page section in a chapter. The first sentence becomes a brief introductory paragraph to give readers an overview. The sentence about Hess serves as the main-idea sentence for five other paragraphs, in which more details are given about Hess's flight. (They tell, for example, how he twisted his ankle in the fall, gave a false name, ended the war in prison, and so on.) The second sentence about Himmler serves as the main idea for four more paragraphs, which discuss the details of the Stockholm conference, give the names of the British and American representatives, describe the steps taken to contact them, and so on. The third sentence about the assassination plot serves as the main idea for a lengthy description of the plotters, their goals, the specific plans they rehearsed, and even the type of bomb used. Clearly, the generalization-plus-examples pattern can be used for more than a single paragraph.

EXERCISE 6

Take each of the following three generalizations and support it with two pieces of evidence. Your evidence does not have to be based on library research. Note the example.

EXAMPLE:

Generalization: Most automobile accidents are caused by teenage drivers.

Support 1:   Open the Sunday papers each week and you regularly find stories of fatalities in which at least one of the drivers was under twenty.

Support 2:   Three of my friends — all of high school age — have been seriously hurt in automobile collisions.

1. Many automotive accidents are caused by older people driving too slowly for prevailing road conditions.

    Support 1:

    Support 2:

2. Large American cars are basically safer than smaller Japanese models.

    Support 1:

    Support 2:

3. Many fatalities can be linked to alcohol.

    Support 1:

    Support 2:

EXERCISE 7

Notice what happens in each of the examples you just completed. If you combined all three sentences you would get a paragraph in which the generalization is the main-idea sentence. Clearly, the generalization pattern lies at the heart of much paragraph writing. Test this by developing a pattern as you did in the previous exercise and rewriting it as a paragraph.

STEP 1   Generalization:

Supporting evidence:

Supporting evidence:

STEP 2   Now rewrite these three sentences in paragraph form. Indent your first or main-idea sentence, and connect it to the others to get a well-organized paragraph.

EXERCISE 8

After you have written a paragraph using this pattern, you should be able to spot such paragraphs more easily in your textbooks.

Find such a paragraph in a course textbook and recopy it here so that it conforms to the basic pattern structure.

Generalization:

Supporting evidence 1:

Supporting evidence 2:

Supporting evidence 3:

Supporting evidence 4:

(You may find fewer, or more, examples of supporting evidence in the paragraph you select.)

EXERCISE 9

Here is an example of the generalization pattern from a college chemistry textbook. As you read it, watch for the main idea and supporting examples and details.

> Compounds containing radioactive isotopes can be detected because of their radioactivity. Using a Geiger counter or other detecting device, it is possible to trace the movement of such radio-isotopes through a plant or an animal. The rate of phosphate intake in plants can be detected by using radiophosphorus; the utilization of carbon dioxide in photosynthesis by using radioactive carbon. The accumulation of iodine in the thyroid gland can be detected by using radioactive iodine, and the absorption of iron by the hemoglobin of the blood can be detected by using radioactive iron. The research into such *tagged* compounds (that is, compounds containing a radioactive isotope) seems unlimited.

1. What is the generalization, or main idea, of the paragraph?

2. What examples are given to support the generalization?

3. How would you outline this paragraph? (Use the space below.)

Cause and Effect

Another common pattern is cause and effect (sometimes called *causal analysis*). In it the writer states a cause and then discusses its effects, or states an effect and gives its possible causes.

Here is a simple example from a paper written by a college freshman:

> I chose this college for at least three reasons. In the first place, it is close to my home. I cannot afford to live in a dormitory and wanted to find a school close enough to home so that I could continue to live with my parents. My second reason is that this college is one of the only ones in this part of the state that offers a program in restaurant management. My part-time job in my father's restaurant has led me to believe that I should seek good training in this field. Someday I might want to play a major role in the family business or in a major restaurant chain. My third reason is simply that many of my best friends are attending this school and I feel more comfortable going to school with people I have known for years.

It is easy to outline such a passage as this. The main-idea sentence is clearly the first: "I chose this college for at least three reasons." The three reasons are then enumerated with clear signals ("In the first place," and so on), thus informing readers which is which. The first sentence here is the *effect* and the three reasons are the *causes*. The writer might have reversed the order of presentation and given readers the three causes for his decision and then said, "Therefore, I chose to attend this college." The basic structure of the cause-and-effect pattern would still be evident.

Usually, writers signal this pattern by using such words and phrases as *because, reason, therefore, as a result, another reason, some consequences*, and so on. When you see such signals you are probably dealing with cause and effect.

EXERCISE 10

The example just given is clear-cut. Here is one from a college psychology textbook. Read it and then complete the outline to show that you can see how the pattern works.

> Researchers are not entirely sure how information gets from short- to long-term memory. Several hypothetical reasons have been suggested. It is said, for example, that repetition plays a role in the process. When learners repeat something over and over again, information is retained. Another explanation concerns relationships: when learners are able to relate new material to what they know, it seems easier to remember it. Another reason for retention comes from simple survival: people remember what they *must* remember.

Outline of pattern

The effect:

Possible cause 1:

Possible cause 2:

Possible cause 3:

EXERCISE 11

Find an example of a cause-and-effect pattern in one of your course textbooks; outline it here.

Effect:

Cause 1:

Cause 2:

Cause 3:

EXERCISE 12

Find an example in a textbook of the cause-and-effect pattern in which a single cause has several effects. Outline it here.

Cause:

Effect 1:

Effect 2:

Effect 3:

Comparison and Contrast

Another useful pattern allows you to better understand one thing by comparing it and contrasting it with another. For example, you want to share with readers your thinking about large urban colleges, so you compare and contrast them with small rural colleges. One student wrote:

> The large city college allows students opportunities to enjoy the excitement and stimulation of city life. They are in constant contact with hundreds of businesses, theaters, banks, museums, musical events, sports activities, and so on. They are exposed daily to the rough and tumble of the large metropolis with its social services, crime, churches, disorder, newspapers, strikes, inconveniences, and conveniences. They are living parts of a gigantic organism composed of millions of fellow human beings. The result: better preparation for living in the modern world.

What the student has done here is answer the question, What are the advantages of going to a college based in a large city? The underlying pattern is basic enumeration. The writer has simply listed the advantages from his point of view.

To develop this paragraph into a short theme, the writer may add a second paragraph focusing upon the advantages of the small college:

> The smaller, rural college, on the other hand, provides other kinds of values. Students can study in an atmosphere free from distracting stimulations. They do not have to worry about getting to and from classes on public transportation, because they live on

campus. They are also in a position to know all their classmates, not just the few who attend certain classes with them. They also have the great advantage of getting to know all their instructors better, because classes are usually smaller and social gatherings more intimate.

The comparison-and-contrast pattern is signaled here by the phrase "on the other hand." This cues readers into the plan used by the writer to organize his information. This paper could have become a cause-and-effect paper if the writer had added another paragraph telling why he chose the city rather than the rural school. After spelling out the advantages and disadvantages of each, he could have used these as reasons to make a decision.

The signal words and phrases used most often in comparison-and-contrast papers are *compare, contrast, between, difference, on the other hand, unlike, similar, whereas, distinguish,* and so on. When you see such signals, watch for comparison and contrast.

Here is an example of comparison and contrast from a college economics textbook.

To protect the public from incompetent practitioners, physicians and attorneys have traditionally tried to establish high professional standards by limiting entry into their professions.

Doctors, for example, have created a number of barriers to entry. These include (1) the difficulties of admission to an approved medical school, (2) the high cost of establishing new medical schools, (3) several years of internship and residency at low pay, and (4) various certification rules. While the need for high standards is seldom disputed, there is little doubt that doctors' salaries and incomes are higher than they otherwise would be because the barriers set up to prevent easy entry into the profession limit competition. Several studies indicate that restrictions on entering medicine are greater than they need be to protect the public and that, as a result, doctors' earnings are the highest of any profession.

Lawyers, by contrast, have been much less successful in limiting entry into the legal profession. It is true that major law schools, such as Harvard, Michigan, and Stanford, admit only a small number of qualified applicants each year and refuse to expand enough to keep up with increasing demands for admission. However, new law schools seem to open daily. In sharp contrast to medical schools which require extensive laboratory facilities and small classes, law schools may be established inexpensively: no expensive facilities are required beyond a library and class size may extend to 200 or 300 students. Because many new law schools have proven to be financially beneficial to universities, more and more have opened throughout the country.

Their graduates do gain access to the profession because even when schools are substandard, their graduates may pass state bar examinations by attending private "cram" schools.

Lawyers, thus faced with their inability to limit competition, have relied on "wage setting," that is, having state bar associations establish and enforce minimum fees for such services as probating an estate, representing a client in court, or drawing a will. Lawyers, through their professional organizations, have also tried to prevent advertising and other forms of competition as unethical.

One result of the legal profession's lack of success in limiting entry into the profession has been that many lawyers are *underem*ployed; that is, they have fewer clients than they can handle. In contrast, many doctors tend to be *over*employed, in the sense that they have more patients than they can handle comfortably.

Notice in this selection that the main idea is stated in the brief introductory paragraph. The authors then present information about doctors and then about lawyers, using the cause-and-effect pattern. The selection as a whole, however, provides a good example of comparison and contrast because each point about one profession is neatly compared or contrasted with a point about the other. The transitional signal, *by contrast*, placed almost in the middle of the selection, indicates the pattern clearly.

EXERCISE 13

The selection about doctors and lawyers was organized logically by its authors, who probably followed an outline as they wrote. To show that you can see the basic comparison-and-contrast plan underlying this selection, prepare an outline for it here. If you need to review outlining order, reread the section on outlining in Chapter 5.

EXERCISE 14

Here is another selection from an economics textbook. Read it thought-fully, and then prepare a brief outline that indicates (1) which two items are compared and contrasted, and (2) the ways in which they are compared and contrasted.

There are two main types of commercial banking systems. One system is characterized by a relatively small number of banks with many branch offices; the other by a large number of independent banks. The first system may be found in the British Isles and in Canada where only a few banks do most of the business; the second in the United States where more than 15,000 individual banks are functioning. In the United States banks have been limited in their efforts to establish branches by various state laws, and interstate banking has been discouraged by law. In only a few states are banks allowed to establish branches statewide; some states allow no branching at all; other states permit branching, but only in areas surrounding the home office of the bank. However, the actual operation of the banking system is essentially the same in both types of systems.

EXERCISE 15

This exercise consists of three steps. First, write an introductory main-idea sentence based on the item you select. Then, prepare an outline for your sentence. Finally, write a short paper on the topic, using the outline.

STEP 1

Choose one of the following items and write an introductory sentence for it. If you choose number 1, your sentence might read: "Although both are popular rock groups, the Rolling Stones and the Beach Boys differ in a number of ways."

1. The Rolling Stones and the Beach Boys

2. Love and hate

3. Poetry and science

4. Japanese and European automobiles

5. USSR and USA

6. Public and private schools

7. High school and college

8. Movies and television

Main-idea sentence:

STEP 2

Now prepare an outline for your topic similar to this:

A. Ways in which they are alike

  1.

  2.

  3.

B. Ways in which they differ

  1.

  2.

  3.

STEP 3

Now write a short paper based on your outline.

EXERCISE 16

Read the following paragraph and then answer the questions about it.

> From the earliest years, boys and girls are treated differently. Children learn what sex they are almost as soon as they learn their names, and even children of 2½ years are aware of the proper sex roles. Boys and girls are dressed differently, given different toys to play with, and rewarded for different sorts of behavior. Young girls are given dolls and encouraged to hold them like "Mother holds baby sister"; young boys are often allowed to get dirty or to be noisy, but girls may be punished, if only by a hard look, for the same behavior.

1. What is the main idea of this paragraph?

2. What single word signals a comparison-and-contrast pattern?

3. What specific items are used to develop the comparison?

Question and Answer

The sixth basic organizational pattern you need to know is the simplest, both for writers and readers. The writer asks a question important for the discussion and then supplies an answer. Here is an example:

> Why do writers use patterns? The basic reason seems to be that they provide a way to pull material together in a sensible plan that readers may readily perceive. For example, the writer may have accumulated a great deal of data on a subject, but knows that if this is presented in a random fashion not only will he lose track of it but readers will not make sense of it. So he uses one of the basic patterns: he puts his data in a list, a sequence, a generalization plus examples, or a cause-effect or comparison-contrast plan. Sometimes he asks questions about the material and answers them.

As you will notice from this example, the answer in question-answer organization may follow a specific pattern. If the writer of the above paragraph stopped with the second sentence, that would be pure question and answer. However, the writer decided to add more information and began using, first, the generalization pattern (notice the ''for example'') and then enumeration of the various kinds of patterns.

This use of two or more patterns in the same paragraph may be seen in the following example from a history textbook:

> Why did the Japanese decide to focus all their attention on the south? At least three reasons have been suggested. Those territories, colonized in the previous century by the British, French, and Dutch, were rich in badly needed natural resources, such as oil and rubber. Second, by concentrating military attack on these areas, they could neutralize the forces of the Chinese Nationalists in southern China, thus keeping them from moving northward. Finally, the final conquest of these territories would provide the first step in the establishment of a great overseas empire for Japan.

This entire paragraph is an answer to the question posed in the first sentence. The answer itself is arranged according to the enumeration pattern. However, within the enumeration pattern you see an example of the cause-and-effect pattern, with the *Japanese focused their attacks on the south* as the cause and the three following sentences giving possible effects of it.

Question-answer paragraphs are usually easy to identify because of the question. However, they may require further analysis by readers when they use other patterns to structure their answers.

USING ORGANIZATIONAL PATTERNS

Writers can write more easily when they follow a plan and use a well-defined organizational pattern. Readers can understand more easily when they, too, can see the plan and recognize the pattern. You — as a reader and as a writer — will benefit from your knowledge of the patterns discussed here. However, there are three points to remember about organizational patterns.

1. Writers do not always use patterns.   Sometimes their material does not lend itself to one of the patterns. Sometimes they express ideas so unusual that ordinary patterns are too confining. As a writer, you may not always be able to fit your information and ideas into one of the structures described here. As a reader, you need to watch for new and unusual ways of arranging material that writers may use.

2. Sometimes patterns run together.   As may be seen from several of the examples, a writer may use more than one pattern in the same chapter or paragraph. For example, when writing a course paper, you may choose enumeration as the basic plan of organization but develop each point by generalization plus example or comparison and contrast. When reading articles or books, be aware of situations in which several plans of organization are used simultaneously.

3. Patterns usually include signal words or phrases.   As you know by now, enumeration and sequence contain signal words such as *first*, *second*, and *next*; generalization uses *for example*; comparison and contrast uses *on the other hand* or *by contrast*. As a writer/reader you need to be sensitive to the signal words and phrases available for each plan of organization.

The following list should help you:

For *Enumeration*

to begin with

then

first, second, third

next

finally

also

more

another

furthermore

in addition

at last

For *Sequence*

first, second, third

next

meanwhile

on (date)

not long after

as

meanwhile

today, tomorrow

soon

finally

at last

now

before, after, while

then

later

For *Generalization*

for example

for instance

in other words

as an illustration

thus

another example

in addition

also

For *Comparison and Contrast*

however

but

nevertheless

unless

similarly

on the one hand

on the other hand

on the contrary

in contrast

although

yet

even though

For *Cause and Effect*

as a result

because

this led to

nevertheless

if . . . then

in order that

unless

since

so that

thus

therefore

accordingly

so

consequently

For *Question and Answer*

who

what

why

which

where

when

how

in what way(s)

EXERCISE 17

To discover how well you understand the use of organizational patterns in writing and reading, complete the following.

1. Indicate in the space provided the name of the organizational pattern you would use to write a paper on the topic. (The first is done as an example.)

Topic	Organizational Pattern
1. Why students drop out of college	(Cause and effect)
2. The development of rock	
3. Setting up a bandstand	
4. A college education is expensive	
5. Five ways to succeed in college	
6. Hitler and Stalin	
7. The stages of growth in clams	
8. How to become a state senator	
9. College and high school	
10. The nine lives of a cat	
11. How to meet girls (or boys)	
12. Common faults of beginning drivers	

Topic	Organizational Pattern
13. Losing weight	
14. Growing old gracefully	
15. Making pizza	

2. Beside the name of each organizational pattern, write five signal words or phrases commonly used with it.

1. Enumeration:

2. Sequence:

3. Generalization:

4. Comparison and contrast:

5. Cause and effect:

POINTS TO REMEMBER ABOUT ORGANIZATIONAL PATTERNS

1. Knowing patterns helps you understand material.
2. Watch for the author's plan.
3. Look for familiar patterns.
4. Check for main-idea sentences.

5. Look for signal words and phrases.

6. Two or more patterns may be used in the same paragraph.

7. Use patterns when you write.

8. Use signal words to help your readers.

9. Outlining helps you see an author's plan.

10. Outlining can help you write better.

6
MASTERY TEST

To show how well you understood Chapter 6, use the space below to write a summary of it. Remember, a summary needs to include the main ideas and, if possible, important supporting examples and details. Try to complete your summary without looking back at preceding pages.

7

Learning to Think and Read Critically

INTRODUCTION AND OVERVIEW

As citizens of a free society where ideas and information flow unchecked, we are all exposed to vast amounts of written and spoken material. Much of this material is probably accurate or, if not accurate, harmless. Well-intentioned speakers and writers try to share ideas and information, explain, persuade, and amuse.

We all need to remember, however, that some of the material we encounter may be inaccurate or misleading. Some is deliberately designed to misinform or propagandize; some is unintentionally false or misleading.

This chapter reviews several basic critical reading skills that you need to use now as a college student and that you will need to use throughout life. It will show you how to evaluate sources of information, recognize bias, distinguish facts from opinions, recognize the purposes behind communications, and most important, how to better make and recognize inferences that underlie spoken and written messages.

SUGGESTED GUIDE QUESTIONS

1. Why do you need to become a critical reader?

2. Why may inferences be dangerous?

3. How are they different from facts and opinions?

4. How can you detect bias?

5. What are the propaganda devices?

EVALUATING SOURCES

All sources of information are not equal. Often we read seemingly authoritative articles and books, only to discover later that they were written by authors lacking background in the fields discussed. Regularly we hear people talk — with assurance and emphasis — about topics they really do not understand.

The author of your textbook on psychology is assumed to be an authority on psychology. You may read the book trusting that what you are told about recent trends and research in psychology is accurate information. The lecturer in your psychology class is assumed to be an authority in the field, so you take notes in the belief that the information is valid. When experts in a field write or speak about their subjects, students may accept the ideas and information as reasonably true.

However, if the author of your psychology textbook wrote an article on, say, the history of submarines, you might want to check out her background in the subject. If your psychology lecturer speaks on "Six Steps for Improving Your Lawn," you may decide to question his lawn-care credentials. These are both instances in which you *can* check: You can, for example, look up the background of the author in appropriate library resource books to discover if she does indeed possess a background in submarines; you can listen carefully to the lawn lecture and compare the information given to what you already know about lawn care and thus form a reasonable judgment about the speaker's background in this area.

Unfortunately, many times credentials are not easy to check. Readers and listeners need to be aware of the problem, asking themselves such questions as: Does this person really know what he is talking about? Does this writer have the necessary credentials to speak authoritatively about this subject? How can I find out the writer's background? How can I test her assertions?

Here are specific suggestions to guide you in evaluating sources of information and ideas:

1. You can check the credentials of many authors by looking at their books. Book jackets often include brief biographical sketches of the author. Here you can find such information as where the person went to school, what degrees he or she obtained, the names of other books written, any honors received, and what experience the person has had in the field. When such information is not given, you can often note the author's degrees or university affiliation on the title page.

2. You can often locate biographical information in the library. Such reference books as *Who's Who* provide necessary background. The card catalog can refer you to other books by the author.

3. You can ask your instructor or other faculty members. If an author is well known, members of the college staff may be able to fill you in on his or her background.

4. You can test an author's background by comparing what he says with what you already know. When statements do not mesh with your knowledge of the world and the way it works, you have some right to question the author's knowledge. It is true that you may not be well informed about a specialized subject, but as an adult, you have sufficient knowledge of life to make some sensible tentative judgments.

5. When still in doubt, you should remain skeptical. Unless you have solid assurances that the author of a questionable work is indeed an authority, assume that there is room for doubt. Many statements in many books have misled people for decades. If more had been critical readers, accurate evaluations of ideas and information would be more common than they are. Here are some examples of misinformation:

   - Countless visitors to Sequoia National Park in California have been led to believe that a giant redwood there (called General Sherman) is "the oldest living thing on the planet." However, the ages of trees can be accurately ascertained, and many other trees are known to be more than 1000 years older than General Sherman.

   - Schoolchildren are often told that Plymouth was the first settlement in New England, yet historians have long known that a colony was established thirteen years earlier in Kennebec, Maine.

   - Many books and articles still refer to Sitting Bull's role at the Battle of Little Bighorn, yet he was miles away when Crazy Horse and others ambushed Custer.

- Some books continue to claim that Henry Ford introduced the assembly line, yet it was actually Ransom E. Olds who boosted production in his company from 425 cars in 1901 to over 2500 the next year.

In these instances, it is doubtful whether speakers or writers were deliberately misleading people. What often happens is that ideas and information continue to circulate without critical examination. An authoritative source — that is, a book or article prepared by a person with the appropriate background — tends not to keep misinformation in circulation. The statements it contains have usually been checked, and sometimes double-checked, for accuracy.

Clearly, it is your responsibility as a thoughtful, critical reader and listener to look carefully at your sources of information.

Exercise 1

Use your knowledge of the world and your common sense to evaluate the following sources of information.

1. Which of the following is the best source of information about the mathematical ability of females?

    a. A column in the daily newspaper

    b. An article in a popular magazine by a mathematician

    c. An article in a research journal by a psychologist

2. Which is the best source of information about smoking marijuana?

    a. Reports from the office of the Surgeon General of the United States

    b. An article in *Rolling Stone*

    c. A chapter in a high school health textbook

3. Which is the best source of information about a particular outbreak of violence in Ulster last week?

    a. An article in an American magazine by a member of the revolutionary Irish Republican Army

    b. A news report by an American reporter in *The New York Times*

    c. A letter from a friend traveling in Europe

4. What is the best source of information about "runner's knee"?

    a. An article in *Runner's World*

    b. A freshman biology textbook

    c. The encyclopedia

5. What is the best source of information about astrology?

   a. The encyclopedia

   b. An astrology magazine

   c. A letter to the editor of a daily newspaper

EXERCISE 2

These items present few challenges. Now examine each of the following statements. Many people believe each to be true. In the space provided, write the name of the source you would go to for accurate information to support or discard each statement.

1. Bagpipes were invented in Scotland.

2. A check for two cents written on a maple leaf must be honored by the bank.

3. The Battle of Bunker Hill was fought on Breed's Hill.

4. A straight line is the shortest distance between two points.

5. Copper bracelets prevent arthritis.

6. A man named D. B. Cooper once hijacked a plane and parachuted out over Oregon with $200,000.

7. Many heroes have been awarded the Congressional Medal of Honor.

8. There are more covered bridges in Ohio than Vermont.

9. Winston Churchill invented the phrase "Iron Curtain."

10. You cannot split an infinitive.

EXERCISE 3

Select an author of one of your textbooks and learn as much informa-tion about him or her as you can. Start with biographical reference books in the library. You may have to do considerable research. One clue: Note his or her college or university affiliation and obtain a bulletin from that institution. Here you may find information about courses this person teaches, his or her college degrees, and so forth. Such bulletins may often be found in the college library or the admissions office.

EVALUATING FACT

In most printed materials, fact and opinion go hand in hand. Factual statements, such as "Dwight Eisenhower was president in 1956," run together with statements of an author's opinion, such as "He was one of our most effective chief executives." There is nothing wrong with this intermingling of fact and opinion; indeed, readers expect and desire to know how authors feel about the information they share. Unfortunately, some uncritical readers accept both fact and opinion unquestioningly. As a critical reader, you need to distinguish between the two kinds of state-ments.

A factual statement can be tested.   "George Washington was our first president" can be checked by going to old newspaper accounts, letters and journals of the time, or public records. There may be dispute about the statement's validity only when confusion exists in the sources.

A "factual" statement may indeed be incorrect.   The definition of *factual statement* accepted by most contemporary logicians is that it is a state-ment that lends itself to verification. The actual process of verification may reveal that the statement is inaccurate, but technically it remains a statement of fact. Thus, "Francis Bacon wrote the plays attributed to Shake-speare" is a statement of fact in the eyes of logicians. Unfortunately for people who say it, the evidence to prove it is inconclusive. Thus, too, a statement such as "Harry Truman was the first president" is factual — although easily disproved.

An opinion statement expresses a value, preference, or feeling.   It may be argued endlessly, but unless it can be proved or disproved, it remains an opinion. Thus, "Mother Theresa is the greatest woman who ever lived" is an opinion statement because it expresses a belief resting in a value system. It is impossible to validate such a statement: How can you prove or disprove it?

Because many people share an opinion does not make it a fact.   "America is the greatest country on earth" is an opinion shared by several million people; however, it is still an opinion. "The Supreme Court has consist-ently upheld the Bill of Rights" is factual; it can be tested by checking the historical record. The first opinion may rest upon many facts such as that cited in the second statement and may be said to be a sound or reasonable opinion, but it remains an opinion. Uncritical readers regularly assume that when they share an opinion with many others it automatically becomes a fact. This is not necessarily true: A few centuries ago, "everyone" believed that the sun circled the earth; only a few decades ago, most people believed that no one would ever actually walk on the moon's surface.

Facts are not necessarily better than opinions.   As a critical reader, you want to know how authors feel about various matters. However, you do not want to confuse their facts with their opinions. Some sources present you with many opinions and few facts; as a result, you end up knowing how authors feel about topics, but you have little specific verifiable infor-mation to use in your own thinking.

Many readers confuse fact and opinion, often basing their own judgments and later actions upon the opinions of others rather than upon factual information. This may be seen when one examines statements and conclusions such as the following:

1. John works in a supermarket every day after classes.
   John is a hard working guy.

2. Bob has never been late for chemistry class so far.
   Bob is extremely punctual.

3. Maria misplaced all her notes and books again.
   Maria is a careless person.

In cases such as these, a person who does not know John, Bob, or Maria may accept the opinions expressed about them — that John is hardworking, Bob is extremely punctual, or Maria is careless. Actually, the other person does not really know whether these statements are true. All that person knows is that someone said so; that someone else had these opinions. The person who expressed the opinions may have based them on facts, but the listener or reader needs these facts too.

Remember, a fact is a statement that can be proven true or false by checking some reliable source. Read the following three sentences and think about the questions that follow them.

José is twenty-one years old.

He is a student, a class officer, and an athlete.

He is the best athlete in the college.

1. Can José's age be proven?

2. Can his status as a student, class officer, and athlete be proven?

3. Can it be proven that he is the best athlete in the college? How?

A reliable source to prove José's age would be his birth certificate or other official records or documents regarding his birth. College officials could supply school records to prove whether he is a student. There are also sources to prove whether he is a class officer and member of a sports group. However, there is no reliable source to prove that he is the best athlete in the college. "Best" is an opinion word.

To support such a statement, both writer and reader must agree about what they mean by "best": Does it mean that José participated successfully in several sports? Does it mean he is a consistent winner in one? Does it mean he scored the most points in a particular game? Does it mean that even though he loses, he does so gracefully? Clearly, readers who do not know what "best" means in this situation are dealing with the writer's opinion, not with a fact that may be checked.

EXERCISE 4

To see how well you understand this important distinction, read each of the following statements and place F before facts and O before opinions.

_____   1. Ronald Reagan was once a film star.

_____   2. He was also head of a labor union.

_____   3. He was once governor of California.

_____   4. He visited China on three occasions.

_____   5. He is the greatest president since Lincoln.

_____   6. The chemistry textbook has 567 pages.

_____   7. It is the world's most boring book.

_____   8. It contains too many diagrams.

_____   9. There are six diagrams in each chapter.

_____   10. Many diagrams are badly drawn.

EXERCISE 5

Here is a comment from a newspaper's letters-to-the-editor page. After each statement is a blank space. In each space tell whether the preceding statement is a fact (F) or an opinion (O).

This business of letting eighteen-year-olds vote is dangerous. _____ Maybe some people that age have a modicum of common sense and some knowledge of the world, but most don't know enough to make sensible decisions. _____ They have no accurate information about world or national events. _____ Most can't tell the difference between a Republican and a Democrat. _____ Give them an opportunity and they'll make their favorite rock star president. _____

EXERCISE 6

Read each of the following statements and mark an F (for fact) or an O (for opinion) after it.

_____   1. One year after the EDB pesticide scare, officials are investigating daminozide, a chemical used by apple growers.

_____   2. Daminozide is now suspected of causing cancer in humans.

_____   3. The Environmental Protection Agency conducted a series of studies.

_____   4. These tended to demonstrate the toxicity of the chemical.

_____   5. An independent agency has denied the EPA charge.

_____   6. This agency is composed of seven of the nation's outstanding scientists.

_____   7. Canceling the use of daminozide could cost apple growers $31 million.

_____   8. The International Apple Institute sets the cost at more than $192 million worldwide.

_____   9. The chemical is used to give apples their red color.

_____ 10. Such apples are mouth-watering.

_____ 11. Studies of carcinogenic substances are too costly.

_____ 12. Yet more studies are needed.

_____ 13. Organic apples are free of carcinogenic chemicals.

_____ 14. The chemical manufacturers should be allowed to police themselves.

_____ 15. Small backyard growers are more responsible than industry-owned orchards.

EVALUATING INFERENCES

As we read and think, we regularly make *inferences*. That is, we note one or two pieces of information and make educated guesses, based upon our knowledge of the particular situation, about things that we do not *know*. We *infer* that if the information we do have is accurate, then something else has happened or will happen, or that something else exists, has existed, or will exist. People say, "If this is true, and this is true, then maybe *this* follows."

Thus, we note that Maria has misplaced her notes and books six times this week. From this observation, we may infer that she has done so in the past or that she will do so in the future. In making the first kind of inference (about the past), we *draw conclusions*; in making the second kind (about the future), we make *predictions*. (Some psychologists, using computer terminology, say that drawing conclusions is *backward inferencing*, and making predictions is *forward inferencing*.) In either case, we have made educated guesses based upon our knowledge of Maria and people in general.

Such inferencing is crucial to all reading and thinking. People must constantly make inferences about life around them because they never have all the information they need. For example, we see a friend walk into a fast-food restuarant and comes out five minutes later unwrapping a hamburger. We do not know what actually happened during the five minutes he was out of sight, but we infer that he (1) walked to the counter, (2) ordered, (3) paid, (4) waited, and (5) received the order. All these inferences are based upon our knowledge of how fast-food restaurants operate. All five are conclusions we draw about past events. If we now infer that he will eat the hamburger, we are making a prediction.

The problem with inferences is that they may be wrong. The ones we make daily about our friends and personal lives may be inaccurate. The ones authors make and share with us may be inaccurate. The inferences we then make on the basis of material we read may be inaccurate. Good inference making is based upon the inference maker's knowledge of the situation; because we all do not possess adequate knowledge of all possible situations, we all may make poor inferences. You can only make accurate inferences about Maria's loss of books and notes if you really know Maria. A foreign student as yet unfamiliar with fast-food restaurants in America may make many false inferences about the friend's skill in obtaining a hamburger so rapidly: "He knew the cook," "He works there," or "He helped himself." Even an American student may make inaccurate inferences about this particular friend's plans for the hamburger. Perhaps he is not going to eat it; he may be going to unwrap it and break it into pieces to feed the pigeons. You can infer this (accurately) because you know your friend's peculiar habits.

Another problem with inferences is that people confuse them with opinions. This is probably because many opinion statements are based upon inferences. Someone notes that John works every afternoon and weekends in a supermarket and infers that he is industrious: "John is a hardworking guy." Actually, John may be working in a particular supermarket to help out a friend or to be closer to a girl he admires.

These distinctions may be explained by the following anecdote:

> A stranger came into our dorm, looked out the window, and said, "There are black clouds in the sky." He looked again and said, "It will rain soon." Then, as he rudely exited, he mumbled, "This part of the country has dreadful weather."

The stranger's first statement is clearly factual. Others can look out the window and verify the existence of black clouds. (Even when they fail to see black clouds, the statement is nevertheless factual because it *is* possible to check it by looking.) The final statement is opinion. The stranger is sharing his personal feelings about the local weather. The second statement is inferential. It is the stranger's educated guess, based upon his observation of the clouds. However, as you can readily see, the quality of the inference is directly related to the person's experience and knowledge of weather in the area. If he had only recently arrived and had little knowledge of local weather patterns, his inference is not valuable. On the other hand, if he had lived his entire life in this geographical area and been a constant observer of weather patterns, perhaps his inference would be worth examining.

Try these examples.

1. Ed received an A in calculus.

2. He always received an A in his math course.

3. He will easily get an A in this course.

4. He is a superb math student.

The first two are verifiable. In each case, the information can be checked; he either received those A's or he did not. The third is someone's prediction, an inference based upon the facts expressed in the first two statements. The third is an expression of opinion.

1. Sue refused to go to the dance with me.

2. Sharon said she was busy when I asked her.

3. I'll never get a date.

4. I'm a disaster when it comes to women.

Again, the first two statements are factual; each can be verified. The second is an inference about the future. The last is opinion statement. Although based upon the factual statements, it expresses a judgment and the feelings of the speaker.

EXERCISE 7

To see how well you understand the inferencing process, complete each of the following statements. Be prepared to explain your thinking about each.

1. We can infer from the frown on the instructor's face that the class research papers were

2. We can infer from looking at all the cars parked in front of the restaurant that

3. We can infer from the negative response from the audience that

4. We can infer from the heavy coat, gloves, scarf, hat, and boots he is wearing that

5. We can infer from his red nose, staggering walk, and slurred speech that he is

6. We can infer from the lack of empty chairs that this particular class is

7. We can infer from the overgrown grass and the pile of newspapers in front of the door that

8. We can infer from the dreamy look in his eyes, the roses in his hand, and the box of candy he is carrying that

9. We can infer from the loud rumbling under the mountain and the billowing smoke and ashes that

10. We can infer from his quick punch, fancy footwork, and success record that

EXERCISE 8

Remember that inferences may be wrong! We often misread the evidence and make inferences that are incorrect.
Go back over the previous exercise and make another inference for each

set of facts given. For example, the instructor's frown may be the result of a toothache or headache.

1.

2.

3.

4.

5.

6.

7.

8.

9.

10.

EVALUATING BIAS AND SLANTED LANGUAGE

Writers and speakers may be biased — that is, they already have formed a strong preference or prejudice. What they say is therefore influenced by their prejudgments. You can spot their bias by looking for loaded words.

For example, your best friend may be overweight. Because he is your friend, you are biased in his favor. You never refer to him as *fat*, *obese*, or *gross*. These are negatively loaded words. Instead, you tend to describe him in positively loaded words such as *plump*, *chubby*, or *robust*. An underweight friend is never *skinny*, *scrawny*, or a *beanpole*. She is *willowy*, *svelte*, *slim*, or *slender*.

Most writers and speakers unconsciously tend to select words that express their feelings and preferences. Unfortunately, some deliberately select loaded words in order to bias readers and listeners. As a thoughtful, critical reader and listener, you need to be sensitive to such *slanted language.*

Read the following pairs of sentences. One in each pair is slanted in favor of the person discussed; one is slanted against the person. Which words are loaded? Which are slanted one way or the other? Which reveal the writer's bias?

1. After Congressman Hinkley wasted as much time as possible, he finally stumbled through his speech.

After Congressman Hinkley weighed every aspect of the important controversy, he made his momentous decision.

(Which of the two is biased in favor of the congressman? Which against? Which words indicate the writer's bias?)

2. Harry ("Killer") Leary, the notorious gambler, was questioned by the police about a gangland slaying.

   Mr. Harold Leary, well known in local racing circles, was asked by local authorities to comment about recent events in the city.

   (Which is biased for Leary? What words are loaded? What else may *police* be called? In what ways do these other words reveal bias?)

3. Jerry's shifty eyes darted suspiciously around the room until he located his accomplice.

   Jerry's eyes moved brightly across the room until he located his long-time colleague and friend.

   (Which is biased in Jerry's favor? Which specific words reveal the writer's feelings about Jerry?)

4. The embassy official courageously maintained his innocence.

   The embassy official stubbornly refused to admit his guilt.

   (Which words indicate the writer's bias? Which statement is clearly biased against the official?)

You may think that these examples of biased language are uncommon. Unfortunately, such examples can frequently be found in daily newspapers and magazines. Writers (and editors and publishers) do have prejudices and well-defined biases, which are often expressed in the material we read in the press. Occasionally, biases are revealed in scholarly books, research reports, and even textbooks. As a critical reader, you need to be constantly alert to slanted language, which may or may not be deliberately introduced.

EXERCISE 9

Locate in a magazine or newspaper a clear-cut example of bias and slanted language. Be prepared to answer the following questions about it:

1. What position, product, or point of view does it support?

2. Which specific words or phrases indicate the bias?

3. How might you rewrite the piece so that it would not be biased? Which words need to be eliminated? Added?

EXERCISE **10**

To check your sensitivity to slanted language, place the following words in the appropriate columns. The first has been done as an example.

1. dictator, strong man, absolute ruler

2. mob, community, people

3. leader of the people, rabble-rouser, party leader

4. go-getter salesperson, high-pressured salesperson, energetic salesperson

5. modern, progressive, crackpot

6. time-tested, outmoded, old

7. venerable, old, antiquated

	Favorable	Neutral	Unfavorable
1.	strong man	absolute ruler	dictator
2.			
3.			
4.			
5.			
6.			
7.			

EVALUATING PURPOSE

Authors write to share ideas and information, to explain, to persuade, and often to amuse. Readers can usually, recognize an author's purpose by the title of the book or article or by the kind of work it is.

However, readers need to look closely at the reasons authors have for writing. Sometimes the purpose is not simply to inform or entertain, but to propagandize or persuade by deceptive means. Critical readers need to ask, What were the author's motives? What's the purpose of this paragraph? This sentence? This phrase? Is the writer using fair means to achieve his or her purpose?

To better understand purpose in writing and critical reading, think about the purposes behind the following five writing situations:

1. A letter to the newspaper editor about school athletics

2. A pamphlet of assembly directions for a VCR

3. A humorous story in a monthly magazine

4. A student's letter home to her parents

5. A full-page magazine advertisement for a new car model

In each case, you should identify purpose rather easily. The letter to the newspaper may be intended to inform or persuade, but it may also serve to bolster the ego of the writer. The second is clearly to inform; the third, to amuse. The letter home to parents may be seen as an attempt to "touch a loved one with words." It may inform and amuse, but its primary purpose is to maintain human contact. The full-page advertisement may be said to inform, but it clearly has another purpose: to persuade potential purchasers to look at — and buy — the car.

Further examination may reveal that there are purposes behind purposes. The writer of the letter to the newspaper may in fact be planning to run for public office; his letter is an attempt to obtain wider visibility in the community. The VCR pamphlet may contain positive references to other products made by the same manufacturer and serve as a subtle advertising tool. The humorous story may actually be used to fill space in a column because the publisher could not sell enough advertisements for that month's issue. Even the student's letter to her parents may have some other purpose: to casually remind them of a coming birthday, to prepare them for unpleasant news, and so on. The full-page ad may in fact be the most straightforward: Its writer simply wants to sell cars.

As you evaluate written and spoken communications, you need always to distinguish between the public or surface purpose and the hidden purpose. Often pieces that seem on the surface to be designed to amuse or share information are also planned to persuade, propagandize, or, unfortunately, misinform.

Evaluating and thinking critically about written and spoken messages seems especially important today. In a democratic society where freedom of speech assures equal rights to both the honest advocate and the unprincipled demogogue, it is possible for skillful writers and speakers to shape public opinion, influence voters, and affect behaviors. Professional persuaders, whether politicians, advertisers, pleaders of causes, even professional educators, can bombard people with words, some of them capable of misleading, distorting, confusing, or corrupting.

Propaganda Devices

In an attempt to educate Americans to the dangers of unscrupulous unfair advocates, the Institute of Propaganda Analysis suggested several years ago that we all watch for uses of propaganda devices. They are:

The glittering generality.   Every item or incident may fit into *some* generalization. Propagandists try to select for their purpose a generality so attractive that people will not challenge the writer's (or speaker's) real point. If a candidate for public office happens to be a mother, for example, the writer may say, "Western civilization could not survive without mothers." The generalization is true, of course, and readers may accept the candidate without asking, Is she a good mother? Does being a mother really have anything to do with the job she's running for?

The testimonial.   To persuade people to strongly favor some person, item, or event, the persuader links it with another that does enjoy prestige and respect. To convince people to like a product, for example, they may associate it with a well-known, well-liked athlete: Charlie Superstar eats Bunko Cereal every morning!

Name-calling.   Here the propagandist tries to pin a bad label on something people are to dislike so that they will unthinkingly reject it. In a discussion of health insurance, for example, an opponent may label the sponsor of the bill a "Communist." Whether the bill has anything to do with communism does not matter to the name-caller. His purpose is to discredit it.

Transfer.   This device, similar to the testimonial, attempts to transfer the prestige and authority of some person or idea to another. For example, it is noted that Mother Theresa favors a certain program, in the hope that her great prestige will somehow be transferred to the program advocated. Politicians like to be photographed with famous athletes or movie stars in hope that some of their luster will rub off on them.

Plain folks. Assuming that most people favor common, ordinary people (rather than elitist stuffed shirts), many politicians like to assume the appearance of common folk. One politician, who really went to Yale and wore five-hundred-dollar suits, campaigned in clothes purchased from a mail-order catalog, and spoke backcountry dialect when soliciting votes in his home district. "Look at me, folks," he wanted to say, "I'm just an ordinary person like you: *I* wouldn't ever sell you a bill of goods."

Card stacking. In presenting an argument where the issues are complex, the unscrupulous persuader often chooses only those items that favor his side of the argument. His readers or listeners get only facts that support his point of view; any other facts are suppressed.

The bandwagon. People are often easily intimidated by numbers. Therefore, persuaders try to convince them that everybody else has joined him or accepts his point of view. If they fail to do so, he implies, they will be left out.

False Argumentation

It is important to distinguish between persuasion and propagandizing. Persuasion is a legitimate purpose for writing and speaking. We often need to explain to others our point of view and encourage them to share it. When you read persuasive material, recognize its legitimacy and value, but also watch for instances of propaganda that may creep into even the most authoritative and legitimate-seeming persuasion.

Some persistent kinds of false argumentation you need to watch for follow.

1. **Post hoc ergo propter hoc** reasoning ("After this, therefore, because of this") occurs when the thinker assumes that because A came before B, A must be the cause of B.

2. **Begging the question** happens when something is assumed proved although the proof is not demonstrated. For example, "The unfair practice of making all students take freshman English should be discontinued at once" assumes that the practice is unfair without offering proof.

3. **Faulty dilemma** presents only two sides of an argument when actually there are more than two. For example, before Hitler came to power, he told voters that they had to choose between his party and communism; they really had several other alternative possibilities.

4. **Ignoring the question** happens when the speaker or writer continues the argument while ignoring the basic issue involved (as when one child says, "Well, you kicked me" when told "You hurt my arm.")

5. **Argumentum ad hominum** is found when the speaker or writer sidetracks the argument by making accusations against a person. It is an argument addressed to the person rather than the issue. For example, a candidate says, "Don't vote for my opponent because his wife is an alcoholic" or "Don't vote for her: Her husband has gangland connections." In such cases, the real issues are ignored while a person's reputation is attacked.

EXERCISE 11

Textbooks rarely contain examples of either propaganda or false argumentation. Magazines and newspapers are seldom entirely free of them. To show that you are alert to such devices, locate five examples from your out-of-class reading. In each case, give the source, date, and writer, and note the kind of false argumentation or propaganda trick used.

	Example	Source	Date	Writer	Type
1.					
2.					
3.					
4.					
5.					

EXERCISE **12**

One of the best ways to make yourself sensitive to propaganda and faulty argumentation is to actually write a paragraph using both techniques.

In the space provided below, write an advertisement for either a product or a political campaigner. Use as many of the "tricks" as you can, and be prepared to explain your use of these techniques.

GUIDES FOR IMPROVING EVALUATION AND CRITICAL THINKING

Becoming aware of aspects of evaluation and critical thinking is the first step in improving these skills. Now that you realize the difference between fact and opinion, you are more likely to make a distinction. Now that you know about inferencing, you are more apt to spot the inferences of others and sense when you are making them yourself. Now that you see how bias is often revealed through slanted language, you are less likely to be taken in by unscrupulous speakers and writers. In time, this awareness can make you a better critical listener, reader, and thinker.

Here are two guides that you can use now. The first, on questioning printed material, may be particularly valuable as you evaluate source material for course research papers, but may be applied to all books and articles you read. The second, for evaluating spoken communications, is useful everywhere, in college and in daily life outside the classroom.

Guide for Evaluating Printed Sources

1. Does the author have the background to write about the topic? Does he or she seem to have the experience and scholarship necessary to discuss the issues?

2. Does the author display any biases? Do you detect overly strong opinion, slanted language, or prejudice?

3. Does the author cite sources? Are these given in full?

4. Have all sides of issues been presented? Does the author seem to be covering up certain aspects?

5. Does the author cite *primary* sources (actual documents) or other authors' references to them?

6. Does the author stand to profit from persuading readers to believe his or her point of view?

7. Why has the author written this particular work? What reasons are given? What reasons might you infer?

8. Is the work a contribution to scholarship or a popularization? Do you think it will be kept on library shelves ten or twenty years from now?

9. Does it have adequate references, notes, index, and bibliography?

10. What are the work's strongest and weakest features?

11. Do you detect the use of any propaganda devices? Which ones?

12. Do you detect examples of false argumentation? Which ones?

Guide for Evaluating Spoken Communications

1. What is the speaker's purpose? (Is he or she just trying to pass the time? Be friendly? Is there a reason for this talk? What is it?)

2. What are the speaker's credentials? (If the talk is social chitchat, credentials do not matter; but if the speaker has a definite reason for this talk, what is it? What is the stated or public purpose? What might be the hidden purpose?

3. Is there evidence of bias? (Can I spot clues that give away possible bias? Is the evidence stacked? Too carefully selected? Does the speaker's background give reason to believe a fair picture is being presented? Does the particular choice of words show prejudice?)

4. Does the speaker use slanted language? (Does he or she favor loaded words? Pat phrases designed to trigger emotions? Is the rhythm,

pacing, or style planned to arouse emotions? Is it the kind of talk where emotive language is acceptable — poetry, drama, ritualistic speech?)

5. Does the speaker make sweeping generalizations? Unsupported inferences? (Are there predictions about the future without the speaker's reasons? Are these educated guesses or unsupported statements? Do I detect "glittering generalities"?)

6. Do opinions predominate in the talk? (Are these opinions backed with facts? Is it the kind of talk where opinions are acceptable?)

7. Does the speaker use any propaganda devices? (Are these examples of card stacking? Plain folks? The testimonial?)

8. Do I accept the message? (Is it true according to what I already know? What reasons are persuading me? Am I being hoodwinked? Do I want to believe for emotional reasons? Am *I* biased? Do I believe the message strongly enough to try to persuade others? Why?)

EXERCISE 13

Prepare an original "All-Purpose Guide for Evaluation and Critical Thinking." On a separate sheet of paper, using the ideas presented in the above two guides and the information given in this chapter, write your own guide. Try to keep it reasonably brief, with as few questions as possible.

POINTS TO REMEMBER ABOUT CRITICAL READING

1. Check the backgrounds of authors.

2. Distinguish between facts and opinions.

3. Watch for inferences made by authors.

4. Inferences can be wrong.

5. Check authors' inferences by examining their backgrounds in the area.

6. Conclusions authors draw are also inferences.

7. Predictions authors make are also inferences.

8. Choice of words can reveal bias.

9. Authors may try to persuade by deceptive means.

10. Authors sometimes use propaganda devices.

7
MASTERY TEST

To show that you have understood this chapter, complete each of the following.

1. Write both a factual and an opinion statement.

2. Write a sentence with an *inference*.

3. Give examples of *positively loaded* and *negatively loaded* words.

4. Give an example of a *glittering generality*.

5. Give an example of the *testimonial*.

6. In two or three sentences, show how a propagandist might use the *bandwagon* device.

7. Give an example of *post hoc ergo propter hoc* reasoning.

8. Give an example of *argumentum ad hominum.*

9. In a brief paragraph, justify the value of persuasion in our society.

10. Why do people need to become skillful critical readers?

8

Learning to Deal with New Vocabulary

INTRODUCTION AND OVERVIEW

One of the chief obstacles to understanding textbook reading assignments is new vocabulary words. Many of these words may be ordinary English words that you have not met before; others may be technical words used by specialists in the fields you are studying. Unless you can figure out their meanings, you may not understand your reading.

This chapter helps you deal with new vocabulary. It first reviews the SSCD approach to unfamiliar words, and then gives more suggestions for using both structural and context clues to meaning. It includes a section on learning technical vocabulary as well as ideas for remembering new words and their meanings.

SUGGESTED GUIDE QUESTIONS

---

1. Why is it important to have meanings for words you encounter in reading assignments?

2. What is the SSCD approach? How does it work in textbook study?

3. What are the signals for getting meaning from context?

4. How may the study of affixes and roots help you?

5. How can you remember new words and their meanings?

WHY IS IT IMPORTANT TO KNOW WORD MEANINGS?

You may have developed a number of useful strategies for getting meaning from reading assignments: finding main ideas, for example, or noting organizational patterns, or reading to answer questions. However, when you encounter new and unfamilar words in assignments, you cannot figure out what the author is saying unless you have some techniques for determining the meanings of the words.

Imagine, for example, coming across this sentence: "His success in this endeavor rested upon his previous experiences as a spelunker." In order to understand the assignment, you need to understand all the sentences within it. If you have no meanings for *endeavor* or *spelunker*, you cannot figure out this particular sentence. You need to know that an endeavor is an attempt and that a spelunker is a person who explores caves.

One page chosen at random from a college economics textbook contains the following words:

fiscal	allocation	subsidies
strategic	analogous	induce
subtle	monetary	conjunction
discretionary	ramifications	implications

You may already know some of these words. Others you can guess by noting how they are used in sentences. Others look like words you know. Some may be completely new. Some are common words used in special ways by economists. You may be a competent reader, but unless you have meanings for these words, you cannot make the best sense of that particular page.

Several research studies have investigated the role played by words in the comprehension process. Each and every one of these studies has shown that the single most powerful factor affecting how well readers understand material is *knowledge of word meanings*. Clearly, if you expect to extract maximum meaning from reading assignments, you need techniques for dealing with unfamiliar words. (For more information on these studies, see References, p. 299.)

THE SSCD APPROACH TO UNFAMILIAR WORDS

Chapter 4 suggested that you use the SSCD approach in your preview of a reading assignment. Because of its value, that approach is reviewed here, using as examples the words taken from the economics book.

First, *sound out* the word.   As noted in Chapter 4, many words you encounter in print for the first time may already be in your listening vocabulary. You know their meanings but have never seen them.

Look at the list of words taken from the economics textbook. Say them to yourself and recall whether you have heard them somewhere. You may have heard, for example, *fiscal* or *strategic*. Once you speak them, you may remember their meanings.

Second, look for *structural* clues.   Words are generally made up of parts, and although you may not recognize a whole word, you may recognize a part or parts of it. As you reexamine that same list, you may note that *strategic* contains *strategy*, a word you do know. You may see *imply* in *implications* and *discrete* in *discretionary*; you may see *money* in *monetary* and in *monetarist*. Often, you can look at the beginnings and endings of words and get help with meaning. For example, the *-tions* in *implications* can help you see that this is a plural noun. The *-ary* in *discretionary* helps you to see that this is an adjective, describing something. All these structural clues help.

Third, check the *context*.   The words surrounding the new word may reveal its meaning. This contextual-analysis approach is probably the most widely used. For example, if the surrounding sentences informed you that the "endeavor" referred to in the earlier sentence involved climbing into an underground sewer system to defuse a bomb, you might guess that spelunking had something to do with undergound explorations. You cannot always arrive at the exact meaning of a word from context alone, but often you can come up with a good enough approximation to help you make sense of the sentence or paragraph.

Finally, when all else fails, use the *dictionary*.   When your interpretation of a paragraph hinges upon one or two strange words and you cannot get their meaning through sounding out, structural clues, or context, then you need to check your dictionary. Such a procedure may slow down your reading time but is essential to understanding.

EXERCISE 1

As you complete one of your textbook reading assignments, list five unfamiliar words. Beside each, tell how you figured out its meaning. Did you sound it out and discover that it was a word in your listening vocabulary? Did you see any familiar parts? Did the context help? Did you have to go to the dictionary? List the words and the approaches you used here.

Unfamiliar Words	Approach Used to Get Meaning
1.	
2.	
3.	
4.	
5.	

USING CONTEXT CLUES TO GET MEANINGS FOR WORDS

Context is the situation or setting in which something occurs. The context of an unfamiliar word would be the sentence or paragraph in which it appears. Context clues are those indications within the sentence or paragraph that can help you define an unfamiliar word. Thus, the single word *dilatory*, standing alone, is either known to you or not. But when it appears in the context of the following sentences, you can guess that it means "late": John kept me waiting for our appointment. He usually comes into the room twenty minutes after the class has started, and he didn't get to today's nine o'clock lab until nine thirty. He's the most *dilatory* person I've ever known."

With practice, you can become increasingly skillful at using context clues. Some of the most common are described here.

1. Direct statement.   Authors often tell readers what they mean by a word: "The *facade* — that is, the face of the building — was tinted red" or "Glandular fever, or infectious mononucleosis, is a serious problem among college students."

2. Example.   Frequently, they provide an example: "*Prefixes*, such as *sub-* and *trans-*, change the meanings of words" or "*Mnemonics* are useful; using one of them, you can easily recall the names of the Great Lakes by thinking of HOMES — *H* for Huron, *O* for Ontario, *M* for Michigan, *E* for Erie, and *S* for Superior.

3. Description.   Sometimes authors will describe a word in enough detail so that you get its meaning: "The *griffin* was a mythological creature with an eagle's wings, head, and beak, but with the body, legs, and tail of a lion."

4. Comparison and contrast.   The meaning of a word may also be revealed by the way an author compares or contrasts it with something better known to you: "Jack was lazy, but Bob was *diligent*" or "In business Harry was *feckless*, while his old friend Joe was efficient and competent."

5. Synonym.   Authors may present the meaning for a word by associating it in context with a more familiar word that means approximately the same: "The *potent* drug's power was felt at once" or "The fishing emporium was stocked with all appropriate *piscatorial* equipment a fisherman might care to purchase." An author may provide several synonyms: "The boys yelled, screamed, jumped, danced up and down, and turned cartwheels. Such *animation* was unusual for them."

6. Summary.   Authors may give a series of items and summarize their meaning in a single word. To understand the word, you need to review the items. Here is an example: "Ted refused to do home assignments. He lacked respect for faculty. He regularly disobeyed rules and regulations. He cut classes more often than he attended them. *Disciplinary* action was taken."

7. **Association.**   Authors frequently provide enough information for you to infer meaning by association: "He studied the front, sides, and back of the new gym and then walked through the front door of the *edifice*."

8. **Situation.**   They may also describe a situation completely enough for you to guess the meaning of a word: "The speed with which he moved across the room, quickly reached the door, and dashed down the steps, showed his great *agility*."

EXERCISE 2

Define each of the italicized words in the following sentences. Then indicate which kind of clues you used. (You may use more than one kind of clue for a word.)

1. *Synonyms*, words that mean the same, provide clues to meanings.

2. *Laconic* Larry never opened his mouth except to eat.

3. As she surveyed the gathering, Sue's eyes and mind missed nothing. Her *perspicacity* was evident to all.

4. His *cravat*, wider than an ordinary tie, had room for more soup stains.

5. *Gregarious* people like Sam are never at a loss at parties. Me — I stand alone in a corner. I never know what to say to people. I like them all right. It's just that I've never learned the social skills.

EXERCISE 3

Here are ten sentences containing words that may be unfamiliar. Indicate their meanings and the clues you used to derive them from context.

1. There are three basic *components* to a personal computer system: the keyboard console, the video monitor, and the software.

   Definition:

   Clue:

2. Both labor and management relied on the expertise of the *mediator*, who settled the disagreements between the two sides.

   Definition:

   Clue:

3. Recent studies indicate a *correlation* between study skills and good grades, thus confirming a relationship that many teachers have always recognized.

   Definition:

   Clue:

4. The ERA amendment includes many *facets*, or aspects, as yet unresolved.

   Definition:

   Clue:

5. The *auditor*, who regularly examines financial records, came to review last year's books.

   Definition:

   Clue:

6. The *dividends* they received — essentially their share of the company's profits — were immediately banked.

   Definition:

   Clue:

7. Sue has *narcolepsy*, a disorder that causes excessive sleep during the day.

   Definition:

   Clue:

8. Many school districts whose computer facilities are limited simply aim for *computer literacy*, hoping to give students at least the basic skills necessary to cope with life in a computer age.

   Definition:

   Clue:

9. The *inquisitive* child's thirst for knowledge was driving her teacher crazy.

   Definition:

   Clue:

10. The three chemical companies *consolidated* their operations to create a corporation.

    Definition:

    Clue:

Exercise 4

An effective way to better understand the use of context clues is to write some sentences that include them. Select five words from the following list, and write a sentence for each that includes one or more context clues.

1. complacent (self-satisfied) — adjective
2. poignant (painfully touching) — adjective
3. chagrin (disappointment) — noun
4. cajole (persuade by pleasant words) — verb
5. laudable (praiseworthy) — adjective
6. facetious (humorous) — adjective
7. aversion (strong dislike) — noun
8. sublime (uplifting, noble) — adjective
9. apathy (lack of feeling) — noun
10. auspicious (fortunate) — adjective

USING STRUCTURE CLUES TO GET MEANINGS FOR WORDS

Many words are made up of other words or word parts. A common word such as *homeless* is easy for beginners to figure out because they already know what a home is and that *less* means "without." *Transcontinental* is also easy because most readers can see the word *continent* and the prefix *trans-*. If they know what a continent is and that *trans* means "across," they can get a meaning. If they also know that the suffix *-al* is usually used to show an adjective, they can figure out that the word *transcontinental* is an adjective to describe something that goes across the continent, like a transcontinental highway or transcontinental flight.

The same process of building larger words from smaller parts can be seen in college textbooks. A psychology book uses both *illegitimate* and *maladjustment* on the same page. Readers familiar with structure clues have no trouble with such words; they know that the prefix *il-* means "not" and the root *legit* means "legal," that the prefix *mal-* means "bad" and *adjust* means "match" or "fit." It is relatively easy for them to figure out that the first word means "illegal" and the second has to do with a "bad match or fit."

Clearly, knowing how to use structure clues can help you get at the meanings of many unfamiliar words. You need to know that many words can be understood when you spot the *root* or *stem*. (In the examples used above, *home*, *continent*, *legit*, and *adjust* are the roots or stems.) You also need to know the most commonly used *affixes*. One type of affix, the *prefix*, comes before a root. The other type, the *suffix*, comes after. (In the above examples, *trans-*, *il-*, and *mal-* are prefixes, while *-less*, *-al*, *-imate*, and *-ment* are suffixes.) Some affixes carry distinct meanings of their own (*-less* means "without" and *trans-* means "across"). Others, like *-al* and *-ment*, simply tell you the part of speech: *-al* tells you the word is an adjective and *-ment* that it is a noun.

The problem for you — and for all those who use the English language — is that there are countless roots and affixes, far too many to memorize conveniently. What you can do is become familiar with those most commonly used.

In the Appendix (on p. 302) you will find a master list of roots, prefixes, and suffixes. This will provide you with examples and meanings for each. You may refer to this list as you study textbook assignments, familiarizing yourself with widely used roots and affixes.

On the following pages are suggestions and exercises to help you get meanings for unfamiliar words by using structural clues.

Roots

The English language developed from an ancient Germanic language called Anglo-Saxon, which combined with an older version of French called

Norman-French. As it grew, it regularly borrowed other words from both Latin and Greek. Many of these words from old German, old French, Latin, and Greek serve today as roots for modern English words.

Here are ten widely used roots, with meanings and examples. Study the list and try to think of other examples of words based on these roots.

Root	Meaning	Example
anthro-	man	anthropologist
astro-	star	astronaut
bio-	life	biologist
cardio-	heart	cardiology
demo-	people	democracy
dict-	speak	contradict
geo-	earth	geology
graph-	write	paragraph
magni-	great	magnificent
psych-	mind	psychologist

Each of these roots serves as a stem for many other modern words. Note the following pictorial display for the root *graph*:

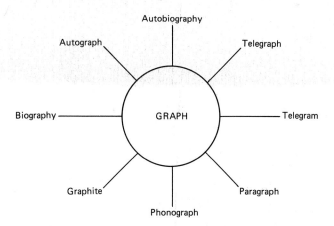

When you see the root *graph* within a word, you can infer that it is related in some way to "write." Sometimes you can see another root such as the *bio* in *biography*. Knowing that *bio* means "life," you can further infer that *biography* may mean writing about someone's life.

To better appreciate the value of this approach to vocabulary study, examine carefully the following diagram. At least twenty-seven words are developed from the root *duc-*, which comes from the Latin word *ducere*, "to lead." Clearly, readers who associate *duc-* with "lead" have a way of figuring out the meaning of many words based upon this root.

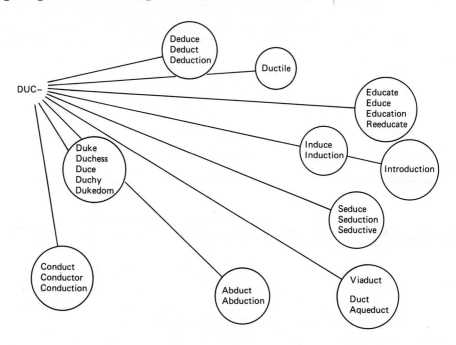

EXERCISE 5

To better understand how individual roots serve as the basis for other words, select one root from the list and write as many words as you can that derive from it.

First, search your memory for examples. Watch for others in your reading. Ask friends. Finally, check a dictionary. Try to locate at least ten words.

1.

2.

3.

4.

5.

6.

7.

8.

9.

10.

EXERCISE 6

Using your knowledge of the ten roots on the list, write out meanings for the italicized words in the following sentences.

1. Statistical data allow scientists to *predict* the behavior of various types of cancer cells.

   Meaning:

2. *Geophysicists* are now able to calculate the age of the oceans.

   Meaning:

3. Woody Allen's new film clearly has some *autobiographical* basis.

   Meaning:

4. In the baroque period the *magnificat* was often treated as a multisectional work similar to the oratoria and other choral works.

   Meaning:

5. After his last breakdown the poet went to a clinic for *psychotherapy*.

   Meaning:

6. The Greek gods were *anthropomorphic*.

   Meaning:

7. Scientists refuse to take *astrological* columns seriously.

   Meaning:

8. The chapter on *biochemistry* is the most difficult in the book.

   Meaning:

9. The *cardiogram* readings were encouraging.

   Meaning:

10. *Demographers* report a slight rise in birth rates.

    Meaning:

Prefixes

Remember, prefixes are affixes that come before roots to change their meaning. *Pre-* and *sub-* are two good examples. Using either, you can make up dozens of words:

Pre-	Sub-
prenuptial (before a wedding)	submarine (underwater)
pregame (before the game)	subway (under the roadway)
predict (tell the future before it happens)	subterranean (under the earth)

Here are ten of the most widely used prefixes with meanings and examples. Examine the list carefully and try to think of other examples.

Prefix	Meaning	Example
anti-	against	antitank
auto-	self	automatic
contra-	against	contradict
micro-	small	microscopic
multi-	many	multimillionaire
poly-	many	polyglot
post-	after	postgame
semi-	half	semiprofessional
super-	above	superhuman
tele-	far	television

Each of these prefixes may be added to other words to change their meanings or to create new words. Note how the prefix *poly-*has been used:

polychromatic — having many colors

polydactyl — having more than the normal number of toes or fingers

polygamous — having more than one wife or husband

polyglot — having several languages

polygraph — an instrument to record blood pressure, heartbeat, and respiration simultaneously

polyphonic — several melodies played at one time

Such a list could extend for pages. Scientific words alone run into the hundreds. Note: *polyester, polyethylene, polygyny, polymer, polymorph, polysaccharide, polysepalous, polyurethane,* and so on.

The following diagram demonstrates how many words use the common prefix *mal-*, derived from the Latin word *malus* or "bad."

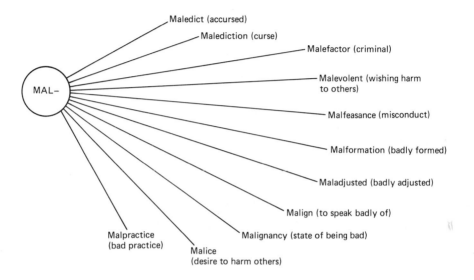

Maledict (accursed)
Malediction (curse)
Malefactor (criminal)
Malevolent (wishing harm to others)
Malfeasance (misconduct)
Malformation (badly formed)
Maladjusted (badly adjusted)
Malign (to speak badly of)
Malignancy (state of being bad)
Malice (desire to harm others)
Malpractice (bad practice)

EXERCISE 7

In a current textbook reading assignment, find five words that include prefixes from the list. Write them here along with meanings.

1. Word:

   Meaning:

2. Word:

   Meaning:

3. Word:

   Meaning:

4. Word:

   Meaning:

5. Word:

   Meaning:

EXERCISE 8

From the list of prefixes in the Appendix select five not introduced in this chapter. For each, write five words that include the prefix. Your examples may come from memory, from a dictionary, or from the glossary of one of your textbooks.

Prefix	Five Examples
1.	
2.	
3.	
4.	
5.	

Suffixes

Suffixes, as noted earlier, usually serve a grammatical purpose: They show verbs (*-ed*, *-ing*, *-s*), adjectives (*-er*, *-est*), and adverbs (*-ly*). *Quick*, *bright*, and *sick*, for example, are adjectives used to describe something. By adding the suffix *-ness* to them, you can turn them into nouns: *quickness*, *brightness*, *sickness*. Some key suffixes that you should know are found in the following list.

Here are ten widely used suffixes with meanings and examples. Study the list and think of other examples.

Suffix	Meaning	Example
-able	can be done	readable
-er, -or	person	actor
-esque	in the style of	picturesque
-ish	to form adjective	clownish
-ism	a belief	naturalism

Suffix	Meaning	Example
-ist	a person	guitarist
-ize	to make	civilize
-ent	full of	fraudulent
-ment	state of	puzzlement
-wise	manner	counterclockwise

This diagram shows how the suffix *-ous* may be added to nouns and verbs to make them adjectives.

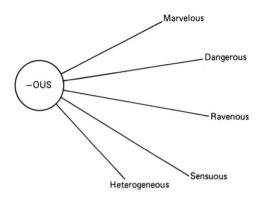

EXERCISE 9

Select five suffixes from the list in the Appendix; for each, write five words that include the suffix. The words may come from memory, a textbook reading assignment, or a dictionary.

EXERCISE 10

Answer the following questions by using the meanings of the prefixes, roots, and suffixes to help you.

1. What is a *monorail*?
2. What is meant by *subzero weather*?
3. What is a *hyperactive child*?
4. What do a *geologist* and a *geographer* have in common?
5. What does a nonscience like *astrology* have in common with a science like *astronomy*?
6. Why are fevers sometimes called *pyrogenic disorders*?
7. What does a *dynamic* person have in common with an explosive like *dynamite*?
8. What does *television* have in common with the *telegraph*?
9. What does a *psychotherapist* try to remedy?
10. What does the word *statuesque* mean?

EXERCISE 11

Again, answer these questions using your knowledge of roots, prefixes, and suffixes. Remember, a list of roots and affixes may be found in the Appendix.

1. What is a *bibliography*?
2. How does *bibliotherapy* try to help people?
3. How does *hydrotherapy* try to help people?
4. What is an example of an *intangible* object?
5. How often does a *biannual* event occur?
6. When you *synchronize* two or more events, what are you doing?
7. When someone *reiterates* a statement, what are they doing?
8. Who rules in a *theocracy*?
9. What is meant by *chronological order*?
10. What does an *orthodontist* do?

HOW TO LEARN TECHNICAL VOCABULARY

Each subject you study in college has its own vocabulary. Just as you need a large general vocabulary to understand and use language effectively, so do you need a large specialized vocabulary of technical terms to understand and perform successfully in each subject area. To be a chemist, for example, you need to have meanings for *element*, *isotope*, *toxicity*, *halogen*, and *matter*. To be a musician, you need meanings for words such as *chord*, *clef*, *transpose*, *theme*, and *note*. To be an economist, you need to know *barter*, *productivity*, *monopolistic*, *differentials*, and *capital*.

Look again at the words given in the examples above and you will see one of the fundamental problems with technical vocabulary. Some of those words are already in your general vocabulary but have special meanings in the technical vocabulary. Every child says and understands, "What's the matter?" but when the chemist uses *matter* the meaning is quite special. It means a specific type of substance, such as *inorganic matter*. Everyone knows what a note is ("I'll drop you a note!") but *note* means something very specific to a musician. Schoolchildren know about capital letters, but *capital* is rather different for an economist.

Some of the words given in these examples are so specialized that most people do not include them in their general vocabularies. Three such words are *isotope*, *halogen*, and *clef*. Many of the new words you will encounter in textbooks are so specialized that you will not even find them in ordinary dictionaries. You will need to check a glossary or a technical dictionary.

The point to remember about technical vocabularies is that you *must* have meanings for the words. Just as you cannot understand spoken or written language unless you have meanings for the words speakers and writers use, so too you must have meanings for words in special fields. You cannot understand the chemistry textbook or the chemistry professor when you lack a meaning for *isotope* or *halogen* any more than you can understand a newscaster on television who discusses the *penultimate* warning when you lack a meaning for *penultimate*.

Six suggestions for learning technical vocabulary are presented here.

1. Make up your mind to learn all technical words.   Some students learn a few new terms as they listen to lectures and read assignments — but "some" isn't enough! To really understand the material in a course, you must know the vocabulary. Words represent concepts; when you fail to learn a word, you cannot know the concept it labels. The vocabulary of the course is your basic handle on the course content. Without it, the content will slip through your mind and be gone when the examination comes.

2. Keep lists. As you encounter new words in courses, write them down with their meanings. This is the most effective single technique for mastering new vocabulary. Short-term memory allows us to retain new information for only a few seconds. Unless we write down new information, it will be lost to us.

We suggest that you allocate a few pages in that section of your notebook where you keep reading and lecture notes for a particular course and label it "Important Words." Make sure that every time you come across a technical word you write it here, either with the meaning you figure out for it using structure or context clues or the meaning you get from the dictionary. The list becomes your chief tool for understanding all lectures and readings in the course. Allow adequate space so that when you encounter each word a second or third time, you have room to jot down new uses or additional meanings for the word. Make sure, too, that you copy the correct spelling. You may need to use the word in an essay-type examination, so as you learn the meaning learn the proper spelling.

3. Check for help in the textbook. Authors and editors of textbooks know that certain words are crucial to understanding the material, and often mark these words in a special way. Sometimes they use boldface type, italics, or even color. Such signals tell you that these words are important and that a definition may be close by. The definition may be spelled out for you or it may be presented in context. Look for such built-in definitions. If you cannot locate them, check the glossary or dictionary. But be sure you have definitions for all such words.

Some textbooks present important words before the chapter text. Under a heading such as "Key Words" or "New Vocabulary," you will find those words authors and editors think may be troublesome. Copy these in your notebook too, even though they are in the book. (The process of copying helps you get them in memory with the proper spelling.) Then, look up the meanings and write them down with the words in your notebook.

4. Look for help during lectures. Words that are important to the course will be used repeatedly in the textbook. They will also be used in lectures and discussions. Some instructors will write new words on the board; some will slow down the pace of the presentation so that the new words stand out. Some will use the new words several times in a lecture so that you have an opportunity to learn them. Make sure you copy all such words into your notebook. When the instructor writes a word on the board, copy it on your list with the correct spelling. When it is said but not written, copy down your best approximation of the spelling, and then go to the textbook after class to locate the word in print and get the spelling. When you cannot catch the spelling of a spoken word, make a phonetic version and later ask the instructor or another student.

5. Use the glossary. Most textbooks include a glossary. This is an abbreviated dictionary listing all technical terms used in the book. It is invaluable (although it is rumored that some students have never actually looked at one!). For your purposes, it can be more useful than a dictionary, because a dictionary will give *all* the meanings of a word, while the glossary will give only the meaning that applies to a particular field. For example, a good general-purpose dictionary may give thirteen or fourteen definitions for *matter*, but the glossary in your chemistry book will give you only the definition that is used in chemistry.

The glossary may be one of the most unappreciated parts of the typical textbook. It can give you precise technical definitions, thus saving you the bother of picking out one from the many provided in a dictionary. It is also wonderfully available. Most students find it irksome to have to put down the textbook they are studying to get another book — a dictionary. The glossary, on the other hand, is right there. By marking the first page of the glossary for easy access, you can always locate your definitions quickly. Another important value of the glossary becomes apparent when you need to review and study for a test. Here are *all* the key words! At the end of a course you can go through the glossary, using it as the basis for a quick self-test. Some students place a check mark beside each glossary word as they look it up. That way, they can review for a midterm or final exam by testing themselves on only the checked words.

Does the glossary approach to new words have any drawbacks? Yes. The words in it have been selected by the book's author and editors, who have chosen words they believe are important for the book or course. Therefore, you need to know all the words they picked. Remember, however, that they do not know *you*. Many words in a typical textbook may not be in your personal vocabulary. An author may use terms such as *element*, *barter*, or *transpose*, but not include them in the glossary, assuming that everyone knows them. You may in fact not yet know them or understand how they are being used in the specific context. This realization should highlight for you the value of the personal word lists you keep in your notebooks.

6. Make use of structure. You have been advised to look at word parts when you want to get meanings for unfamiliar words. Often, roots and affixes provide clues to meaning. Sometimes they indicate meaning so directly that you do not need to check the glossary or a dictionary.

The use of structural clues becomes even more important when dealing with technical vocabulary. Most scientific words, for example, are relatively recent. They were created to fit specific needs, and are often made up of old parts! For example, when scientists discovered various drugs that could be used to reduce the physiological effects associated with histamine production in allergies and colds, they simply took a widely used prefix that meant "against" and coined the word *antihistamine*. Because so many scientific words have been constructed from old Latin and Greek roots plus common affixes, the study of word structure can pay you big dividends as you learn technical vocabulary.

SUGGESTIONS FOR REMEMBERING NEW VOCABULARY

Here are eight suggestions for remembering the new words you learn as you read and study.

1. Copy down new words.   Keep one section of your notebook for new vocabulary, where you will write each new word with a synonym or brief definition. This is your *record of personal vocabulary growth*. As the semester moves along, you should see this record expand; as your college years go by, the list will serve as a permanent record of your vocabulary development.

2. Use each in a written sentence.   Words by themselves are not valuable; it is as tools for thinking and communication that they help you. In your notebook, after your synonym or definition, write out a sentence that uses the word effectively. The process of writing the sentence helps to secure the word and its meaning in your memory. It later will provide you with an example of how the word is actually used.

3. Use the words in conversation and writing.   The new words need to become part of your basic speaking and writing vocabularies. One way to insure that they become firmly entrenched is to use them as often as you can in speaking and in writing letters, notes, and course papers.

4. Relate new words to what you already know.   As you record these items in your notebook, think of how each relates to the knowledge you already have of the world. Ask yourself: How does this fit in with my present information? For example, when you want to learn *habitats*, think of the living environment of a favorite pet, of worms that you may use for fishing, or of house mice. The process of relating helps you better define the new word while at the same time placing it more securely in your memory.

5. Use different forms of the words.   Try changing suffixes to make a word function as an adjective, a noun, or some other part of speech. For example, as you learn *frugal* (an adjective), make up some sentences in which you use *frugality* (a noun). As you learn *emulate* (a verb), try it in sentences as the noun *emulation*. Such practice shows you the possibilities each new word offers for general use.

6. Try index-card drills.   Write each word you want to learn on one side of an index card and its definition on the back. You can flip the cards at spare moments and make sure you are adding the words to your permanent vocabulary.

7. Make crazy associations.   Many students say that they remember difficult words by associating them with odd personal recollections. For example, you might remember *cardiologist* by linking it with a doctor you once met who always told jokes: He was a real card. You might better remember *polygamy* by linking it with a fictional Polly who had four husbands. The possibilities are endless.

8. Pace yourself.   As you read and study, your list will grow. Experience shows that it is unwise to learn an entire list of new words (thirty or forty or more!) all at once. When you want to review your new acquisitions, take them five or ten at a time. More learning will result.

EXERCISE 12

This chapter describes several strategies for figuring out the meanings of unfamiliar words, as well as suggestions for remembering word meanings. Review the chapter and choose the strategy or suggestion that you think can help you most as you read. In the space below, describe your choice and tell why you made it.

POINTS TO REMEMBER ABOUT NEW VOCABULARY

1. You need word meanings to understand assignments.
2. Sound out words to see if you already know them.
3. Look for familiar roots and affixes.
4. Try to get meanings from context.
5. Use the dictionary when necessary.
6. Take advantage of the glossary.
7. Keep word lists.
8. Use new words as often as you can.
9. Practice with index-card drills.
10. You can increase your vocabulary.

8
MASTERY TEST

To discover how well you have understood Chapter 8 select the best answer for each of the following questions.

1. What is the primary reason for learning word meanings?

    a. To improve scores on vocabulary tests

    b. To impress interviewers when applying for a position

    c. To better understand reading assignments

2. Which of the following are types of context clues?

    a. Direct statements and examples

    b. Prefixes and suffixes

    c. Roots and affixes

3. Which of the following are widely used roots?

    a. *dict-* and *geo-*

    b. *sub-* and *pre-*

    c. *-ous* and *-able*

4. Which of the following are commonly used prefixes?

    a. *-ment* and *-ent*

    b. *graph-* and *magni-*

    c. *poly-* and *super-*

5. Which of the following words belong in your technical rather than general vocabulary?

    a. *dilatory* and *potent*

    b. *isotope* and *halogen*

    c. *diligent* and *auspicious*

6. What is a *bibliotherapist*?

    a. A librarian

    b. One who treats mental disorders

    c. One who cures with books

7. What is a *glossary*?

   a. An example of meaningless speech
   b. Shiny page used on book covers
   c. A specialized vocabulary

8. Which of the following is a way to learn and remember new words?

   a. Get their spellings correct.
   b. Place a check mark beside them in a dictionary.
   c. Use index-card drills.

9. What is a good way to identify technical vocabulary words?

   a. They tend to be polysyllabic.
   b. They have Latin or Greek roots.
   c. They are often highlighted in textbooks

10. Which of the following is a good approach to getting the meanings for unfamiliar words?

   a. SQ3R
   b. STEP
   c. SSCD

9

Learning to Remember and Recall Information and Ideas

INTRODUCTION AND OVERVIEW

Much of the material we read and hear in courses is soon lost to us. It remains in short-term memory just long enough for us to assume that we have learned it. Even material that does get into long-term memory is not always readily retrievable.

To succeed academically, you need to gain as much control as possible over your memory. You need to know how it works and how it can be improved. You need effective strategies for getting information and ideas into long-term memory, as well as techniques for more efficient recall.

This chapter examines how data is stored and retrieved from memory and provides suggestions for memory improvement.

SUGGESTED GUIDE QUESTIONS

1. What is memory? What are the different kinds?

2. Why do people forget?

3. What are the best ways to get new learnings into long-term memory?

4. How does note taking help us remember?

5. What are mnemonic devices? How do they help?

WHAT IS MEMORY?

Memory is the ability to store and recall previous experiences. You may store information and ideas for a brief time in *short-term memory* or for much longer periods in *long-term memory*.

All data coming into your mind remains in short-term memory for a few seconds while the mind assesses its value and significance. While it is held in short-term memory, you tend to believe that you possess it permanently because your attention is focused on it and you can recall it easily. An instructor notes, for example, that $S = K \log W$ is Ludwig Boltzmann's response to the second law of thermodynamics and that "S stands for entropy, K is a universal constant known as Boltzmann's constant, W has to do with the number of ways in which parts of the system can be arranged, and log is, of course, logarithm." As a good student, you listen, take in that information, and assume that you have it in memory. You may actually test yourself by repeating what S, K, and W stand for. The problem with short-term memory, unfortunately, is that people can deceive themselves. Because data is available in short-term memory, they assume they have it; they can recall it and say it. They do not always realize that as much as 90 percent of data held in short-term memory is lost after a short time.

The information and ideas that are retained in long-term memory seem to remain for a very long time indeed. Some say long-term memories are retained until the brain finally expires. The data that the mind stores permanently is not only available but often easily recalled. Some, while available, is not readily retrievable. For example, you may learn the second law of thermodynamics — that is, store it in long-term memory — but be unable to recall it a year (or a day!) later. The problem, then, with long-term memory is that you need to store information in such a way that it will be retrievable when you want it.

Psychologists say that more has been discovered about human memory in the past decade than has ever been known. Many of the ways the mind stores and retains data are now beginning to be understood. As a student, you need to know as many strategies as you can to help you store ideas and information so that you can retrieve them when you want them. The more control you have over your memory, the more successful you will tend to be in college and in life. (For more information about your memory and the way it functions, see References, p. 299.)

EXERCISE 1

Complete all three parts of this exercise to gain insights into the workings of your own memory.

PART I

Write down here:

1. Your telephone number:

2. Your area code:

3. Your Social Security number:

4. Your zip code:

5. Your mother's maiden name:

6. The name of your first grade teacher:

7. The name of the football coach in the high school you attended:

8. The number of your high school homeroom:

9. The name of the first boy or girl you ever went with to a movie:

10. The name of your seventh grade English teacher:

PART II

Now go back over each answer and think about *why* you remembered that specific information.

Indicate here the reason you believe you have retained that information.

1.

2.

3.

4.

5.

6.

7.

8.

9.

10.

PART III

Can you see any patterns here? Do you remember some information because you use it all the time? Some because of strong personal or emotional associations? Some because you simply need it to function in life? Why do you think you have forgotten other information?

Use the space provided here to answer these questions before continuing the chapter.

HOW DO WE GET NEW MATERIAL INTO LONG-TERM MEMORY?

The central concern of this chapter is How do we get the new ideas and information we study in college into long-term memory so that we can use them later? This question has been intensively studied in recent years and some answers are available.

Drill, Practice, or Review

Students and teachers have known for a long time that doing something over and over again seems to help us remember it. Children in school write a spelling "demon" one hundred times correctly and seem to remember how it should be spelled. Dancers practice a movement thousands of times until they have made it part of their regular physical response. Pianists and athletes drill on certain body actions until these have been thoroughly internalized. Recent research indicates that such drill is certainly one of the ways we can use to store important data in long-term memory. How can you use this tried-and-true method as a college student?

Flash cards. Elementary teachers often write important facts on cards and flash them before their classes so that the children will respond with the correct answers, printed on the reverse sides. Thus, children read "7 × 7 is ____" or "The capital of Maine is ____," and check their answers over and over again with the information on the backs of the cards. This technique is valid for college study. There are many kinds of material you can learn quickly and efficiently using flash cards. (See Chapter 8 for a suggestion for using index cards to learn new vocabulary.)

Repetition. Just as children frequently learn correct spellings or their multiplication tables by repetition, college students can force data into their long-term memories by repeating over and over again. A new technical word can be learned by using it several times in different sentences written in a notebook: "X is ____," "One feature of X is ____," "X is made up of ____," and so on. A new word of a more general nature may be forced into memory by introducing it in conversation several times after learning it. A formula, an important name, or a key date may be retained by similar repetitions.

Question and answer. As you study course material (especially for a test), make up questions about it. Write these down the left side of a piece of paper; then write the answers on the right side of the same sheet. If you fold the sheet down the middle, you can quiz yourself repeatedly, checking the answers until you have made sure all material is in long-term memory.

Association or Relating

Most people learn early in life that they can remember new material when they associate it with material they already know. One student remembers his friend's license plate number because it contains the same numbers as popular TV channels. Another remembers correct spellings of certain words by focusing on smaller words within each. (She always gets *piece* right because she thinks of a *piece* of *pie*.) However, there is more to association than these examples indicate. Psychologists tell us that association is one of the basic ways of learning: People learn by relating the new to the known. We can find instances of this kind of learning in almost every aspect of life. Children learn the vast number of facts they need by relating them to the ordinary things in their lives: a *tuba* is like a trumpet, only bigger; a *dentist* is like a doctor, but he treats teeth; a *bus* is like an automobile, only it holds more riders; and so on.

This way of learning — and remembering — continues throughout adult life. As a college student you easily learn that a *professor* is like a teacher, a *dean* like a principal, a *word processor* like a typewriter, and so on. As you have more experiences with professors, deans, and word processors, you begin to see the ways in which they are distinct from teachers, principals, and typewriters, but the original learning came about because of the association you made. Most of the new knowledge you acquire through the rest of your life will probably come about in this same way: You relate the new to the known.

How can you make use now of this important truth? You can force yourself to see connections. As you study your lecture notes and reading assignments, look for relationships between the new material and things you already know. When you see *capitalism* defined in your book, stop and think of examples of capitalism in your experience. You may think of a yard service a friend started, in which he invested money to buy equipment and sought neighbors who needed lawn and garden care. You may think of a person you read about who started a record store. As you study the concept of *capitalism*, it begins to make better sense to you when you relate it to what you know. You can start to look for differences between the textbook definition and the "real thing" as you know it. Seeing the differences helps you better understand the concept.

One strategy (recommended earlier in this book) is to list in your notebook the major terms and concepts in the course, the ones highlighted in textbooks and lectures. Then, as part of your study process, connect each with knowledge you already have acquired, either through direct experience or through your reading, televiewing, or film-viewing experiences. Once you establish connections, you will understand the item better and remember it more easily.

Mnemonic devices

Related to association are *mnemonic devices*. There are deliberate tricks learners use to remember key information. Schoolchildren learn the names of the Great Lakes by using the first letter of each to spell HOMES (*H*uron, *O*ntario, *M*ichigan, *E*rie, and *S*uperior). The student referred to earlier remembers the spelling of *piece* by using a mnemonic device (*pie*ce of *pie*). Many children remember how many days in each month by memorizing a simple jingle: "Thirty days hath September" and so on. Some students distinguish a Bactrain camel from a dromedary by turning the initial letters on their sides: Bactrain (B) has two humps, while dromedary (D) has only one. Some remember the reciprocal of pi (0.318310) by simply remembering the phrase "Can I remember the reciprocal?" in which the number of letters in each word indicates the numbers! Some professional students of memory have become exceedingly skillful at making up mnemonic devices. They can remember vast amounts of material by creating associations.

How can you use this information in your study? If you have specific blocks of data to learn, spend some time trying to devise personal mnemonic devices. You may find that learning comes easier for you and that the devices help you remember information far beyond test time.

Personalization

Related to both association and the use of mnemonic devices is personalization. Most people have noticed that they remember information about people more readily than information about things. People remember one another's physical appearance and personality characteristics long after they have forgotten names. This is probably because most of us are people-oriented: We like and enjoy, dislike or detest, are comfortable with or uncomfortable with, other people. We may say we watch certain television programs for the scenery or the action, but we really follow the people. We remember the characters of a favorite novel long after we forget the plot or the scenes. This may be because people are essentially curious about one another. Certainly, people and their personalities play a role in remembering.

How can we make use of personalization in studying? Napoleon is remembered long after the names and dates of his battles are forgotten. We know much about our great presidents after we have lost from memory the details of their administrations. Even in subjects like science and economics, we often recall easily the great people in those fields although we sometimes forget the details of their work. When we are studying we can use this feature of human memory; we can deliberately try to relate data to people. For example, while studying American history, make a point of learning as much as possible about the actual people involved. When you study, say, the military activities of the opposing armies in the American Revolution, learn all you can about people like Generals Clinton and Gates, Henry Knox, Nathanael Greene, Baron von Riedesel, Mad Anthony Wayne, and others. When your book fails to give you specific information about individuals, look them up in other books, check out biographies, and note the entries in the biographical dictionaries. You can use your natural interest in other human beings to help get important data into long-term memory.

Interest

Many students have noted that we all remember what we are interested in. When the instructor uses an example in a lecture that refers to one of your favorite pastimes or hobbies, you sit up and take notice. You may remember that particular item in the lecture and forget all else! Some children who cannot remember the multiplication tables can remember batting averages. College students who cannot recall dates from a history chapter can easily recall specific details and specifications for various classic automobiles. Clearly, interest plays a role in memory.

How can you use your interests to better remember course material? You can carry the steps suggested under Association or Relating a bit further. When you study your notes, try as suggested to relate each item to knowledge you already have. That is a valuable study technique, one proven effective by countless students. Now, however, examine each of those items to discover if it in any way relates to one of your interests. At first, the fact that Henry Knox carried the captured British cannons across mountains to Boston in 1776 does not interest you. When you think about the situation, you may realize that it does. For example, you may personally be interested in hiking and mountain climbing. When you reflect on the terrain Knox and his men faced, you begin to think of your own experiences, and the otherwise uninteresting material becomes interesting. An academic fact goes more easily into long-term memory because (1) you have related it to what you already know, (2) personalized it by thinking of the historical figures as actual men doing something you have done, and (3) connected it with one of your personal interests.

Visualization

Some people remember pictures better than words. They can shut their eyes and "see" scenes that they cannot recall in words. Such people are said to have strong *visual memories*. (Some of them have such strong visual memories that they are said to have *photographic memories*.) Everyone has the ability to remember through visualization; you can use and strengthen this ability to help you learn. For example, you may have difficulty remembering the verbal description of a historical event, but can picture it in your mind's eye.

How can you make better use of your ability to visualize? One way is to make visual maps of the material you study. (Refer to Chapter 3, Learning to Listen to Lectures and Class Discussions.) As you read assignments, draw maps on the new ideas and information. This is like outlining as a note-taking technique, but it allows you to "see" the new material in relation to what you know and other new material you are learning. If you had been mapping this chapter so far, you might have a drawing something like this in your notebook:

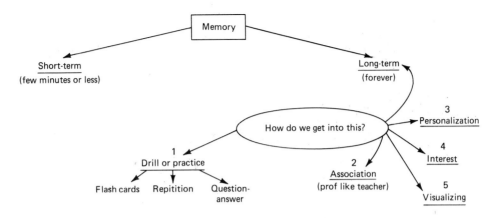

Such maps present you with a picture of relationships involved in the new learning. Often, you can remember the pictures better than the words alone.

There are other ways you can make use of visualization. For example, you can look for pictures of people and places, of events and objects. As you study the names and terms, check the pictures (photographs or paintings, drawings or old etchings). Try as you study to make connections between the verbal levels (that is, the words and terminology) and the pictorial levels (all your visual representations). This approach has proven successful for many students. They find that at test time they can easily "see" significant points in their mind's eye and retrieve necessary data from long-term memory more readily.

Physicalization

Many psychologists who have studied this area believe that there is a powerful physical element in memory. People seem to remember what they do. You may or may not remember points you read in the textbook or hear in the lecture, but when you actually *do* the actions associated with them, you find the ideas going into long-term memory. For example, as you read certain directions in a laboratory manual, they may or may not go into memory. Then you actually do the steps described, with maximum bodily involvement, and discover that the steps are now part of your permanent memory. You may read certain procedures in another textbook and forget them. But when you read and write them out in your notebook, you find that they have gone into memory. Evidently, the act of writing (which involves physical movement by the hands and arms) helps you retain the new information.

How can you make use of this physical element in learning and remembering? You can look for ways to physicalize your learning. Take each new block of study material and see if you can do something physical with it. Can you act out an event? Mimic a word? Draw a picture? Write out information? Go through a sequence of events?

You cannot always take advantage of this approach to memory, but you can investigate it. Here are some possibilities:

Acting out.   When you want to remember a scene from a novel, a history book, or even a poem, try to go through the motions described in the text. It is valuable to do this with friends, but it can be done alone. For example, you need to remember the climax of a novel you are studying in English class. With friends, choose roles (the characters in the book) and go through the actions described by the author. It takes a bit more time than the actual reading, but you'll never forget the scene.

Mimic.   Many students have learned that they can recall particular words by mimicking a person described by the word. For example, you want to remember *insouciance*. You look at the definition (indifference or lack of concern) and then act out insouciance by greeting a friend with indifference. After you have done this once or twice, you'll never forget the word.

Drawing.   When you have a particularly troublesome idea to remember, try drawing it out on a piece of paper. For example, in history class, you need to know the details of a major battle. On your notebook page, draw the details described verbally in the book. The act of physically drawing the battle plan will aid you in recalling the battle later. Using your hands to make visual representations in this way is valuable, especially in many science classes. What puzzles you in print makes sense as you draw out a rough representation. The act of making the picture helps get the data into memory.

Note Taking

Throughout this book note taking has been emphasized. It is one of the most valuable tools a student has — in lecture classes, in textbook reading, and elsewhere in college. Note taking can help focus your attention on the subject at hand; it can help you better understand the material; and it can aid in remembering. Note taking is a way of making all learning physical in that you must use your hands, eyes, and arms. It forces you to engage your body in the learning — and remembering — process.

EXERCISE 2

An effective note-taking technique that helps you organize material for retention and easier retrieval is the use of the *retention block*. This is simply a block drawn on your notebook page which is then divided into an upper, or *topic*, section and a bottom, or *data*, section.

Retention blocks help you learn and remember the main and supporting facts in a chapter or section of study material. They help you organize and arrange the material so you are getting clear and concise facts as you learn to distinguish between significant and insignificant supporting material. They may serve, too, as summaries of important points in each section of a chapter.

Here is how you use a retention block. First, read the passage; then fill in the top of your block with your answer to the question, "What is this about?" You now have the topic. Next, reread to fill in the bottom section with supporting ideas, examples, and details. This is your data.

To better understand this technique, read the following passage and note how the retention block below it has been filled in.

The free market rests upon the premise of voluntary association and exchange. Anyone with wares and services to vend takes them voluntarily to market, hoping to make a profit from the sale. Other people looking for things to buy go voluntarily to the market, hoping to find what they need or want. Those who go with wares and services as well as those who go to satisfy needs or wants are not forced to buy or sell. Producers are attracted voluntarily to the market by their wish to make a profit. Consumers also go by choice, hoping to fulfill their needs and wants. The two (producers and consumers) then do business together, which usually leaves them both receiving economic benefit from the exchange. The producers receive a profit, and the consumers receive either wares or services that are worth more than the cost.

RETENTION BLOCK

TOPIC: WHAT IS THIS ABOUT?	Free market — voluntary association and exchange
SUPPORTING IDEAS, EXAMPLES, FACTS	anyone can buy or sell no one forced to buy or sell producer attracted by hope for profit consumer attracted by needs and wants both receive economic benefit producer receives profit consumer receives wares and services

Now try to use a retention block on the following paragraph selected from an economics textbook.

Poverty in the United States has many causes. Many of the poor are people over age 65, forced out of the labor market by age and illness. Two other groups are the rural and urban working poor, the first striving to earn a living from marginal or even submarginal farmlands and the second often lacking basic skills needed to make a living wage. Another group is the immobile poor. These are the people trapped by their age and training into occupations for which demand no longer exists. The largest group by far is made up of Puerto Ricans, American Indians, blacks, Chicanos, and Asiatics — the minority poor. These people, taken together, constitute only one-eighth of the total population but one-third of America's poor.

EXERCISE 3

Many students like retention blocks because they give a pictorial representation of the printed material.

Make one now with a section from one of your assignments. Remember, you can make a retention block for an entire chapter or from a longer section of a chapter.

EXERCISE 4

Specific suggestions are made here for getting new ideas and information into your long-term memory. It's your turn now to add to the list.

1. Flash cards, repetition, and questions and answers are ways of making use of drill. In the space provided, name five other ways you can take advantage of drill in your present college courses.

2. Associating new material with what you already know is a valuable trick for remembering. Tell of five recent occasions when you have used this approach to remembering.

3. Describe five mnemonic devices that you regularly use or have heard other people use.

4. You may be able to remember course material better by personalizing it. Give five examples of how personalization may work for you in your present courses.

5. Interest is extremely important in memory, because we all tend to remember things we are interested in. Give five examples here of how you can make a connection between course assignments and areas of your personal interest.

6. Pictures often stay in memory when words don't. Give five examples of mental pictures that have remained in your memory from recent course activities.

7. "Doing" is often better than "reading about." Give five examples here of times when you have remembered something because you have actually done it.

8. Of all the approaches to long-term memory described in this chapter, which works best for you? Use the space provided to tell about your experiences with this approach.

WHY DO YOU FORGET?

There are several answers to this question. Read each and try to relate it to your own recent experiences as a college student.

1. Decay through disuse.   Many people uncritically accept this explanation without knowing what recent research says about it. It is based upon the belief that when you learn something new there is a *memory trace*, an actual physical change in the brain cells. They say that as the body and brain grow and change, the trace may disappear. Today most psychologists say this probably does not happen. They point out that once people have learned to cycle or drive with a standard shift, they can remember all the necessary skills even after *not* cycling or using standard shift for twenty or more years. They also note that most people can remember events, names, and places from childhood after fifty or sixty years! This explanation is often used as an excuse: When you forget, you are tempted to say that the memories have decayed through disuse.

2. Interference.   This is a better explanation for forgetting. When you learn several things at once, the learning of the newer facts may interfere with remembering what you learned earlier. For example, you learn about philosophical systems in an introductory philosophy course: first Plato, then Aristotle, then Roman thinkers, medieval philosophers, and so on. When you try to recall specific details of Aristotle's beliefs, you find "interference" from later study. Researchers have shown that when you memorize two lists of nonsense words, the learning of the second interferes with recalling the first. However, they have also discovered some encouraging information: When the earlier learnings really mean something to you, there is less likelihood of interference. For example, when you memorize data that is unrelated to what you know about the world, later learnings may erase it; but when you learn something of importance to you — something meaningful — later learnings have no effect.

3. Motivated forgetting. Put simply, some forgetting takes place because you want it to! Information may have unpleasant associations or be too painful to recall. In such cases, you do not have much control over the forgetting process, but you should realize that such forgetting exists.

4. Poor retrieval systems. Most experts in this area say that you usually forget because the system you use for retrieval is inadequate. Look back at the methods suggested earlier for getting data into long-term memory. Each has a built-in retrieval system. For example, when you put information into memory by association, you are using the associated material as your "hook" to later retrieve that information. Mnemonic devices require some association. Visualization, interest, personalization, even drill and note taking assume some association. When a specific association is missing, you may not remember. The best way to insure remembering is to build a strong association when you put data into long-term memory.

EXERCISE 5

Here are some practical situations to think about. In each, you have to remember certain definite pieces of information. You do not want to forget them because you are sure they will be included on your examination. In each case, tell how you would learn the information in such a way that forgetting will be difficult.

1. A history assignment asks you to list the major conflicts in the Pacific during World War II. You go through the textbook carefully and arrange them in chronological order. How can you learn them in such a way that you will not forget them?

2. You must learn twenty new words in a foreign-language course. What is the best way to avoid forgetting them later?

3. In a music appreciation course you are asked to learn all the instruments in a symphony orchestra. How can you learn them so you will not forget them two weeks from now?

4. In a child development course you must remember the stages outlined in the book that the author highlights. How can you best remember these?

5. In preparing for a biology examination you list twenty words that appear in the textbook. You want to learn the definitions for an exam. What can you do to insure remembering?

MEMORY AND MEMORIZING

Some students occasionally use memorization as a way of getting new material into long-term memory. Knowing that they have a test scheduled on a certain day, they deliberately set out to memorize sections of the textbook or their lecture notes.

What's wrong with memorizing? By saying something (a poem, a formula, a set of dates, and so on) over and over, we can remember it. It appears to be a viable technique. However, it has major drawbacks for a college student. It is based completely on drill, and as we have seen, drill is only one way of getting new information into long-term memory. There are many better ways. When you want to store material for a test, you will have more success when you relate the new to the known, make associations, and look for meaningful connections. Personalization, physical responses, and visualization all work more effectively than straight memorization. Memorization can also be dangerous. Being able to rattle off a list of words or numbers is not the same as knowing that material. You can too often trick yourself into believing that you know something when actually you have simply memorized it.

Should you ever memorize in college? The answer is only once in a while, under special circumstances. Most of the material you are asked to learn should go into your long-term memory in a systematic, meaningful way. When you tie the new data to material already organized and understood, you can get at it more easily. When you force data in by incessant drill, you are taking a chance that you may not be able to recover it when you need to. Maybe sometimes you can use memorizing — when learning a poem, a complicated formula, a sequence of dates, and so on. Be wary, however, of what you choose to memorize; you may be wasting valuable study time on a technique of limited effectiveness.

One important final point should be made about memorization. Some people still talk of memory as a "muscle," implying that constant use will improve parts of the brain. Most research today contradicts such claims. Memory cells in the brain store memories. To get information into long-term memory is a matter of associations, of establishing meaningful relationships between the new and the known, as well as of visualization, personalization, and physicalization. Interest plays a role in the process, and drill often helps. To think of memory as "muscle building" limits you in your choice of effective study techniques.

SOME FINAL TIPS ON MEMORY IMPROVEMENT

The theoretical discussions in this chapter ought to help you understand how your memory works. Here are some practical tips that have helped many students.

1. Intend to remember!   In Chapter 1 we talked about attitudes toward college learning. Your attitude toward memory is important. When you set out to learn new material, you can make a personal decision: *You will remember*. Often the attitude you take toward the learning experience influences what you remember. Students who study with a negative attitude ("I'll *never* remember all this!") tend not to remember. Those who study with a positive belief that they can remember will tend to remember.

2. Space your work over several study sessions.   The line separating short- from long-term memory is fuzzy and not thoroughly understood. Most students find that when they study intensely for several sessions much of the new material does get into long-term memory. If you use different approaches (such as associations, visualizations, personal relationships, and so on) in different sessions, you increase the chances that you will be able to recall the material later.

3. Use several approaches.   Eight ways to get data from short- into long-term memory are given in this chapter. Use all of them. Try to make associations one day. When you come back to the material a second time, try to make up original mnemonic devices. At another session, use pictures or drawings. The more approaches you can use, the more successful you become.

4. Keep testing yourself.   Even when you seem to have mastered the new material, test yourself. Questions in the margin or on a separate page of your notebook can provide you with quick testing opportunities. Cards with questions on the front and answers on the back can be carried with you for brief reviews. Overlearning is your insurance for examinations.

5. Review before sleep.   Psychologists are not sure about how the mind works when sleeping, but they know that considerable mental activity goes on when you are asleep. Many students say that when they try to learn and review new material before bedtime, the new learnings seem to go more readily into long-term memory. Perhaps the mind continues its work without your conscious knowledge. A quick review the following morning (especially before the test) pays dividends too. After you have reviewed the material before falling asleep, go over it the first thing in the morning.

EXERCISE 6

Do you have other tricks you use to remember? In the space provided here, describe any approaches that have proved successful for you. Be prepared to share these with the group later.

EXERCISE 7

To discover how well you have understood this chapter, in the space below write a brief summary of its main ideas.

POINTS TO REMEMBER ABOUT RETENTION SKILLS

1. Short-term memory is short!

2. You need to get data into long-term memory.

3. Drill and repetition help.

4. Make associations.

5. Relate the new to the known.

6. Review regularly.

7. Make sure you understand the material.

8. Use retention blocks.

9. Space your work over several study sessions.

10. Use several approaches.

9
MASTERY TEST

To check your understanding of Chapter 9, fill in all the blanks in the following passage with appropriate words or phrases.

Memory plays a crucial role in college learning. You must be able to store and recall data from lectures and reading assignments. As a college student, you must be aware that new information is stored for only a few seconds or minutes in (1)_____ . The best way to make sure that the new material you hear in lectures is not lost later is to (2)_____ . Unless you do, you may forget approximately (3)_____ percent of what the speaker says.

The same problem exists when you read textbook assignments. You need to identify important new information and try to get it into your (4)_____ . Some effective ways to do this are: drill, (5)_____ , the use of mnemonic devices, visualization, physicalization, personalization, interest, and, of course, note taking. As you study for tests, try (6)_____ the new information to what you already know, go over some of it repeatedly until you have it in memory, or make use of a (7)_____ such as HOMES (to remember the names of the Great Lakes).

You may forget for a number of reasons. Some people still think that "decay through (8)_____ " is an explanation of forgetting, although most psychologists no longer accept this theory. Today forgetting is most often explained in terms of poor retrieval systems, motivated forgetting, or (9)_____ . One point most psychologists agree upon is that memory is *not* a (10)_____ that gets better with more and more use.

10

Learning to Take Tests

INTRODUCTION AND OVERVIEW

Throughout your college career you will take tests. Some will be true-false or sentence-completion tests; others will be multiple-choice or essay-type tests.

There are skills you can learn now to help you better prepare to take all kinds of tests and assist you in the actual process of test taking. You should not be a passive test taker, but rather one with considerable control over the entire testing system.

This chapter tells you what specific materials you need to focus on as you prepare for examinations, as well as giving suggestions on how to study for all kinds of tests. It provides many valuable tips for taking multiple-choice, true-false, and sentence-completion tests, and concludes with ideas you can use to write more effective essay tests.

SUGGESTED GUIDE QUESTIONS

1. What are the best ways to prepare and study for an examination?

2. Why is it valuable to create your own questions while studying?

3. What are the values of studying with others? The drawbacks?

4. Why is it crucial to read all directions carefully?

5. Why is proofreading important when taking an essay-type exam?

WHAT SHOULD I STUDY?

In the days or weeks prior to an examination you may have read hundreds of pages in books and listened to many hours of lectures. This adds up to a great deal of material. Do you need to reread all of it for the exam? Is it possible to zero in on certain parts? How can you increase your learning efficiency as you prepare for an exam?

The best way to prepare for an exam (whether quiz, midterm, or final) is to (1) review everything, but (2) focus on what counts most. First, review all your material quickly to gain an overview. This means looking at all assigned readings, plus all reading and lecture notes. You will rarely have enough time to carefully reread everything, but you will have enough time for a review that will allow you to see the topics in perspective. Next, you need to focus on those points in the material that can help you most on the actual examination.

Definitions of specialized terms. In order to understand the material you are studying, you need definitions for the words used in that material. When your instructor and textbook author regularly use certain words and specialized terms, make sure you have meanings for them.

Go through the textbook chapters and supplementary readings to identify all words and phrases that you do not know, especially those that seem important. One way to do this is to look first at titles, subtitles, and headings. For example, one economics textbook includes the following subtitles and headings:

The Commercial Banking System as a Whole
  The banking system's lending potential
  Some modifications
    Other leakages
      1. Currency drains
      2. Excess reserves
  Willingness versus ability to lend

Your first step in preparing for an exam on this chapter is to make sure you know these words. Do you know *commercial, banking systems, lending potential, modifications*? How about *leakages, currency, drains, excess, reserves*? Some of these words (such as *currency* and *reserves*) have special meanings in the field of economics. When you come across such terms, you may find them in the book's glossary. Some may be words in common use but not in your personal vocabulary (such as *potential* or *modification*). You can look these up in your dictionary. Write down the meanings, and then check the book to see how the words are used. It is especially helpful when you locate examples that show the meanings. Can you find an example of *lending potential*? *Currency drain*? *Excess reserves*?

While defining specialized terms, it is a good idea to get the spelling in your memory. You may have an essay exam that forces you to write these words.

Lists.   As you review your material, watch for lists. Usually, these are labeled somehow, appearing as subtitles or headings:

Four Effects of the Stamp Tax

The Stages of Human Development

Four Reasons Why Study Skills Are Important

Eight Points to Remember about Intelligence Tests

In lectures, speakers may say:

"The Stamp Tax had four effects."

"Let's look at the stages of human development."

"There are four reasons why study skills are important."

"Here are eight points to remember about intelligence tests."

Whether you note them in your textbook or your lecture notes, such lists are important. They guide you in study preparation because they tell you, in no uncertain terms, exactly what to learn. They also provide enormous aid in writing essay exams because they give you an outline to follow as you write.

Watch for such lists and place them high on your priority schedule. When study time is limited, you may use it to better advantage by focusing on those specialized terms and the lists you find in the material.

Ideas stressed in book and class.   As they speak, instructors frequently stress particular ideas. They may repeat them; they may write them on the chalkboard. They may simply raise their voices or emphasize key points by gesturing. If you have taken good lecture notes, you probably caught these important ideas and recorded them in your notebook.

In books, authors also stress main ideas. They do this in print by using a different type (capital letters or italics), color, or boldface. Sometimes the key ideas are highlighted in titles, subtitles, or headings. Sometimes they are repeated in different words. Watch for these print signals just as you watch for the speaker's raised voice or dramatic gesture. They cue you into the central points of the chapter.

Remember, if an idea is important enough to stress in class or by some visual device in the book, it must be important enough to be on the test. When an idea is repeated several times in lectures or reading assignments, it needs attention during your test preparation time.

Ideas noted as "test possibilities."   Often, instructors actually tell you what material will appear on a test. They point to certain information and say, "This is important and won't be overlooked on the test." Often, too, they will point to certain sections of the course text and tell you that these may appear in an exam. When you catch such warnings, mark your notes: underline, star, circle, block in. Such information is priceless!

Previous exams and quizzes.   Take time to go back and review exams and quizzes you have already taken in the course. These can be an invaluable source of guidance. Individual instructors have personal preferences for certain approaches and types of test items. By examining old test papers, you can get some clues to the ways the next test will be constructed. One person may favor lists ("What four factors influenced Hitler's decision to invade Russia?") or definitions ("What is meant by *excess reserves*?") Once you become acquainted with the testing approach favored by certain professors, you have a distinct edge that you otherwise might lack.

Study guides, handouts, and reviews.   Clearly, when an instructor goes to the trouble of typing, duplicating, and distributing additional material for the class, that material must be important. Don't neglect it when you study. By confining yourself to the textbook and the lecture notes, you may miss topics that may appear on the test. Review all handouts — just because this material was distributed informally in class does not mean that it is of lesser importance.

Lecture notes.   If you have taken effective lecture notes, devote a large proportion of your study time to them. They are a vital source of information for you at the test preparation stage. Go through them looking for possible test questions, specialized words, and lists. Look for ideas that stand out and ideas that are also discussed in handouts. In some courses, your lecture notes are your best source of possible test questions.

Textbook assignments.   Some students study only the textbook when preparing for an examination. Reviewing textbook assignments is important and must be done; however, you will profit more by reviewing reading assignments as you focus on the other points suggested here. Read the necessary chapters, but also check for the definitions of specialized words, look for lists, note ideas stressed in lectures and readings, review all handouts, and study lecture notes. This combination of approaches is essential to insure that you have touched base with all possible testing possibilities.

EXERCISE 1

Prepare for an actual examination by following the steps outlined here. Keep a record noting how you handled each of the steps.

1. What specialized words have you selected to define and learn? Write them here:

2. What vocabulary words used regularly in the lectures and readings are unfamiliar to you? Write them here:

3. What are the definitions of these words? Write them beside the words to remember them:

4. What lists are included in your reading assignments? Write them here:

5. What lists were noted in your lectures? Write them out:

6. What ideas were stressed in both readings and lectures? List them:

7. What ideas were noted in class as possible questions? List them:

8. Have you reviewed previous tests and quizzes? What do you observe about the instructor's testing style and preferences? Write your answers here:

9. What have you discovered from your review of handouts, study guides, and other supplementary materials? What specific information do you get from these that was not given in lectures and readings? List this information here:

10. What questions have you created during your exam preparation that may be included on the exam? Write them here:

HOW SHOULD I STUDY FOR AN EXAMINATION?

Once you have identified what to study, you need to think about how best to study it.

Here are seven suggestions:

Make a list of what you plan to study. Write down all the points discussed in the previous section of this chapter. For example:

vocabulary

lists

key ideas stressed

possible test items

previous exams and quizzes

handouts

lecture notes

textbook reading assignments

Go through the list systematically.   First, check to make sure you have meanings for all specialized words and words unfamiliar to you. Next, identify all lists mentioned in class and in the book. Then, learn all the key ideas stressed in the course. Continue through your list in a systematic manner.

Make up questions as you go along.   If you note that the term *lending potential* is used several times, make up a study question, such as "What is lending potential?" If you see a heading, The Stages of Human Development, write out a question, "What are the stages of human development?" If the instructor stressed *molecular transfer*, ask "What is molecular transfer?" The process of writing out and answering your own questions is one of the best ways to prepare for a test. The questions, too, may serve as the basis of quick review in the hour (or minutes) before the test actually begins.

Summarize particularly difficult points.   As you review the material using the system suggested here, you will encounter topics that are difficult to understand. An effective strategy for dealing with such points is to write a summary. Summary writing in itself is difficult, but it pays big dividends. For example, you find you are unable to answer the question, "What is molecular transfer?" Try writing out a one-paragraph summary of the pages in the book that explain the idea. You will find that you must read and reread many times as you write. This process helps you shape the basic concept in your head. In most cases, this writing-reading-writing activity will help you better understand the troublesome idea.

Go to other sources.   Often you find that you cannot prepare a summary. You read, write, reread, and so on, but the summary refuses to shape itself for you on paper. At such times, go to other books, other references, or other people. For example, your textbook may not be helpful to you on certain points (*molecular transfer* or *commercial banking systems*). They are mentioned over and over again in the book and in class, but are not defined. Check other textbooks in the library. Some are written at a less sophisticated level. High school books that you can find in the public library sometimes treat the same topics in a manner that is easier to read and understand. Sometimes you can locate a magazine article that discusses difficult course material in simple language aimed at the nonspecialist. Many times when you have difficulty defining a technical term, you should simply ask someone. Other students, graduate students in the departmental offices, or instructors may be able to explain key words and ideas in language that you can more readily understand.

Use common sense about studying with others.   Studying with other students is not necessarily the best way to prepare for an exam. First, you should go through the five steps outlined here. You cannot do these as effectively when you work with others, as each requires your total concentration. You may later profit from reviewing the material with others. For example, you can later compare vocabulary terms to discover if you all have the same meanings for certain words; you can also compare your lists of words, lists, stressed ideas, and so on. You can later test one another, using the questions each person has created. The danger with group study sessions is that they too often become social sessions that divert attention away from the material and onto more pleasant topics.

Remember the basics.   When you study for an exam, remember the advice given before in this book: Choose an appropriate place, one that is quiet and comfortable; make sure the lights are arranged properly; assemble all your materials beforehand; and attend to your physical needs before studying.

EXERCISE 2

Now is the time to try some of these approaches. In this exercise, take each of the topics given and turn it into a question you can use to guide your study.

Topics	Your Questions
1. The sun and solar energy	
2. Reading is a complex skill.	
3. Jean-Paul Sartre	
4. Differential equations	
5. 1944	

EXERCISE 3

When studying for an exam, the questions you create guide your study by providing a purpose for rereading and review of the material. Try creating some more questions using real headnotes. Select a textbook assignment and copy here all the subtitles and headings. Then write out the questions you invented for each.

Subtitles and Headings	Your Questions
1.	
2.	
3.	
4.	
5.	
6.	
7.	
8.	
9.	
10.	

EXERCISE 4

Summarizing is a powerful tool for understanding. Take one difficult idea or concept from an assignment and write a brief summary to explain it. Remember that you will have to go back, read, and reread as you write.

The idea or concept:

Your summary explanation:

EXERCISE 5

Apply the techniques recommended here to an actual examination. Keep a brief record of exactly how you studied for an examination.

1. **Did you make a list of what you plan to study?** Include it here.

2. **Did you go through the list systematically?** Make check marks by each item on your list to show that you did cover it.

3. **Did you create your own study questions?** Write them out and include them with this exercise.

4. **Did you have to summarize any difficult ideas?** Include the summaries.

5. **Did you go to other sources for help?** Indicate the sources here. Tell what you asked and what you learned.

6. **Did you study with others?** Explain: With whom? When? Was the experience helpful? Include your responses with the exercise.

HOW CAN I TAKE TESTS MORE EFFECTIVELY?

Deciding what to study and doing the actual studying are only half the battle. Once you start the test, you have to remember certain points about test taking itself. Here are some tips for you for the different kinds of tests you will encounter.

Multiple-Choice Tests

Remember, multiple-choice test items consist of (1) a stem, (2) a statement to complete the stem, and (3) two or more misleading statements that appear to complete the stem but do not.
For example:

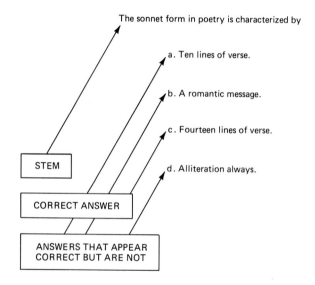

The sonnet form in poetry is characterized by

a. Ten lines of verse.

b. A romantic message.

c. Fourteen lines of verse.

d. Alliteration always.

STEM

CORRECT ANSWER

ANSWERS THAT APPEAR CORRECT BUT ARE NOT

How can you best handle multiple-choice items? You need to use reasoning skills and tactics that can help you out of possibly troublesome situations. Here are some approaches:

1. Turn the stem into a question. This approach is especially useful if you have been using a question-answer system in studying. If you have turned headnotes and lecture statements into questions in your notebook, you have been studying to discover and write down answers. In a case such as this one, you ask yourself, "What's a sonnet?" You should recall that one part of the answer refers to its length, fourteen lines.

2. Try elimination. From your reading in the literature course, you remember that some sonnets are not at all romantic. You can eliminate answer b. You also remember that some of the sonnets you read in the course did not have any alliteration; you therefore eliminate d. Sometimes the process of elimination allows you to arrive at the correct answer even though you did not have it in memory.

3. Watch for qualifiers.   Absolutes, such as *never, only, always,* or *all* are dangerous. They usually indicate a wrong answer. In the example on the sonnet, you may become suspicious of answer d because of the *always.* Watch, too, for qualifiers such as *probably, usually, generally,* and *often.* Chances are greater that these indicate correct answers.

4. Watch for incomplete items.   An answer may appear at first glance to be correct, but check to make sure it is complete. If a phrase or term has been omitted, the answer is probably incorrect.

5. Of two opposites, one is probably correct.   When you find two possible answers that are exactly opposite in meaning, one of these may be correct. Go back to the first suggestion made above about turning stems to questions. Turn the stem into a question when this situation happens and see which of the two provides the most reasonable answer.

6. More words tend to be right.   Because the correct answer must account for all possible information, it tends to be the longest. This is not always true (a sonnet has fourteen lines), but is true often enough to insure that when you are in doubt, go for the longest!

7. The most complete answer is probably correct.   In order to cover all possibilities, the writer of the test may have had to put in more information. Just as you need to be alert to long answers, you need to watch for long, *complete* answers. They tend to be correct.

True-False Tests

Frequently, you are asked to complete simple true-false tests. These are relatively easy for instructors to make up for short quizzes and are easy to correct. Here are some tips for handling them:

1. All parts must be true.   Read the statement carefully, watching for words or phrases in the sentences that may not be entirely true. If you spot such a problem, reject the statement as false.

2. The more included, the better the choice.   As you have seen in multiple-choice tests, a completely accurate statement usually requires more words. When you encounter longer statements, mark them *true* unless you are sure they are not. The long ones *tend* to be true.

3. Absolutes are dangerous.   When you see words such as *never*, *only*, *always*, or *all*, be suspicious. Statements that include them are probably false.

4. Items that give a reason are probably false.   An item that gives a reason to justify itself may be false. Ask yourself why the writer bothered to give one reason. It may be that there are *many* reasons to account for the statement; singling out one looks suspicious! For example, "Leaves of deciduous trees change color in the fall because of the cold" is true but suspicious. Your reading in the textbook informed you that there are a number of reasons why these leaves change color.

5. Watch for negatives.   Negatives tend to confuse the issues, so be careful when you see them. For example, "Consistent study makes for a well-prepared student" is easy; "Inconsistent study does not make for a well-prepared student" is difficult. Translate all negative statements into positive ones to make sure you understand them before responding.

6. Watch for qualifiers.   Words such as *probably*, *surely*, *generally*, *sometimes*, *often* or *usually* may be dangerous. Read the sentence to yourself *without* the qualifier to see if the sense changes before you respond.

Matching Items

Another type of test used frequently consists of matching. You must connect items on one list with items on another, either by drawing lines from item to item or by placing a number or letter identifying words on one list beside those on another. In most cases, the items on one list are related to those on the other. For example, on the matching test below, the names of famous inventors appear in the left list; various inventions are named in the right list. You must write the letter of each invention next to the name of its inventor:

_____	1. Gatlin	a. phonograph
_____	2. Whitney	b. machine gun
_____	3. Colt	c. automobile
_____	4. Edison	d. revolver
_____	5. Diesel	e. cotton gin
		f. engine

The best way to approach matching questions of this kind is to choose *one* of the columns and match as many items as you can with those in the other column. You can start with either one, although you may have more success if you start with the column providing the most information. (In this example, it would be the right-hand column.)

While you are doing such test items, cross out the words you have used as you go along, to avoid confusion. Do all those you are sure of before you start guessing!

Sentence Completion

These test items require you to supply either a missing word or phrase. Some tips for handling these are:

1. Make sure your answers fit logically into the statement. (Say them to yourself to hear how they sound.)

2. Make sure your answers fit grammatically. (Again, listen to your answers to determine whether they sound grammatically sensible.)

3. The article *an* before a blank indicates that the word or phrase needed must begin with a vowel.

4. The article *a* indicates the needed answer begins with a consonant.

5. If the blank is longer than that required for a single word, you may very well need a phrase.

Essay-Type Exams

These may range from a single paragraph to a full blue book. Because you are graded on your writing and organization as well as your knowledge, this type of exam can be especially tricky. Some tips for taking essay exams follow.

Read directions carefully. Note the *topic*, the *guide word*, and any *limiting words*. For example, "Trace the events that led to the Boston Tea Party." That seems simple, but watch out. The *topic* is "Boston Tea Party." That's what you are supposed to write about. The *guide word* is "trace." That tells you exactly what to do. You are not supposed to describe it or explain it; you are supposed to trace the events that led to it. "Led to" are the *limiting words*. In this case, they tell you that you need concern yourself only with those events that took place before the event.

Guide words are very important. Study the following list to make sure you know how to handle each when you see it on a test.

Common guide words are:

- **Compare.** Look for similarities between two items and note them in your answer.

- **Contrast.** Look for differences between two items and highlight these in your answer.

- **Define.** Tell what the word means to you by explaining what general class of things it falls into and the specific ways it differs from that class.

- **Discuss.** Tell all you possibly can about the topic; try to present your information in some logical order. If told to "discuss" the Boston Tea Party, plan an outline first so that all your data is arranged in sequence. On a scrap of paper, write out an outline such as this to guide you:

  I. What it was

  II. When and where it happened

  III. Why it happened

  IV. What were the consequences

  Such a quick guide enables you to discuss in a sensible manner without omitting important details.

- **Describe.** Again, tell all you can, but give emphasis to actual, observed events. For example, if asked to describe the Boston Tea Party, focus on what happened. You still need an outline, but your outline will be concerned more with the sequence of events. It might look like this:

  I. What it was

  II. What happened first

  III. What happened next

  IV. What happened finally

  V. In what ways it was different from similar events

  You need an outline to guide you as you write a description, just as you need one to "discuss."

- **Evaluate.** Here you give positive and negative features. For example, if asked to evaluate the success of the Banking Act of 1933, give all the reasons why it helped the economy, plus reasons why it may have had a negative effect on aspects of the economy. When you finish, come to a conclusion based on your evaluations of these pros and cons.

- **Illustrate.** Give specific examples. If asked to illustrate the effects of a certain law, describe specific examples of how the law affected certain groups. The more specific examples you can give, the better. You are drawing a picture with words, so the more details you put in, the better the picture.

- ***Analyze.*** Break down the topic into segments. If you are asked to analyze a process in history, chemistry, or any other subject, make an outline and use it to discuss each separate part of the larger process. Make sure as you write that each segment is related to those coming before and after.

- ***Justify.*** Give reasons to support a statement. For example, if asked to justify the amendment that repealed Prohibition, give each reason you can to explain why it needed to be repealed. In such essays, you are *proving* a case as if you were a lawyer in court.

- ***Trace.*** Follow a time sequence. If asked to trace the development of the National Socialist Party in Germany in the 1930s, tell about each event in sequence.

- ***Summarize.*** Give the ideas of a topic in as few words as you can. In a term paper you may be required to put a large amount of information into several pages; in a summary you must condense it into a paragraph or two. When asked to summarize for an essay test, remember that you still need an outline to guide you as you write.

- ***Relate.*** Show connections. Tell how the topic connects to another topic, stressing the points the two have in common. Usually, the directions tell you what is to be related to what. Read them carefully.

Outline or map.   After you have read the essay test directions and decided (1) what the topic is, (2) what the guide words tell you to do with it, and (3) what words limit you in certain ways, then you need to make an outline or map. For example, if you are asked to trace something, list the steps on your outline in chronological order, noting any limitations in time. (Remember, "Trace the events that *led to* the Boston Tea Party.") If asked to analyze, outline the parts of the problem or process so that you can discuss each separately, without running back and forth from idea to idea. The importance of outlining to successful performance on essay tests cannot be overemphasized. (For a review of mapping techniques, see Chapter 3.)

Look for the question implied in the directions and answer it in your first sentence.   "Trace the events that led to the Boston Tea Party" implies a question: What events led to the Boston Tea Party? "Evaluate the effects of Rommel's African victories on the war in Europe" implies the question, What effects did Rommel's African victories have on the war in Europe? Once you have turned the directions into a question, you can answer the question in a single sentence which becomes your opening sentence for the essay. For example, you can start your American history essay by saying, "Four separate events led to the Boston Tea Party." You can start your European history essay by writing, "Rommel's African victories had both positive and negative effects on the war in Europe."

In each of these cases, your first sentence sets up a plan for writing. Once you have mentioned "Four separate events," you can build an outline with a I, II, III, and IV. In the second case, you have constructed a plan with positive effects grouped in one section and negative effects in another.

Spend some time thinking about your first sentence. It informs the reader of your plan and predicts the kind of information you will provide. Most important, it gives you a skeleton to fill out as you write.

End by restating your conclusions.   In formal essays of a more literary nature (the kind you may do in an English class), you may not want to be obvious and tell readers what you have already told them. However, in a test you cannot be too obvious! Make sure your reader knows what you have said.

Proofread.   Many excellent essay responses are penalized because writers fail to check their work. When you have completed the essay, double-check for the following:

- The essay should make sense, moving from point to point in a logical manner.

- Each paragraph should have a clearly defined topic sentence to tell the reader what the paragraph is about. (It may be wise to place it first.)

- There should be no run-on sentences. Be sure you have separated each sentence with appropriate punctuation.

- There should be no fragments. Read each sentence to yourself to be sure it has a beginning (a subject) and an end (a predicate).

- Each sentence should make sense. You can often detect grammatical as well as logical problems by saying each sentence to yourself.

- Each sentence must begin with a capital letter and end with the proper punctuation mark.

- Check your spelling. You cannot always run to the dictionary in a test situation, but you can use synonyms. Don't ruin a good answer with misspellings.

- The entire essay should follow your original plan. Before you hand in the paper, be sure your plan is logical, that one part relates to another, and that the essay achieves what you wanted it to.

For many students, essay-type examinations are the most difficult. You are expected to give information in an organized manner, using language that is acceptable and sensible. You are also expected to do all this within a limited time framework. This is difficult, but you can learn to master the techniques.

Here are five other helpful suggestions:

1. Use a pen. Pencil smudges and may give your final paper an unattractive appearance.

2. Write on 8½-by-11-inch paper if no examination booklets are distributed.

3. When using separate sheets of paper, put your name on each and clip them all together.

4. Draw neat lines through errors. Parentheses are inappropriate and confusing.

5. Allow enough time to double-check your work. You may need to rewrite or add more information.

EXERCISE 6

Answer the following, using information learned in this chapter. Be prepared to tell why you chose certain answers and which of the suggestions you followed in each case. All are true-false type.

1. A university computer center will usually have several hundred prewritten subprograms either developed by the center or obtained from an outside supplier.
   T   F

2. Generally, the longer a volcano is dormant, the more potentially dangerous it becomes.
   T   F

3. Sometimes "fools' gold" is better than the real thing.
   T   F

4. Scientists have found that all plants have distinctive, measurable reactions to various pollutants.
   T   F

5. Red blood cells never spend any time in transit.
   T   F

EXERCISE 7

Now use what you learned to answer these multiple-choice items. Again, be prepared to tell why you chose your answers and which of the suggestions guided you.

1. *Melaphyre* refers to

    a. rock.
    b. an igneous porphyritic rock with a dark groundmass.
    c. volcanic rock.

2. Volcanology has been

    a. a white art.
    b. dormant.
    c. a black art.

3. The mature personality is

    a. always the product of early parent-child relationships.
    b. sometimes the product of early parent-child relationships.
    c. never the product of early parent-child relationships.

4. To find out if next spring will be wet or dry, you can

    a. dig a hole thirty inches deep.
    b. dig a hole fifty inches deep.
    c. dig a hole forty inches deep and take the ground's temperature.

5. Nineteenth-century American novels tend to

    a. always be realistic.
    b. be realistic because of the materialism of the society.
    c. be longer than nineteenth-century English novels.

EXERCISE 8

To prepare for a possible essay examination, complete the following exercise on a separate sheet of paper. First, choose a course that may be likely to have an essay exam. Predict four possible examination questions you may be given. Next, outline two of these, using as much course information as possible. Finally, write out an essay following one of the two outlines.

EXERCISE **9**

On a separate sheet of paper, write out a well-constructed short essay on the subject, "Discuss reasons why it is important to learn to manage your time." Outline the essay, using the information provided in Chapter 2, Learning to Make the Best Use of Your Time.

SOME FINAL POINTS ABOUT TEST TAKING

Here are some general suggestions to guide you as you take various college examinations:

1. In addition to the time you set aside for study, go over the main points the night before the examination and, if possible, early the next morning.   Here is where your own self-created questions can help: Go through these to make sure you have all the answers.

2. Get to the testing room early.   You start with a handicap when you start breathless and disoriented. Make sure you arrive with time to spare in order to settle yourself in and get organized.

3. Read all directions before writing anything.   Nothing can do you as much harm as starting a test (multiple-choice or essay) without knowing exactly what is expected of you. Read every direction carefully; *ask for assistance if you are still puzzled.*

4. Answer the easier test items first.   Some are easy when you really know your material and spot the answers at once. Do them right away; you will then have more time to concentrate on more difficult items.

5. Don't spend too much time on any one question.   If you do those you know first, you'll have more time for the hard ones. But even then you can get bogged down on a troublesome item and lose time that could be spent improving your total score.

6. Reread before you turn your paper in.   This is clearly important for essay questions: You need to check spelling, punctuation, sentence sense, and so on. It is also important for objective items. You may find you have omitted an item or confused the order. Double-check before you leave the testing room.

WHAT ABOUT "EXAM ANXIETY"?

One hears regularly of students who know their material but "just can't take examinations." Such people are prone to a state called "exam anxiety," in which they grow tense and forget much of the material they studied so hard to learn.

The best way of dealing with this problem is *systematic preparation*. When you have carefully defined what you need to study and systematically gone through the process of review and restudy, you should not tense up in the test situation. An intensive session the night before the exam, a good night's sleep, proper nourishment, and a quick review the morning of the test should put you at ease. Some feelings of anxiety are normal. After all, success in college is your goal, and success is determined to a large extent by examination performance. (A famous theatrical director once said that she did not respect actors who were *not* nervous before a performance. Nervousness was a sign of caring and a precursor to success in performance!)

What can you do on those occasions when you have prepared well physically and mentally and yet find yourself tense and anxious on test day? Some psychologists and college counselors suggest the following:

1. Behavior rehearsal. Sit quietly for a few moments before the exam and picture the actual test situation in your mind. Try to see yourself entering the room, sitting down, reading the test, and so forth. In your "mind picture" you are completely calm and in control of yourself. Rehearse your behavior step-by-step during the test, and then go over the entire test-taking experience with yourself always as a successful student coping with individual test items and finishing satisfactorily. When you encounter the real situation, such a positive mental run-through may give you support and release from tension.

2. Breathing exercises. Breathing exercises can also provide help in a stressful situation. Inhale deeply through your nose, hold the air in your lungs for a few seconds, then exhale slowly through your mouth, making your stomach contract as you breathe out. Repeat such an exercise three or four times, relaxing between times.

3. Muscle relaxation. When you are stressful, certain muscles tense in a painful way. You may find that you grip your pencil tightly with your fingers or that your neck or shoulder muscles contract. Progressive relaxation loosens these muscles and decreases the stress that their tension causes in the body. Stretch out on the floor and focus your attention on the identified muscle area. First, increase the tension in these muscles as much as you can, then relax the tensed area. Continue to tighten and relax; then, if necessary, focus on another set of tensed muscles.

4. Visualization. Some students have had success with visualization. While in a quiet, relaxed position, they close their eyes and imagine a peaceful place (the beach in winter, a pasture, a mountain forest). Sometimes they try to imagine themselves in this place, relaxing and quietly enjoying the beauty of their surroundings. Five or ten minutes of visualization often relieves them of the anxieties prevalent before examinations.

Other techniques recommended for the relief of exam anxiety are biofeedback, self-hypnosis, meditation, and others. If you find yourself too frequently anxious and tense before tests, consult with a college counselor or physician. Some nervousness before exams should be expected; too much may indicate related problems that you should check out.

POINTS TO REMEMBER ABOUT TEST TAKING

1. Prepare by focusing on key points.
2. Study definitions, lists, ideas stressed in class, and all lecture notes.
3. Make summaries of material as you go along.
4. Try to predict test questions.
5. Watch for qualifiers and absolutes in both multiple-choice and true-false items.
6. In a multiple choice test, the longest answers, especially when in the middle, tend to be correct.
7. Start with the longer statements when doing matching items.
8. Look for *a* and *an* when answering fill-in items.
9. Outline or map essays so that they are logical and clear to the reader.
10. Carefully edit all essays for sense and logic as well as grammar and spelling.

10
SELF-EVALUATION

Instead of a Mastery Test, this chapter ends with a Self-Evaluation that will give you an opportunity to assess your own test-preparation habits and test-taking skills.

	Always	Sometimes	Rarely
Items I Review for Exams			
1. Definitions			
2. Examples			
3. Summaries			
4. Previous tests and quizzes			
5. Study guides			
6. Lists			
7. Stressed ideas			
8. Specialized vocabulary			
9. Unfamiliar words			
10. Illustrations, maps, charts, and tables			
11. Review questions in book			
12. Lecture notes			
13. Reading assignments			
14. Self-created questions			
15. All handouts			

	Always	Sometimes	Rarely
Suggestions I Follow Before Exams:			
1. Review all material the day before			
2. Use my own questions for a quick review			
3. Get a good night's sleep			
4. Eat properly			
5. Arrive early			
6. Bring adequate supplies			
7. Skim textbook headings and summaries			
8. Reread my own summaries			
9. Make a last-minute check of technical vocabulary			
10. Read all directions carefully			
Suggestions I Follow During Exams:			
1. Examine the entire test before starting			
2. Plan a time budget for the test			
3. Check off the items that will require more time			
4. Do all easier items first			
5. Ask the instructor when directions are not clear to me			
6. Make sure all questions are answered			
7. Turn multiple-choice item stems into questions			

	Always	Sometimes	Rarely
8. Watch for qualifiers			
9. Watch for negatives			
10. Outline essays in advance of writing			
11. Watch for guide words in essays			
12. Watch for limiting words in essays			
13. Proofread all essays carefully			
14. Reread all test items for accuracy			
15. Make necessary changes			

11

Learning to Write Papers for College Courses

INTRODUCTION AND OVERVIEW

As a college student, you will be asked frequently to submit written assignments. Some of these will be brief reports or even briefer response (or reaction) papers that can be completed in one or two sessions. Some will be longer papers that demand in-depth investigations of course topics and require days of preparation and writing. Some will be even longer research papers involving considerable library research time and many days or weeks of actual writing.

This chapter examines the process of writing all course papers. It focuses primarily, however, on the shorter reports and course term papers. Your major research papers will be developed using the same approaches but, because they require specialized library research, they are treated separately in the next chapter.

Here you will learn important prewriting, writing, and editing techniques. You'll learn how to collect material for your papers, how to organize the material for writing, how to narrow down topics and focus on a specific theme or main idea. You'll be given suggestions for the actual writing and for preparing your work for presentation.

SUGGESTED GUIDE QUESTIONS

---

1. What do you need to do before you start to write?
2. How can you overcome "writer's block"?
3. Why do you need to identify your readers before you write?
4. What three techniques can help you organize your material?
5. Why is editing crucial to writing success?

WHAT ARE THE PURPOSES OF WRITTEN ASSIGNMENTS?

College writing assignments serve at least three important educational purposes:

They allow your instructors to better evaluate your course learning. When you write, you show how much information you have and how well you relate it to previously acquired knowledge. A short paper can reveal a great deal about your present level of understanding in a course.

They give you opportunities to learn more. As you gather information to write, you learn material not always given in the course textbook. You are also forced to look at this new information in relation to everything else you know, thus helping you organize it in your mind for later use. The writing may become a powerful learning experience in itself.

They give you further practice in writing. Writing plays a role in almost all careers — sometimes a major role. People who know how to write well tend to succeed: They can write reports, evaluations, proposals, directions, bulletins, memos, and so on. Learning to write well should be a major objective for all college students.

HOW CAN I LEARN TO WRITE BETTER PAPERS?

Some students mistakenly believe that writing consists of taking ideas from their heads and putting them on paper. For them, writing is a slow and painful process. They spend hours trying to get those ideas from their heads onto paper — and rarely succeed. The papers they eventually present in courses are often jumbled, unfocused, and ineffective.

Other students learn early in their college careers that writing is a process of *thinking on paper*. They discover that successful writing is successful thinking. They know, too, that it is what writers do before they begin to write that makes for success — not the actual writing itself. They are aware of the separate steps in the writing process and the separate substeps involved. What are these steps?

First comes *prewriting*. Here is where you:

1. Get yourself organized.

2. Get into the right frame of mind for writing.

3. Zero in on a well-defined topic.

4. Gather material by brainstorming.

5. Gather more material by researching.

6. Define your thesis, or main idea.

7. Identify your readers.

8. Organize your material for writing.

Second comes the actual *writing*. This is where you:

1. Write the first draft.

2. Revise it.

3. Get an outside opinion.

4. Rewrite if necessary.

5. Revise again.

Third comes the *editing*. Here is where you:

1. Check for purpose, organization, and clear thinking.

2. Check for spelling, punctuation, sentence structure, and grammatical problems.

3. Evaluate the entire paper from the point of view of your reader.

4. Prepare the final copy.

These steps are described in the following pages. As you read them, complete as many of the exercises as possible. After you have read them, try out the step-by-step process by completing an actual college paper. You'll find, as have many students, that writing a paper is less of a chore and, most important, that your completed paper will be better than it would have been if you hadn't gone through the process systematically.

Prewriting

Professional writers will tell you that it is the time spent *before* you write that is most important. The time you spend preparing yourself for the first draft pays the greatest dividends in quality. In other words, the extra hour or so you spend in preparation will contribute more to your final grade than the time you spend in actually writing or typing. What steps are involved in this important prewriting stage?

1. Get physically organized. Professional writers do their work at a table or desk, surrounded by the tools they need. Just as automotive mechanics or dentists do their best work in carefully prepared surroundings, so do writers. You can, of course, do some writing in the library or the locker room (just as a mechanic can do emergency repairs on the highway), but to produce most effectively, you need a comfortable base — a table or desk in a room at home or in your dormitory, with pencils, pens, typewriter, an adequate supply of paper, dictionary, and so on at hand.

2. Get psychologically organized. To do your best work, you need more than work space and equipment: You need to be in the right frame of mind. Many students complain of "writers' block": "The paper is due on Friday but I just can't get started." They lack the proper psychological frame of mind.

How can you put yourself in the right mood for writing? How can you overcome "writers' block"?

- Don't try to begin when you are overly tired, hungry, or worried about other matters. (See Chapter 2, "Learning to Make the Best Use of Your Time.")

- Don't plan to complete a writing assignment in a single sitting. Break down the writing task into smaller, more manageable pieces. Tell yourself that you'll write the opening paragraph or one page. You'll find that you *can* complete segments of an assignment, block or no block.

- Schedule your writing assignment sensibly. When you must complete a course paper by a certain date, make up a reasonable schedule so that you need do only one chunk at a time:

  Monday — Research and brainstorming to gather material
  Tuesday — Outline

Wednesday — First draft

Thursday — Revision and second draft

Friday — Have someone else read it

Monday — Rewrite

Tuesday — Revision and editing

Wednesday — Type

Thursday — Check final copy and changes, and prepare cover page

Friday — Ready to submit

EXERCISE 1

You need to be both physically and psychologically prepared to write. What steps have you taken in the past to prepare yourself? What steps will you take in the future? Complete the following in order to better evaluate your preparation.

Steps I have taken in the past to prepare myself physically to write:

1.

2.

3.

4.

5.

Steps I plan to take in the future:

1.

2.

3.

4.

5.

Steps I have taken in the past to prepare myself mentally for written assignments:

1.

2.

3.

4.

5.

Steps I plan to take in the future:

1.

2.

3.

4.

5.

   3. Narrow down the topic.   Students usually start with a general topic, one assigned or one they choose. For an English class theme, for example, one student decides to write about rock music. That is a general topic, much too large to discuss intelligently in less than a 300-page book! It needs to be narrowed down. The student decides to focus on punk rock. That is still too large a subject for a paper, so she decides to narrow it down still further. In the process of narrowing down the topic, she has hit upon a *thesis* and a possible title. She decides that she will explain how recent records from well-known groups have tended to be less wild. Her main idea is that this particular kind of rock music has become more and more like other kinds of rock and less distinctive. Her thesis is "Punk rock has become domesticated." Her title becomes, "The Taming of Punk Rock."
   One of the most important jobs you need to do before you actually write the paper is to narrow it down to manageable size. As you do this, you will discover exactly what you want to say (that's your main idea or *thesis*) and what your title will be.
   Here is a good way to help you narrow down your topic:

- Write the topic on your notebook page. For this example, we will use "Witchcraft."

- List all the possible questions that come into your head about the topic over a period of days. For "Witchcraft," you might get: What is it? What are some examples? Who does it? Where do these people supposedly get their powers? Can it be controlled? How has it been depicted in films, novels, television? Is there any rational explanation for it?

- Study your questions to discover *one* that might help you focus your paper. You might choose "How has it been depicted in films, novels, and television?" and then decide to narrow your investigations to television alone. You now have a handle on the topic — a place to begin your search for material and a peg to hang it on.

In your attempts to narrow down your topic, remember three points:

1. Try to choose a topic that interests you. Sometimes you have no choice, but when you do, select a topic that will hold your interest for what may be a long period of time.

2. Try to choose a topic you already know at least a little bit about. Writing provides opportunities to learn, but it is advantageous to have some prior knowledge to guide you through the planning stages of a project.

3. Choose a topic that can be handled in a course paper. You have only a few days or weeks to collect data, organize it, prepare a first draft, revise it, and write the final copy. Don't be overly ambitious.

4. Brainstorm.   When you write out questions about the topic in order to narrow your focus, you are brainstorming. You need to continue this activity once the topic has been narrowed.

Brainstorming is best done in small groups, but you can do it alone. In a typical writing situation in college you will probably work alone. Sit down in a quiet place and jot down everything that comes into your head about the topic, especially your narrowed-down version. You'll probably be surprised at how much information you already possess. Often you can fill an entire notebook page with items. For *witchcraft*, one student wrote down: Salem, witchcraft trials, *Carrie*, rituals, secret curses, symbols, evil, medieval times, Joan of Arc, dunking, spells, charms, occult, ceremonies, sacred dances, chants, covens, sacrifices, familiars, images, and on and on.

Brainstorming has two values: It activates your memory, reminding you of many things you already know about the subject, and it also gives you a starting place. Once you have gone through the process and filled a page or more, you have something to work on as you start the first draft. Sometimes, too, as you brainstorm, you get more ideas for further narrowing your topic. The list on witchcraft might help the student who made it decide she wants to focus more closely on specific kinds of witch-craft or upon a historical view of the subject.

5. Research.   For the most part, brainstorming relies on searching through memory for ideas you already have. Sometimes such searching fails to provide sufficient data for a paper, and other sources need to be examined.

How do you research your topic? Here are three ideas to get you started:

- Go to the card catalog in the library and see what books are available on your topic. You do not have to read all these books from start to finish. Go through the tables of contents and check the index of each. You can gather further information to add to your brainstorming list. You probably need to keep track of all this new information on cards so that you will have the names of authors, publishers, and titles.

- Check magazines and journals. Your library will have a copy of the *Readers' Guide to Periodical Literature.* Ask the librarian. In it you will find a list of articles that have appeared in magazines and journals, among which will be some to provide you with more information on your topic. Again, keep track of the information on cards (with authors, titles, page numbers, dates, and names of the magazines).

- Talk to people. One good way to research a topic is to ask people who may know more then you do. Sometimes friends, acquaintances, and relatives have knowledge of a subject that they will share. Add all this to your personal data bank. You will need all the information you can get once you actually start writing.

Remember to keep track of your new information, either by noting it on cards or in a section of your notebook. Keep track, too, of the sources of that information: book titles, journal articles, authors' names, dates, and so on. You will need that information for your bibliography. (More suggestions for recording research data are found in the next chapter.)

EXERCISE 2

As you see, it is important to narrow down your topic. Large, vague, too-general topics lead to writing problems and unsuccessful papers.

To gain further practice in narrowing down a general topic, take each of the general topics given on the left and tell how you would bring them down to manageable focus.

EXAMPLE:

Witchcraft	becomes	Witchcraft in the 1980s
Punk rock	becomes	The death of punk rock

1. Exploration of space

2. Our right to free speech

3. The values of education

4. Computers and American life

5. The impact of television

6. Learning to write

7. Listening to lectures

8. Recent developments in biology

9. Japanese technology

10. Travel by jet

EXERCISE 3

Often a writer already knows a great deal about a topic without realizing it. Personal brainstorming sessions pay off. By jotting down in your notebook all the information you already have in memory, you can begin to see the scope of your general topic, start the process of narrowing it down, and collect data for your first draft.

Try brainstorming with yourself on any one of the following topics:

1. television
2. computers
3. writing
4. space exploration
5. free speech
6. public education
7. Japanese automobiles
8. Mexican food
9. the Jet Age
10. modern sculpture

EXERCISE 4

When you have one or two (or three) people brainstorming together, you can come up with long lists of data. If possible, try brainstorming one of the above topics with others. Keep track here of the information you accumulate together.

6. Select your theme.   By this point, you should have collected much information. Brainstorming and researching should have produced a vast number of notes. You can't just write this down on paper and consider the job done! You have to have something to say about all this data, a *message*, or as writers call it, a *theme*.

When you narrowed down your topic, you began the important process of developing a theme, but now you need to spell it out in a clear-cut sentence. For example, a student may have started to gather material on punk rock and narrowed the search down to "the demise of Punk Rock." At this stage, she needs to state her theme: "Punk rock is dying." Another student may have started with the theme witchcraft and narrowed it down to "witchcraft in America today." At this time, he needs to state in a sentence the theme that will guide him through the writing stage: "Witchcraft in America is alive and thriving."

Your theme becomes the main idea for your entire paper. It is reflected in the title you choose and is probably stated clearly in the opening paragraph of your paper. After your readers have read your paper, it is the main idea, message, or theme that they will remember, not all the details you used to support and develop it.

EXERCISE 5

Once you have narrowed down your topic to manageable size, you begin to see the theme or main idea of the paper. For example, witchcraft is a general topic; witchcraft in the 1980s is an idea you can handle in a short paper. The narrowed-down version may become your theme: "Witchcraft is still alive in the 1980s."

Notice that the theme is always stated as a sentence. It is the main-idea sentence for the entire paper.

To gain further practice in stating themes, take each of the general topics in column 1 and show how you narrowed it down in column 2. In column 3, write the theme, or main-idea sentence.

1. General topic	2. Narrowed-down version	3. Theme (main idea)
1. American cars		
2. College lectures		
3. Part-time jobs		
4. Fast food		
5. Airports		
6. Religion		
7. Drinking places		
8. Shoes and boots		
9. Pro football		
10. Anger		

7. Organize your material.   After assembling all your material and zeroing in on a specific message, you need to organize this data in some sensible way. You'll need some kind of outline.

Some professional writers prepare a formal outline (see Chapter 5, "Learning to Note and Use Main Ideas"). They actually divide their notes into Roman numerals for the main points of the paper, and then further divide these into capital letters for the subpoints. Some writers develop detailed formal outlines with Arabic numbers and lowercase letters (again, see Chapter 5). You don't necessarily have to do this in such detail, but you should make some kind of outline. Divide your notes so that you have your major points with pertinent examples and details under each.

One sensible way to do this is as follows:

- Note your general topic (witchcraft, for example)
- Write down your specific area within this topic (in other words, the result of your narrowing down; in this case, it may be witchcraft in the 1980s).
- Also note your theme or message ("Witchcraft is alive and thriving in the 1980s").
- Examine all your notes to discover the natural breakdowns for this theme. You may find headings such as these:

  I. What is witchcraft? (a definition)

  II. Where did it begin?

  III. Its history through the ages

  IV. Its place in the modern world

  V. Why it has survived.

- Reexamine your headings to make sure they fit the theme. (You can see that roman numerals IV and V are the most important in the above outline. Therefore, these two will be highlighted. I, II, and III, however, provide your readers with important background and need to be included.)

You may or may not end up with a formal outline, but you will need some kind of rough breakdown to provide you with a structure for the paper. The simple outline given above for "Witchcraft is alive and thriving in the 1980s" gives the writer some guidance as the paper is written. After the actual writing has begun, it may become apparent that changes are necessary (maybe a separate introductory paragraph or five separate paragraphs to give examples of "Its place in the modern world"). However, it is easier to make changes from a rough outline than to begin redoing large sections of a half-finished paper.

One excellent way to organize your paper is to *follow a format*. A format is simply a *plan* or *model* that you use to guide you as you write. It can be compared to a blueprint. It allows you to take the material you've collected and arrange it systematically in a way that will make sense to readers.

Here is an example of the five-paragraph essay format:

- *Paragraph 1.* Tell your readers exactly what your main idea or thesis is in a single clear-cut sentence. Explain why you are writing about this topic and how you intend to develop it. Try to begin with a sentence that will catch the attention of readers, a vivid example or detail, or an appealing anecdote or story.

- *Paragraph 2.* Give one piece of evidence to support your thesis. Make sure your language fits the situation, that it is appropriate for your readers. Check again to be sure this evidence really supports your thesis; if it does not, discard it and find better evidence.

- *Paragraph 3.* Give another piece of evidence to support your thesis. Put yourself in the reader' place; ask: Does this make sense? Does it convince me?

- *Paragraph 4.* Give a third piece of supporting evidence. Again, check to be sure it supports your thesis. Would you be won over to the point of view of the writer if you were a reader?

- *Paragraph 5.* Briefly restate your main point. Put yourself again in the readers' place: Do you follow the message so far? Do you agree with what is being said? Is the language sensible and appropriate? Is the final sentence a logical wrap-up? Does it add a sense of closing? What is still missing?

How might you use this simple plan in writing a short paper on witchcraft in the 1980s? In the first paragraph, you would present your thesis, "Witchcraft is alive and thriving in the 1980s." You might actually start with a story of a recent event (perhaps taken from a recent magazine or newspaper). You surely would need to define what you mean here by the term *witchcraft*. Point out that "Startling evidence exists to show that witchcraft did not die in the Middle Ages." (This shows readers that you are planning to offer more "evidence.")

In your second, third, and fourth paragraphs, give examples to prove your thesis. These come, of course, from your brainstorming and research. They must relate to witchcraft in modern times and demonstrate that it is "alive."

Your final paragraph restates your main idea, although perhaps in slightly different words (you don't want to bore your readers). You might end with another brief story that in addition to further supporting your thesis, provides an interesting ending.

At this organizational stage of writing, you need to be thinking of the functions of your different paragraphs. Each paragraph does a different job in the paper. (In the five-paragraph essay format described above, the second, third, and fourth paragraphs were *explanatory*; they gave examples to support the thesis.) When you outline and select a workable format, you also need to be thinking ahead and making decisions about what each of your paragraphs is supposed to do in the total paper.

What are *paragraph functions*? What purposes do individual paragraphs serve in the total paper?

- *Introductory paragraphs.* Writers usually indicate their topic and point of view in a well-defined introductory paragraph. Sometimes they spell out their purposes and set limits on the discussion to follow. In reports and scientific papers, authors will not only say, "The purpose of this paper is _____" but define its scope as well: "It will do the following but not attempt _____." Good writers often provide readers with background so they can relate the new information to what is known. A reader should be able to answer questions such as these: What is this paper about? What plan is the writer going to follow? What is the writer's point of view?

- *Explanatory paragraphs.* These inform, tell about, explain, or provide evidence to support the writer's thesis or main idea. They are usually organized by the generalization pattern, with a main-idea sentence, and are usually marked by words and phrases that signal their purpose, such as *for example, for instance, to illustrate,* and so on.

- *Narrative paragraphs.* Although narrative paragraphs are usually found in stories, writers sometimes use them in expository prose — to relate historical events in sequence, capture reader interest, or provide supporting evidence in story form as anecdotes. Narrative paragraphs use signal words such as *first, next, then, finally,* and so on. Readers may ask: Why is the writer using this story here? What is the point? Does it help or hinder?

- *Descriptive paragraphs.* Sometimes writers have to stop and describe something. They need to give additional information so their readers can make better sense of the paper. Sometimes you may need to describe a person, an event, or an object; sometimes descriptions are inappropriate. Be aware of how your descriptive paragraph relates to the total paper.

- *Definitional paragraphs.* In many papers, writers must define terms. They sometimes do this by referring to a dictionary definition, by showing how the term is alike and different from terms familiar to readers, or simply by saying "By _____, I mean this _____." As you outline your paper, think about the problems your readers may have if they do not understand some of your terms. Do you need a definitional paragraph? Do you need two or more?

- ***Transitional paragraphs.*** Often writers need to let readers know that they are moving into a new area — into, for example, a subdivision of the paper or into an explanation. Rather than shift abruptly, they may use a separate short paragraph. When writing the witchcraft paper, a student may want to tell about her personal experience with witchcraft; she could lead into it by saying:

    Well-documented examples of witchcraft in recent time have been reported from contemporary newspapers. One startling example occurred in our own community recently.

- ***Concluding paragraphs.*** A successful paper gives the readers a sense of closure, a feeling that the end has been reached. Usually writers signal readers by terms such as *finally, in conclusion,* or *in summary,* but not always. They can also achieve a sense of closure by pulling together the main subpoints and reviewing the ways these supported the thesis.

As you organize your notes from brainstorming and researching, you will need to outline and look for a format, or plan. As you tidy up your outline and format, think of the ways each individual paragraph will contribute to your overall plan. The more time and effort you put into this organizational stage, the easier the actual writing will be for you later.

EXERCISE 6

One way you can become better at organizing your material is to study the way professional writers organize theirs. Take an article in a magazine and read it carefully, looking for the author's plan of organization. What are the article's main points? Its supporting points? Can you detect a format? Introductory paragraphs? Explanatory paragraphs? Definitional paragraphs?

In the space below, make an outline of the article from your point of view as a reader. If the article is successfully organized, you can assume that its author followed a similar outline when writing.

8. Identify your readers. Now you have collected material and organized it into a rough outline. Before you actually start writing, you need to think of readers. Who exactly is going to read the paper? Professional writers tell us that this is one of the key questions writers ask themselves as they write. Once you know who will read your paragraphs, sentences, and words, you begin to shape them to fit the readers. For example, if you are writing for children, you do not use overly difficult words or long, involved sentences. On the other hand, if you are writing for college-educated readers, you do not use short sentences or simplified vocabulary. Good writers try to think of the people who are to read their work as they write it.

In your case, you are probably writing for a college instructor or professor. The general rule still holds: Write for your readers. When developing a college paper for a course, aim your language (your words and sentences) at the person who will read it. Your reader or readers will tend to be looking for straight forward, sensible language organized in a logical manner. Write accordingly.

Writing

The actual writing of your paper is a five-step process. You need to:

1. Write the first draft.
2. Revise it.
3. Get a second opinion.
4. Write it again.
5. Revise it again.

Once you have organized your material in a sensible plan, you can begin the *first draft*. Be concerned at this stage with getting your ideas down on paper. What you write this first time around is rarely what you will eventually submit as a finished product. Remember about writer's block: Some students cannot get started because they expect their first run-through to be perfect; when you know that this first attempt is just that — a first attempt — you will be less apt to block up.

After you have written the first draft, read it carefully, trying to put yourself in the place of your reader. Ask yourself: Am I getting my message across? What seems right? Wrong? Which terms and vocabulary words need explaining? Is the organizational plan reasonable? Note all changes in pencil. Don't hesitate to cross out words, sentences, or whole paragraphs if they don't do the job.

Now, *revise*. Take your corrected first draft and rewrite it carefully so that all problems are eliminated. This second version ought to be much better than the first. However, as the author of the paper you are too close to it to judge it fairly. You need a second opinion. The writer of a paper is rarely its best reader: You may fail to see problems in sentence structure, word choice, or in the overall plan. You already know what you want to say and assume that you've said it. Your paper can profit at this point from a careful reading by another person.

The third step in the actual writing, therefore, is to *show your work to someone else*. This reader may be another student, a friend, or a relative. The person you choose should be someone more or less like yourself and your potential readers. In other words, you would not ask a child or a person unfamiliar with your topic and your ideas. Get this person's opinion. Ask: Do you understand the paper? What parts are puzzling? What needs to be changed? Ask the reader for a short summary: "Tell me in a few words what the paper means to you." The reader's summary should be comparable to one you might make.

What if you cannot find another reader? Then you play the role. Pretend that you are a stranger, unfamiliar with the material. Ask yourself similar questions: What is the main idea? Do the pieces fit together? What needs to be changed?

On the basis of this "outsider's" point of view, you write again. Make all recommended changes. Incorporate into this second version all the suggestions you have derived from the second opinion. Sometimes the changes will be minor; sometimes they may necessitate a completely new writing. Don't, however, hesitate.

Once you have rewritten the paper, you need to subject it to the same revision process. Go through it carefully, checking for sensible organization, good choice of words, comprehensible sentences, and so on. Even though you are sure at this stage that the paper looks satisfactory, you may locate problems to be rectified.

Many writers suggest that some time should elapse between revisions. If time allows, let a day or more pass before you begin to look again at the paper. You tend to reexamine your own work more objectively and from a different perspective after a short interval.

Editing

After completing these five steps, you have another important responsibility. Before you hand in the paper to your instructor, you must *edit*. This means that you must check again to be sure that the paper fulfills your original purpose and that all problems in spelling, grammar, and punctuation have been eliminated. You need to put yourself in the place of a professional editor who carefully examines and reexamines each line prior to publication.

Here are some basic guide questions for editing:

1. What was my purpose in writing this paper?

2. In what ways have I succeeded? Failed?

3. Are my sentences complete? To test for complete sentences, read each aloud. Does it sound right? Does it have a subject and a predicate? Does it begin with a capital letter? Does it end with a period, exclamation point, or question mark?

4. Are my paragraphs complete? To test them, check to see if the sentences all relate. Is there a main-idea sentence in each paragraph? Do the other sentences relate to it? Are paragraphs indented? Does each separate paragraph serve a purpose in relation to your overall plan?

5. Can I explain every punctuation mark? Each mark is used for a reason. If you can't explain why you used a comma, semicolon, or colon, maybe you shouldn't use it.

6. Is each word spelled correctly? Spelling counts. Readers don't really trust a message when it contains misspelled words; they assume the writer is not an informed person. If you have any doubt about the spelling of a word, check it in the dictionary or with another student.

7. Will readers be able to read my writing? There's no point in going through all this trouble if readers cannot decipher your writing. When a page looks really difficult to read, don't hesitate: Do it over again neatly and legibly.

8. Is the final paper good looking? Neatness counts, too. Readers assume that you don't care when you give them a messy, unattractive piece of writing. Check your margins, spacing, titles, and other features. Your final product should appeal to readers' eyes.

When your paper passes such an inspection as this, you may need to check for other matters. Some of these include the following:

9. Have I followed an appropriate plan of organization? Do I have a clear-cut plan that readers can follow with a minimum of effort? Are my introductory paragraphs really introductory? Do I follow a basic organizational plan, such as cause and effect or comparison and contrast? Do I have a concluding paragraph?

10. Do I use appropriate transitional devices? Do I signal readers to my plan by using the right devices? *First, second, next,* and so on for sequence? *Because* for cause and effect? *On one hand, on the other hand* for comparison and contrast? Such transitional signals help readers detect your plan and follow more easily.

11. What about levels of English? Is the language too formal? Too slangy? Too colloquial? Inappropriate in any other way?

12. Have I used technical language, jargon, foreign words, or some private "in-group" language that may cause readers problems in understanding? Such language choices should be changed because all readers do not necessarily know special words that you know.

13. Do I have grammar problems? The ones to watch out for are these: (a) incomplete sentences, (b) run-ons, (c) misplaced modifiers, (d) lack of agreement between subjects and predicates, (e) pronouns without antecedents, and (f) ellipses, or places where you left out parts of the sentence. Read each sentence aloud to double-check its grammatical sense.

14. Is there anything in this paper that seems to strike a wrong note? The most routine paper reflects the writer's thinking and personality. Is there a sentence, phrase, or word in this paper that may cause readers to question my good sense or reasoning powers?

Exercise 7

As you edit your papers, be wary of spelling errors. Many otherwise acceptable papers receive lower grades because their writers failed to make that one final check for misspelled words.

Students sometimes ask, "If you don't know how to spell a word, how can you spot it as incorrectly spelled when you edit?" There are at least five answers to that question:

1. When you do know the beginning letters, you can check a dictionary. You may not be sure, for example, whether *receive* has *e* before *i* or *i* before *e*. But you do know that it begins with *re*, so go down the dictionary page column until you find the word.

2. You can ask someone. Don't hesitate to ask a friend — or stranger!

3. Have someone check your final draft for spelling as well as sense. Even professional writers know that they frequently misspell common words. Do what they do; have another person read your paper and mark misspellings so that you can correct them before you type your final copy.

4. Use a substitute word. On those occasions when you cannot use the dictionary and another person is unavailable, think of a good synonym. It is wiser to rewrite a phrase or sentence than to knowingly submit misspelled words.

5. Be aware of the most commonly misspelled words. Keep a list handy of words often spelled incorrectly by writers. Become familiar with these words by reading through the list occasionally.

Such a list follows.

One Hundred Words Most Commonly Misspelled on Student Papers

1. accommodate	16. convenience
2. accumulate	17. coolly
3. achievement	18. criticism
4. all right	19. curiosity
5. argument	20. decision
6. athlete	21. definite
7. benefited	22. desirable
8. bulletin	23. desperate
9. business	24. disastrous
10. cemetery	25. disease
11. committee	26. division
12. comparative	27. eighth
13. conceive	28. efficiency
14. conquer	29. eliminated
15. conscientious	30. embarrassed

31. especially	66. occurrence
32. existence	67. omission
33. existent	68. omitted
34. experience	69. opinion
35. familiar	70. optimistic
36. fascinating	71. opportunity
37. forty	72. original
38. friend	73. outrageous
39. grievance	74. parallel
40. height	75. particularly
41. immediately	76. permissible
42. incidentally	77. persuade
43. indispensable	78. phenomenon
44. intelligence	79. physically
45. interfere	80. possess
46. interpreted	81. preceding
47. interrupted	82. preference
48. irresistible	83. preferred
49. laboratory	84. prejudice
50. laid	85. privilege
51. leisure	86. probably
52. lightning	87. procedure
53. loneliness	88. proceeded
54. maintenance	89. prominent
55. mathematics	90. quiet
56. minute	91. quite
57. mischievous	92. quizzes
58. mysterious	93. received
59. necessary	94. recommend
60. niece	95. rhythm
61. ninety	96. ridiculous
62. ninth	97. sacrifice
63. noisily	98. separate
64. occasionally	99. similar
65. occurred	100. tragedy

EXERCISE 8

What if your particular spelling demons are not on the list of commonly misspelled words? Then start your personal list today. In the back of your notebook, begin keeping track of words that you have trouble spelling.

When you add a word to your list, try to learn it as soon as possible. A good way to do this is to follow this four-step plan of attack:

1. Look carefully at the word that causes you trouble.

2. Copy the word exactly, noting the visual features and the way letters relate to one another.

3. Cover the word (with hand or card), try to see it in the mind's eye, and write it from memory.

4. Uncover the original and check your reproduction. Make corrections if necessary and repeat until you have mastered the correct spelling.

EXERCISE 9

How well do you follow the step-by-step procedure for successful writing? Here is a Checklist for Writing to use on your next written assignment.

CHECKLIST FOR WRITING

Name of course: _____

Date: _____

Specific directions for the assignment:

Prewriting Stage	Date	Steps Taken
1. Getting yourself organized		
2. Getting into the right frame of mind		
3. Narrowing topic		
4. Brainstorming		
5. Researching		

	Date	Steps Taken

6. Defining thesis

7. Identifying readers

8. Organizing material

Writing Stage

1. Writing first draft

2. Revising

3. Getting another opinion

4. Rewriting

5. Revising

	Date	Steps Taken

Editing Stage

1. Checking for purpose

2. Checking for organization

3. Checking for thinking

4. Checking spelling

5. Checking punctuation

6. Checking sentences

7. Checking grammar

8. Reading from point of view of another person

9. Preparing final copy

10. Evaluating for appearance

POINTS TO REMEMBER ABOUT WRITING
COURSE PAPERS

1. Writing provides opportunities to learn more about a subject.

2. What you do before you write is extremely important.

3. Define your topic carefully.

4. Gather material by brainstorming and research.

5. Identify your readers.

6. Organize your material carefully.

7. Write a first draft.

8. Rewrite when necessary.

9. Edit for spelling, punctuation, and grammar.

10. Reread for logic and clear thinking.

11

MASTERY TEST

To check how well you understood this chapter on writing papers for college courses, complete the following true-false test. (Before you begin the test, you may want to go back to Chapter 10 and reread the suggestions for taking true-false tests.)

1. The chief purpose for writing course papers is to gain additional practice in writing skills.   **T   F**

2. Writing is simply putting ideas from your mind on paper.   **T   F**

3. The writing process includes several steps or stages.   **T   F**

4. One way to overcome writers' block is to get enough rest.   **T   F**

5. All writing assignments should be completed in a single sitting so that the completed paper will have unity.   **T   F**

6. A thesis in a paper is like its main idea.   **T   F**

7. Brainstorming a topic is more like researching a topic than it is like narrowing down a topic.   **T   F**

8. Outlining is a good way to organize your material before writing.   **T   F**

9. Editing is more like proofreading than it is like revising.   **T   F**

10. The prewriting stage is more important than either the actual writing or the editing.   **T   F**

Writing the Research Paper

INTRODUCTION AND OVERVIEW

Many college courses require a research paper. What you learned in Chapter 11 about writing applies to writing research papers. For example, you need to spend more time in preparation than in writing: gathering information, defining the theme, organizing material, and so on. You need also to write a first draft, revise, and edit. However, the college research paper is different in a number of ways from regular course papers: It is longer, requires documentation, and, as its name implies, is based on research.

This chapter examines characteristics of the research paper and suggests techniques to help you write better ones. It includes a detailed review of library research methods and concludes with a guide to follow as you research and write.

SUGGESTED GUIDE QUESTIONS

---

1. What is a good research paper?

2. How do you find a topic?

3. What steps can you take to make sure you have collected all pertinent data?

4. Why is it important to organize your material systematically?

5. What are the key steps in writing? In revising? In editing?

WHAT IS RESEARCH?

Research consists of finding answers to questions. You start a research project with a question or a group of related questions and search the available sources of information to discover answers. Your questions may be *specific* ("Who actually invented the automobile?" or "Does vitamin C prevent the common cold?") or *general* ("What are the causes of an economic depression?" or "How has *truth* been defined through the ages?"). As you search for information you may discover that your question has been answered by others but you were not aware of the answer. You may find that your question has never been answered and seems unanswerable. You will certainly discover more information than you knew before you started your search.

In many areas (physics, biology, sociology, psychology), researchers actually do experiments to discover answers to their questions. For example, a chemist may test a certain substance to discover its effect upon another substance, or a sociologist may conduct a poll to learn how many Americans actually accept a certain point of view. In these cases, library-type research is conducted by the investigators before they do their studies in order to learn what previous researchers have reported on their topic. When you read studies in science and the social sciences you usually find a section at the beginning called "Review of Research," where previous research in an area is summarized.

Your research papers in college will tend to be library research. Rather than conduct actual experiments, you will be expected to critically examine data collected by others and stored in the library and then report on your findings. In some courses, you may be encouraged to conduct an experiment and report on your findings, but even in such reports it is expected that you will review other pertinent studies in the library. In all research, however, you will be *seeking answers to questions*. If you remember this, your work in the library or elsewhere will make more sense to you.

WHAT IS A RESEARCH PAPER?

The research paper is *a report on your findings*. Usually it is composed of certain well-defined parts:

- An introduction, in which you tell exactly what question you are seeking to answer, as well as your reasons, or justification, for singling out this question.

- A review of all the sources you examined to find answers, in which you carefully document the names of authors and provide accurate bibliographical information so that readers may check out your sources.

- Your conclusions, where you explain to readers how you interpreted the findings of previous studies.

Your completed research paper will tend to be longer than an ordinary college course paper because of your need to report fully on all the sources you examined. The need to provide readers with bibliographical data such as the names of authors, titles, publishers, and dates of publication also adds to the length of the completed paper.

The values of writing a research paper are many. In the process of conducting your library search, you will add to your store of knowledge. You will gain information and ideas not included in the basic course textbook. You will also discover points of view different from those of your college instructor and the author of the textbook. Another great value of writing a research paper is that *you are on your own*. You create the questions. You seek out the answers. You make sense of the answers you find. You come to your own conclusions. As countless students will testify, writing a good research paper can be a high point in your college career. Long after you have forgotten the lectures and reading assignments, you will remember your search and the answers you found.

Research paper writing is also one of the most practical experiences you have in college. In business, science, the various professions and many jobs you may have later in life, you will use the techniques learned in research paper writing. You will have to pose questions, locate answers, come to conclusions, and report results to others. Training in such skills can help you in many areas in our complex society.

Before we examine steps in the development of your paper, here are four suggestions:

Start thinking about your topic early.   Once you know that a research paper is required in a course, start a page in your notebook headed "Ideas for Research Paper." Jot down areas of interest and particular topics that you might like to explore further; especially, write down questions that come to mind about the course topics. These can be extremely helpful when you begin the project.

Begin collecting material.   As you identify points of interest, watch for sources of information about them. When you browse in the library, copy down titles of books and articles that relate to your possible topic. In your newspaper and magazine reading, watch for possible sources. Keep track of all these possibilities in your notebook. You can save time later if you begin the project with some good leads.

Start as soon as possible.   Once you have identified a topic, start working. It takes a great deal of time to do a successful research paper. By starting early, you gain an advantage over other students: More books will be on library shelves, research periodicals will be available, and so on. Students who wait until the end of the semester to begin often find themselves competing with other students for scarce resources.

Plan on interlibrary loans.   If you start early, you can take advantage of interlibrary loan systems. Some of the books you need may not be in your college library, but you can borrow them from other college libraries.

WHAT DO YOU WRITE ABOUT?

Sometimes your instructor will assign you a topic in which case the question of selection will not arise. Most often, however, you will be told to develop a course research paper, and the task of selecting a topic and narrowing it down will be yours.

You, need, first, to choose an *area* of the course that interests you. Then you need to select a *topic* from within that area. Once it has been selected, you need to narrow it down to manageable size. Here it is recommended that you work from a *question* so that your research and writing activities will be guided by your search for an answer. This sequence may be shown as follows:

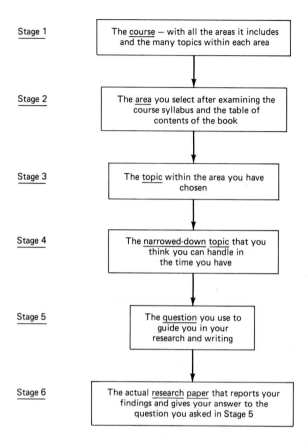

Stage 1 — The <u>course</u> — with all the areas it includes and the many topics within each area

Stage 2 — The <u>area</u> you select after examining the course syllabus and the table of contents of the book

Stage 3 — The <u>topic</u> within the area you have chosen

Stage 4 — The <u>narrowed-down topic</u> that you think you can handle in the time you have

Stage 5 — The <u>question</u> you use to guide you in your research and writing

Stage 6 — The actual <u>research paper</u> that reports your findings and gives your answer to the question you asked in Stage 5

How does this process work in a particular course?

You are required to do a research paper in general psychology. First you open your textbook to the table of contents and find the following twelve chapter titles:

1 Psychology: Understanding Human Behavior

2 The Biological Foundations of Human Behavior

3 Perception: How We See the World

4 Learning: How We Learn about the World

5 Memory: How We Remember

6 Language: How We Communicate to Others and Ourselves

7 Motivation: Why We Behave the Way We Do

8 Human Information Processing: An Engineering Approach to Behavior

9 Human Development: From Child to Adult

You check this table of contents with the course syllabus your instructor distributed the first week of the course and find that it lists the same twelve headings but includes assignments and dates. These twelve headings are your *areas*. Your instructor has not discussed them all yet, but you decide now that information processing is the one that interests you most.

Now you move into Stage 3 of the chart: selecting a topic within your area. You go back to the table of contents and find this detailed breakdown of the chapter:

Chapter 8   Human Information Processing: An Engineering Approach to Human Behavior

1. Tools for studying information processing
   Flowcharts
   Feedback
   Information
   Hierarchical structures
   Comparing information

2. Attention and reaction time
   Reaction time
   Attention

3. Computer simulation of human behavior
   Problem solving
   Decision making

At this stage, you decide to look ahead at the chapter and note the subheadings given in the book. You also decide to read some sections of the chapter to be sure that this is an area that really interests you. You may decide at this time that the material is not quite as interesting to you as you first believed, in which case you may choose another area.

The next step is to choose a *topic* from this breakdown of headings within the chapter. "Tools for studying information processing" looks interesting, but you decide to read it rather than research it. You choose

"Computer simulation of human behavior" because you have already read some magazine articles on the subject and find it especially interesting. This is now your topic.

How do you narrow it down? You can use the table of contents to guide you and zero in on "Problem solving," or you can think about articles you have read and try some personal brainstorming. (See Chapter 11 of this book.) Once you have narrowed down the topic (Computer simulation) to "Problem solving," you need to think about a question to guide your research. An obvious one occurs to you at once: "Can computers solve problems?" As you work, you may discover that this is too broad and change it to "What kinds of problems can computers solve?" or "Can computers solve problems faster than people can?" At this point, you have a working question to guide you — even though you may change it later. The important point is that you are now ready to begin.

HOW DO YOU BEGIN A RESEARCH PAPER?

The steps in beginning to write a research paper are much like those you go through in writing any college paper. (Again, see Chapter 11.) They are:

Get yourself organized, physically and psychologically.

Zero in on a well-defined topic.

Gather material by brainstorming and researching.

Define your thesis or main idea.

Identify your readers.

Organize your material for writing.

Because research papers are not quite the same as other course papers, a special set of suggestions is presented here:

1. State your topic and guide question. In those pages of your notebook reserved for this project, note down exactly your narrowed-down topic ("Computer problem solving") and your question ("Can computers solve problems?"). After you start to work, you may shift or change these, but write them down now to give yourself a firm beginning place.

2. Brainstorm. On another page, do some personal brainstorming. Write down everything you already know about the topic and question. This activates knowledge you already possess and sets your mind for further exploration. If you have an opportunity, try to brainstorm with another person, because others can often suggest ideas for your notebook that you might not think of at this stage. The longer your brainstorming list, the better your tentative outline.

3. Prepare a tentative outline. At this stage, you cannot develop a working outline because you do not yet have enough information. You *can* prepare a tentative, or temporary, one. As you brainstorm "Computer problem solving," for example, you find many ideas that fall into a sequence and others that appear to be related. Your tentative outline for that topic might look like this:

I.   What is "computer problem solving"?
   A.   What is a computer?
   B.   What is problem solving?
   C.   Definitions to be used in paper
II. History of early efforts to solve problems by computer
   A.   With vacuum computers
      1. successes
      2. failures
   B.   With transistor-type computers
      1. successes
      2. failures
III. Problems encountered by researchers
   A.
   B.
   C.
IV. Recent developments
V.   The future of computer problem solving

Your rough outline will contain blanks because you are still unfamiliar with the material. Working on the basis of your brainstorming alone, you cannot yet prepare a true working outline.

4. Collect your data. This is the primary activity in the project. You now need to supplement the material listed on your brainstorming pages with actual research information, most of which you need to obtain from books and journals.

HOW DO YOU COLLECT MATERIAL?

First, you need to find good sources of information. The college library is probably your best single repository. You need, therefore, to know: (1)

how the library is organized, (2) how the card catalog works, (3) the call number system, (4) the location of periodicals and special reference books, (5) how to use the photocopy machine, and (6) how to take out books you need. Here are some basic steps to get you started:

1. Become familiar with the physical layout of your library. Spend some time walking around the rooms noting where various services are located. If your library has a guide or map for distribution, obtain one. You need to know the exact locations of:

The card catalog (in order to locate the specific books you need)

The reference desk (in case you have questions)

All reference books (encyclopedias, dictionaries, etc.)

The periodicals and the guides to periodical literature (to find magazine and journal articles)

The photocopy machine (to copy pages from books and journals)

The checkout desk (so that you can take material out for special examination)

2. Know how the card catalog works. Every book in the library is noted on three separate cards, all filed alphabetically. One card is filed under the book's title, another under the author's last name, and the third under the subject of the book. Because you probably do not know the names of authors of books on your topic, the best starting place for your search may be under the subject. For example, if you began to look for books about computer problem solving, you would start with "Computers" and "Problem solving." On these cards you will also find *tracings*, cross-references from your subject to related ones. "Computers" may refer you to "Artificial intelligence" or "Information processing." You can use these tracings to locate other books dealing with your topic.

Each card (title, author, or subject) will also give you other important information: the complete title, full author's name, subtitles, publisher, city where published, and date of publication. It also gives you the *call number*.

3. Know the call number system. The call number on the card tells how to locate the book on the shelves. Sometimes you can go directly to the shelf and find the book you need. Sometiems you must give the number to a member of the library staff, who will locate the book for you.

Two systems of call numbers are used in libraries; you need to find out which is used in your college library. It is not necessary to memorize either system, but you should be familiar with both. Here is how they operate.

The Dewey Decimal System arranges all books in the library according to the following plan:

000 General works — books about books, magazines, newspapers, and lists of books

100 Philosophy and psychology — human behavior but not psychiatry

200 Religion — history of religion and mythology

300 Social sciences — economics, sociology, occupations

400 Language — linguistics, grammar, dictionaries

500 Pure sciences — botany, physics, chemistry

600 Useful arts and applied sciences — engineering, medicine (including psychiatry), farming

700 Arts and recreation — music, sports

800 Literature — plays, poetry, speeches

900 History — geography, travel books, biography

Each of these categories is further subdivided according to the system. The 600s, for example, are divided as follows:

610 Medicine
620 Engineering
630 Agriculture
640 Home economics
650 Business

660 Chemical technology
670 Manufacturing
680 Mechanical trades
690 Building construction

The Library of Congress System has the advantage of a broader base because it uses the twenty-six letters of the alphabet; this system is more flexible and capable of greater expansion. Here it is:

A   General works

B   Religion and philosophy

C   History and related sciences (such as coin collecting and genealogy)

D   Universal and old world history

E–F American history

G   Geography and anthropology

H   Social sciences (such as economics or sociology)

J   Political science

K   Law

L   Education

M   Music

N   Fine arts

P   Language and literature

Q   Science (including mathematics)

S   Agriculture (including hunting and fishing)

T   Technology (including engineering and manufacturing)

U   Military science

V   Naval science

X   Bibliography and library science

Remember, you do not have to memorize these systems. The library staff usually posts notices so you can locate particular kinds of books in open-shelf libraries; in the others, the books will be obtained for you.

4. Know where periodicals are located and how to find specific articles.   For information and ideas more recent than can be found in published books, you need to know how to locate material in current journals and magazines. You do not need to go through hundreds of back or new issues to find what you want. You can refer to one of several guides such as the *Readers' Guide to Periodical Literature.* In it you look up your topic (or author or specific article title) and quickly locate information. Under the heading "Computers" you may discover hundreds of recent articles with authors' names, names of magazines or journals, the dates of publication, and even the page numbers. Two other excellent guides are *Access* and the *Popular Periodic Index.* If you cannot locate the issues of the journal you need, a member of the library staff can steer you in the right direction.

5. Know the reference books.   While most students are familiar with the dictionary and the encyclopedia, many do not realize that there are many dictionaries and many encyclopedias, and that some are better suited to certain purposes than others. There are dictionaries of literature, science, technology, philosophy, and so on. There are also specialized encyclopedias in these and other fields, as well as a wide variety of biographical sources (such as *Who's Who in Finance* or *Who's Who of American Women*). In the reference section of the library you will also find such useful books as *The World Almanac,* atlases, dictionaries of foreign terms, and statistical handbooks. One good way to start your search on a subject is to go to the main entry in a major encyclopedia. Here you will find general explanations and definitions of terms, as well as suggestions for further reading.

After you have written a tentative outline and become familiar with the library, you are ready to begin looking for specific sources. There are two more important suggestions you should follow.

6. Work from the general to the specific.   Start with general reference books (such as an encyclopedia or specialized encyclopedia) to get an overview of the subject. You will also acquire background in the area because these entries tell you what most scholars and researchers currently agree is basic knowledge in the field.

Next, proceed to the card catalog and check books on your topic. Take a few of the most promising home to read more carefully. You can gain much good background from a rapid reading of some books; other books demand more careful examination. After this, go to the periodical index to find recent articles. These will provide you with up-to-date information and more modern points of view.

7. Record your findings.   In other words, keep notes. It is not enough to read the material; you must keep a detailed record of your discoveries.

The best way to do this is to use cards, either 5-by-8- or 4-by-6-inch size. On them write (1) the name of the author or authors, (2) the exact titles of the books or articles, (3) the information you need. For books you must also write the names of the publishers along with the cities in which they are located and the dates of publication. For periodicals you need the exact names of the magazines or journals, the dates of publication, the volume and number information, as well as page numbers.

Use a separate card for each reference. If you copy a great deal from one source, you may have to use two or more cards, which you should staple together. Write on only one side of each card.

A sample card is shown below:

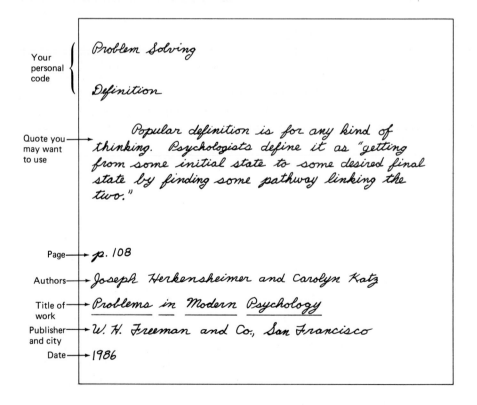

Here are some tips for making good notes on your cards:

- **Get all necessary information.** The book or periodical may not be on the shelf when you come back later. You can save time and effort by recording *all* the important information when you find it.

- **Use a personal code.** Your tentative outline tells you roughly what you need. Use a line or phrase from that outline in the upper left-hand corner of the card so you can arrange your findings later.

- **Use your own words for the idea.** In Chapters 6 and 7 of this book you learned that one way to understand new material is to say it in abbreviated form in your own words (paraphrase and summarize). When you copy new material for your paper, copy the ideas in your own words and you will understand and remember them better.

- **Use quotation marks for exact quotes.** In your paper you will often need to support a point by giving readers the exact words an author used. The way to distinguish between the author's words and yours is to place quotation marks around the author's words. (See sample card, above.)

8. **Don't neglect material on microform.**   Much of the material you need may be found in books and periodicals. However, many libraries now save space by photographing material in reduced size. You will need to read it on special machines that enlarge the photographs for you on a larger screen. You may need assistance when you first try one of the machines, but with practice, you can learn to use them with a minimum of effort.
How do you know what is on microform?

- Beside the call numbers for books (in the card catalog), you will see the abbreviations *mc*, *mf*, *mfc*, or *mic*. These indicate that your library has the book on microform. (Many old or rare books are now stored this way.)

- One of these same abbreviations will appear beside the name of the periodical in the Linedex or the Holding List. (Many popular magazines, such as *Time*, are now filed this way.)

- Newspapers on microform may be located through *Newsbank*. This reference will help you locate articles in newspapers, but it only goes back to 1970. By using the *Newsbank* index, you can locate articles on your topic that may have appeared in many newspapers throughout the country since that time.

- The *New York Times Index* goes back to 1851, but it refers you only to articles published in that newspaper. You need to look up your topic by date (at the time it was news), because articles are arranged by topic in chronological order. *The New York Times Index* may be especially valuable to you because it provides summaries of articles as well as the microfilmed articles themselves.

- Indexes for local and other national newspapers are often available in the college library. When searching for information about a regional or community issue, you can check a local newspaper. You can also locate business and world news articles in the indexes for the *Wall Street Journal* or the *Christian Science Monitor*. Some libraries may also have an index to the London *Times*; this index goes back to 1785.

EXERCISE 1

To show that you can use the card catalog in your library, tell under what subject heading you would look to find books containing information on the following subjects.

1. Growing tomatoes
2. Yo-yos
3. Repairing refrigerators
4. Selling real estate
5. Scrimshaw
6. Life after death
7. ESP
8. Famous magicians
9. Cold remedies
10. Notary public

EXERCISE 2

To show that you can use the microform resources in your library, locate the front page of a local or national newspaper of the day you were born. Note some of the major news stories that day.

EXERCISE 3

To show that you have learned how to obtain information in your library, answer each of the following questions. Indicate the source of your answer.

1. Who invented the zipper?

2. Why are some words spelled differently although they sound the same?

3. What was the name of the plane that dropped the bomb on Hiroshima?

4. What is an acoustic guitar?

5. When was the piano invented?

6. How does television work?

7. What was the weather in Washington, D.C., the day John F. Kennedy was inaugurated?

8. Where was basketball first played?

9. What is a "blurb"?

10. When and where was Fidel Castro born?

EXERCISE 4

Just as mathematicians and scientists use their own symbol systems, so do scholars and researchers. Here are some common abbreviations used in books and articles. Read the list to become better acquainted with them, and as you work in the library, watch for examples of each. (You might put a check mark beside an abbreviation when you come across it in your research to learn which seem to be used most frequently.)

ab. — abridge

anon. — anonymous

bul., bull. — bulletin

© — copyright

ca. — *circa* (Latin for about)

cr. — confer or compare

ed. — editor

e. g. — *exempli gratia*, for example

et al. — *et alii*, and others

et seq. — *et sequentes*, and the following

f. and ff. — pages following

ibid. — ibidem, in the same place

i. e. — *id est*, that is

infra — below

loc. cit. — *loco citato*, in the place cited

ms — manuscript

n. b. — *nota bene*, take careful note

n. p. — no place

op. cit. — *opere citato*, in the work cited

p. and pp. — page(s)

pass. — *passim*, here and there

pseud. — pseudonym

q. v. — *quod vide*, which see

rev. — revised

seq. — *sequentes*, the following page

tr. — translator

v. or vid. — *vide*, see

viz. — *videlicet*, that it to say, namely

v., vol. — volume

WRITING THE RESEARCH PAPER

Once you have narrowed down your topic (usually to answer a specific question) and collected material, you still have two matters to consider before you write: You need to identify your readers and organize your material. The first task is easy in this case; your readers will be your fellow students and the course instructor. You are writing for educated adults. This means that you cannot use slang or colloquial expressions; that you will adopt in your writing a serious, professional tone; and that you will follow the accepted research paper style.

How can you best organize your material? One approach is to group all your cards according to the personal codes in the upper left corner. You can spread these out on a large table and see patterns emerge. You begin to see that you have adequate information about one point but not enough on another. You will see certain sequences and subgroupings. With your tentative outline before you, you can begin to make a preliminary organization of the material.

At this stage you may begin to develop your working outline, which will include all the main headings and subheadings for the paper. If your tentative outline guided you through the data collection stage, its basic structure may resemble that of the working outline. As you work, you may discover serious omissions in your data that necessitate return trips to the library. You may find that you have too much material on some points, more than you can possibly use.

Once your material is organized and you have a working outline, you can begin to write. The suggestions given in Chapter 11 for writing course papers apply here:

1. Write a first draft.

2. Revise it after a careful reading.

3. Get an outside opinion by showing it to another person.

4. Rewrite or make necessary changes.

5. Revise again if still not satisfied.

6. Edit carefully for

    purpose, organization, and quality of thinking.
    correct spelling, punctuation, sentence structure, grammar.

7. Evaluate the entire paper from the point of view of your readers.

8. Make any final changes.

9. Prepare your top copy for submission.

Remember, your thesis statement (the main idea of the entire paper) is the answer to your research question. It should be reflected somehow in your title and be made clear to readers. If you started your quest with the intention of answering the question "What kinds of problems can computers solve," the answer you discovered is the focus around which the whole paper revolves.

As you write, you must also concern yourself with two other important matters: *plagiarism* and *documentation*. Both are major concerns for student writers.

Plagiarism

Plagiarism is the theft of material from another writer. You can never use material from a source without proper acknowledgment. If you reproduce sentences, phrases, or paragraphs from a book or article without crediting the author, you are open to the serious legal charge of plagiarism. If your work is published, you could be sued. If plagiarism is discovered by your instructor, you could fail the course and sometimes be dismissed from college.

You may quote someone else by using quotation marks around the sentence and providing a reference. You may even use an entire paragraph from another source, but you must indent it and give proper credit.

For example, you may quote a sentence or two as follows:

> For his study of children's thinking, Russell accepted this definition of thinking: "a determined course of ideas, symbolic in character, initiated by a problem or task, and leading to a conclusion."[1]

You may also use an entire paragraph:

> The Gestalt psychologist Wertheimer wrote,
>
> > Many are of the opinion that men do not like to think; that they will do much to avoid it; that they prefer to repeat instead. But in spite of many factors that are inimical to real thinking, that suffocate it, here and there it emerges and flourishes. And often one gets the strong impression that men, even children, long for it.[2]

You may also paraphrase. But here, too, you must give credit. You may write,

> As Smith says, "Anyone who tells you he understands the financial situation of Nationalist China in the 1930s is lying."[3]

Or you may paraphrase,

> As Smith has pointed out, no one really can understand the complex financial situation of Nationalist China in the 1930s.[4]

When is it unnecessary to quote? When information is widely known and appears in most books on the subject, there is no need for you to either quote or give a source. If all the books you examined agree that the financial situation in China in the 1930s was indeed complicated, you do not need to give a reference.

Documentation

It is generally agreed that when you mention a source of information, you must document that source. You must tell your readers where you found the information in such a way that they can also find it. In the examples noted above, you would need to tell exactly where you found the definition of thinking you quoted from Russell and where readers may locate the book from which you took Wertheimer's paragraph. In practice, this means that you must give (1) the authors' full name, (2) the title of the book or article, (3) the publisher and date of publication of the book, and (4) the name of the journal that published the article, as well as the date of publication, volume, and number. For both articles and books you must give page numbers.

How do you include this documentation in your paper? Unfortunately, there are several systems used in American colleges and universities, some allowing for a simple date after the author's name in the text and a complete reference in the bibliography, and some insisting upon a footnote, with a number after the item on the page, documentation on the bottom of the page, and further documentation in the bibliography. You need to check with your instructor to learn which system is preferred by your college. The department or college may follow a specific handbook that spells out the documentation system favored. If you have kept accurate records of bibliographical data on your index cards, the task of documenting and preparing a bibliography will be less difficult.

GUIDE SHEET FOR WRITING
THE RESEARCH PAPER

The following guide sheet is designed to assist you as you go through the various steps needed to complete a good research paper. You may note your decisions and the dates you completed each step.

1. Area selected:

2. Topic selected:

3. Topic narrowed down to:

4. Question underlying paper:

5. Brainstorming conducted on:

6. Preliminary library search conducted on:

7. Tentative outline prepared:

8. Study of library facilities on:

9. Call number system used in library:

10. Check of possibilities in card catalog:

11. Check of periodical index:

12. Check of appropriate reference books:

13. Card system begun on:

14. Size of card chosen:

15. Name of reference system used in college:

16. Handbook used for reference system:

17. Thesis statement for paper:

18. Guide question to be answered by research:

19. Title of paper chosen:

20. Working outline prepared:

21. Material organized for writing:

22. First draft completed:

23. Outside opinion obtained:

24. Revised version completed on:

25. Careful check to avoid plagiarism made on:

26. Editing for spelling, punctuation, and grammar:

27. Editing for purpose, organization, and clarity of thinking:

28. Last-minute changes made on:

29. Paper completed:

30. Submitted:

POINTS TO REMEMBER ABOUT RESEARCH PAPER WRITING

1. Start with a question you want answered.

2. Define your topic carefully.

3. Become familiar with the library.

4. Know how the card catalog works.

5. Know basic tools such as the periodical indexes.

6. Be familiar with various reference books.

7. Keep accurate records of your search.

8. Work from a detailed outline.

9. Understand and avoid plagiarism.

10. Stick with an appropriate system for documentation.

12

MASTERY TEST

To show that you understood this chapter, complete the following multiple-choice test.

1. Research is defined here as

    a. statistical analysis of data.

    b. finding answers to questions.

    c. a collection of data.

2. A research paper is

    a. a report on your findings.

    b. statistical in nature.

    c. a collection of findings.

3. Learning to write research papers is valuable training for many positions in

    a. government.

    b. science.

    c. many occupations and professions.

4. You can borrow books not in your library through

    a. the college bookstore.

    b. interlibrary loans.

    c. checking publishers' catalogs.

5. One good way to begin your paper is to

    a. ask your librarian for assistance.

    b. brainstorm your topic.

    c. examine papers done by previous students in the course.

6. The card catalog lists

    a. all books in the library.

    b. all books copyrighted in the United States.

    c. all book and magazine articles.

7. Letters of the alphabet are used as the basis of the

   a. Dewey Decimal System.
   b. Library of Congress System.
   c. all library classification systems.

8. Which of the following will not help you locate a magazine article?

   a. *Access*
   b. *Readers' Guide to Periodical Literature*
   c. *Who's Who in the East*

9. Plagiarism is

   a. using someone else's material without giving credit.
   b. charts and graphs.
   c. documentation.

10. The necessary data for your bibliography may be found in

   a. *Readers' Guide to Periodical Literature.*
   b. your index cards.
   c. books from interlibrary loan.

References

The theory underlying this book is derived from a variety of sources, particularly from research findings about study-skills instruction, reading comprehension, vocabulary development, and learning theory.

Fifteen books that provide discussions of recent research are noted here. In them readers may locate additional information about specific topics treated in these chapters. (See Topic Key below.)

1. ANDERSON, JOHN R. *Cognitive Psychology: Its Implications.* San Francisco: Freeman, 1980.

2. ANDERSON, THOMAS H., AND BONNIE B. ARMBRUSTER. "Studying." In *Handbook of Reading Research*, edited by P. David Pearson. New York: Longman, 1984.

3. DALE, EDGAR, AND JOSEPH O'ROURKE. *Techniques for Teaching Vocabulary*, 3rd. ed. Palo Alto, Calif.: Field Educational Publications, 1971.

4. DEVINE, THOMAS G. *Teaching Reading Comprehension: From Theory to Practice.* Newton, Mass.: Allyn and Bacon, 1986.

5. DEVINE, THOMAS G. *Teaching Study Skills: A Guide for Teachers*, 2nd ed. Newton, Mass.: Allyn and Bacon, 1987.

6. GRAVES, MICHAEL F. "Selecting Vocabulary to Teach in the Intermediate and Secondary Grades." In *Promoting Reading Comprehension*, edited by James Flood. Newark, Del.: International Reading Association, 1984.

7. HENDERSON, EDMUND. *Teaching Spelling*. Boston: Houghton Mifflin, 1985.

8. KOLESNIK, WALTER B. *Motivation: Understanding and Influencing Human Behavior*. Boston: Allyn and Bacon, 1978.

9. MEYER, BONNIE J. F. "Organizational Aspects of Text: Effects on Reading Comprehension and Applications in the Classroom." In *Promoting Reading Comprehension*, edited by James Flood. Newark, Del.: International Reading Association, 1984.

10. MURRAY, DONALD M. *A Writer Teaches Writing*, 2nd ed. Boston: Houghton Mifflin, 1985.

11. PETROSKY, ANTHONY R., AND DAVID BARTHOLOMAE. *The Teaching of Writing*. Chicago: University of Chicago Press, 1986.

12. ROBINSON, H. ALAN. *Teaching Reading and Study Strategies: The Content Areas*, 2nd ed. Boston: Allyn and Bacon, 1978.

13. RUMELHART, DAVID E. "Schemata: The Building Blocks of Comprehension." In *Theoretical Issues in Reading Comprehension*, edited by R. J. Spiro, B. C. Bruce, and W. F. Brewer. Hillsdale, N. J.: Lawrence Erlbaum Associates, 1980.

14. TIERNEY, ROBERT J., AND P. DAVID PEARSON. "Toward a Composing Model of Reading." In *Composing and Comprehending*, edited by Julie M. Jenson. Urbana, Ill.: ERIC Clearinghouse on Reading and Communications Skills, 1984.

15. VACCA, RICHARD T., AND JOANNE VACCA. *Content Area Reading*, 2nd ed. Boston: Little, Brown, 1986.

TOPIC KEY TO REFERENCES

Information on specific topics may be located in the numbered sources on the preceding list by using the following key.

Topic	Sources
Academic aptitude	1, 5, 8
Attitude	1, 5, 8
Critical reading	4, 5, 12, 15

Topic	Sources
Editing	5, 10, 11
Intelligence	1, 5, 8
Listening	5
Main ideas	4, 5, 10, 12, 15
Mapping	4, 5, 15
Memory	1, 4, 5, 13
Note taking	4, 5, 12, 15
Organizational patterns	4, 5, 9, 12, 15
Outlining	4, 5, 12, 15
Prewriting	5, 10, 11, 14
Research papers	5, 12, 15
Self-questioning	1, 4, 12, 15
Spelling	5, 7
Study skills	2, 5, 12, 15
Summarizing	1, 4, 5, 12, 15
Test taking	5, 12, 15
Textbook reading	4, 5, 12, 15
Time management	5
Writing skills	5, 7, 9, 10, 11, 14
Vocabulary	3, 4, 5, 6, 12, 15

Appendix

TWENTY WIDELY USED ROOTS

Root	Meaning	Examples
1. agri	field	agriculture
2. anthro	man	anthropologist
3. astro	star	astronaut
4. bio	life	biology
5. cardio	heart	cardiology
6. chromo	color	chromatics
7. demo	people	democracy
8. derm	skin	epidermis
9. dyna	power	dynamite
10. geo	earth	geology
11. helio	sun	heliocentric
12. hydro	water	hydroelectric
13. hypno	sleep	hypnotic
14. magni	great	magnificent
15. mono	one	monolithic

Root	Meaning	Examples
16. ortho	straight	orthodox
17. psycho	mind	psychology
18. pyro	fire	pyrotechnics
19. terra	earth	terrace
20. thermo	heat	thermometer

TWENTY MORE WIDELY USED ROOTS

Root	Meaning	Examples
1. cept	take	accept
2. cess	go, move	recess
3. dict	say, tell, speak	contradict
4. duc	take, lead	introduce
5. graph	write	paragraph
6. gress	go	digress
7. mit	send, let go	transmit
8. path	feeling	sympathy
9. pend	hang	impending
10. port	carry	portable
11. psych	mind	psychic
12. script	write	inscription
13. sist	stand	resistant
14. spec	look	retrospect
15. tang	touch	tangible
16. tract	draw	attract
17. vers	turn	reversal
18. vid	see	videotape
19. voc	call	vocalize
20. zygo	connect	zygomorphic

TWENTY WIDELY USED PREFIXES

Prefix	Meaning	Examples
1. anti-	against	antitank
2. auto-	self	automatic
3. bene-	good	benefit

Prefix	Meaning	Examples
4. circum-	around	circumscribe
5. contra-	against	contradict
6. hyper-	over	hypertension
7. inter-	between	interval
8. macro-	large	macroscopic
9. micro-	small	microscope
10. multi-	many	multimillionaire
11. neo-	new	neolithic
12. pan-	all	Pan-American
13. poly-	many	polygamy
14. post-	after	postgame
15. proto-	first	prototype
16. pseudo-	false	pseudonym
16. retro-	backward	retrospect
17. semi-	half	semiprofessional
18. super-	above	superhuman
19. tele-	far	television
20. trans-	across	transport

TWENTY MORE WIDELY USED PREFIXES

Prefix	Meaning	Examples
1. a-	in, into, on, at	aboard
2. ad-	to, toward, addition	adjoin
3. ante-	before	anteroom
4. bi-	two	bipartisan
5. co-	together with	cooperation
6. com-	with, together	combine
7. de-	down, remove	depress
8. dis-	apart, away	dismiss
9. ex-	forth, from, out	exit
10. extra-	beyond	extraterrestrial
11. il-, im-, in-, ir-	not	illegitimate, impassable, incompetent irregular

Prefix	Meaning	Examples
12. mal-	bad	maladjustment
13. mis-	wrong	misunderstand
14. mono-	one	monotheistic
15. pro-	before, forward	proceed
16. re-	again	reappearance
17. sub-	under, below	submarine
18. syn-	together with	synthesis
19. trans-	across	transform
20. un-	not	unable

TWENTY WIDELY USED SUFFIXES

Suffix	Meaning	Examples
1. -able	can be done	readable
2. -ade	thing made	lemonade
3. -ana	collection of	Americana
4. -arian	person who	librarian
5. -ate	to make	fascinate
6. -ation	process	visitation
7. -ent	inclined to	fraudulent
8. -er, -or	person	actor
9. -esque	in the style of	picturesque
10. -gram	something written	telegram
11. -ic	to form nouns	plastic
12. -ical	to form adjectives	comical
13. -ion	state of	ambition
14. -ish	to form adjective	clownish
15. -ism	a belief	naturalism
16. -ist	a person	guitarist
17. -ize	to make	civilize
18. -ment	state of	puzzlement
19. -some	like	troublesome
20. -wise	manner	counterclockwise

TWENTY MORE WIDELY USED SUFFIXES

Suffix	Meaning	Examples
1. -age	makes a noun	usage
2. -ance	makes a noun	vigilance
3. -ancy	state of	truancy
4. -ard	person who	drunkard
5. -ency	quality of	frequency
6. -ery	makes a noun	drudgery
7. -ful	makes an adjective	fanciful
8. -ice	makes a noun	malice
9. -ify	makes a verb	terrify
10. -less	without	fatherless
11. -or, -ore	person who	donor, commodore
12. -ory	place where	laboratory
13. -ous	in the nature of	tempestuous
14. -ry	collection of	jewelry
15. -ship	makes a noun	leadership
16. -ster	one belonging to	gangster
17. -ward, -wards	makes an adverb	forward
18. -wright	workman	playwright
19. -y	inclined to	dreamy
20. -yer	person who	lawyer

Index